FASCINATING STORIES
OF
FORGOTTEN LIVES

REDISCOVERING SOME OLD TESTAMENT CHARACTERS

Profiles in Character from

CHARLES R.
SWINDOLL

THOMAS NELSON
Since 1798

NASHVILLE   DALLAS   MEXICO CITY   RIO DE JANEIRO

FASCINATING STORIES OF FORGOTTEN LIVES

Published in Nashville, Tennessee, by Thomas Nelson. Thomas Nelson is a registered trademark of Thomas Nelson, Inc.

Thomas Nelson, Inc. titles may be purchased in bulk for educational, business, fund-raising, or sales promotional use. For information, please e-mail SpecialMarkets@ThomasNelson.com.

Published in association with Yates & Yates, LLP, Attorneys and Counselors, Orange, California.

All Scripture quotations, unless otherwise indicated, are taken from the *New American Standard Bible* (NASB) © 1960, 1962, 1963, 1968, 1971, 1973, 1975, 1977 by the Lockman Foundation, La Habra, California. Used by permission.

Other Scripture references are from the following sources:

Quotations designed TEV are from the Good News Bible: The Bible in Today's English Version, © 1976 by the American Bible Society.

Quotations designated MSG are from the *Message* copyright © by Eugene H. Peterson, 1993, 1994, 1995, 1996. Used by permission of NavPress Publishing Group.

Quotations designated NET are from the NET Bible®. Copyright © 2003 by Biblical Studies Press, L.L.C. www. netbible.com. All rights reserved. Used by permission.

Quotations designated NLT are from the Holy Bible, *New Living Translation* (Wheaton, Ill.: Tyndale House Publishers, 1996). Used by permission.

Editorial Staff: Shady Oaks Studio, 1507 Shirley Way, Bedford, TX 76022.
Cover Design: Gearbox; Illustration: PixelWorks
Page Design: Inside Out Design & Typesetting, Fort Worth, TX 76180

ISBN 978-1-4002-7823-7 (tp)

Library of Congress Cataloging-in-Publication Data

Swindoll, Charles R.
    Fascinating stories of forgotten lives / Charles R. Swindoll.
        p. cm.—(Great lives series)
    Summary: "Portrait of twelve lives from the Old Testament whose lives have great lessons to teach us"—Provided by publisher.
    ISBN 978-0-8499-0016-7 (hardcover)
    1. Bible. O.T.—Biography. 2. Christian life. I. Title.
BS571.95   2005
221.9'22—dc22

Printed and bound in the United States of America
11 12 13 14 15 — 5 4 3 2 1

Fascinating Stories
of
Forgotten Lives

Publications by Charles R. Swindoll

BOOKS FOR ADULTS

Active Spirituality
Bedside Blessings
Behold . . . The Man!
The Bride
Come Before Winter
Compassion: Showing We Care in a
    Careless World
Cultivating Purity in an Impure World
The Darkness and the Dawn
David: A Man of Passion and Destiny
Day by Day
Dear Graduate
Dropping Your Guard
Elijah: A Man of Heroism and Humility
Encourage Me
Esther: A Woman of Strength and Dignity
The Finishing Touch
Five Meaningful Minutes a Day
Flying Closer to the Flame
For Those Who Hurt
Getting Through the Tough Stuff
Getting Through the Tough Stuff
    Workbook
God's Provision
The Grace Awakening
The Grace Awakening Devotional
The Grace Awakening Workbook
Growing Deep in the Christian Life
Growing Strong in the Seasons of Life
Growing Wise in Family Life
Hand Me Another Brick
Home: Where Life Makes Up Its Mind
Hope Again
Improving Your Serve
Intimacy with the Almighty
Job: A Man of Heroic Endurance
Job: Interactive Study Guide
Joseph: A Man of Integrity and Forgiveness
Killing Giants, Pulling Thorns

Laugh Again
Leadership: Influence That Inspires
Living Above the Level of Mediocrity
Living Beyond the Daily Grind,
    Books I and II
The Living Insights Study Bible,
    general editor
Living on the Ragged Edge
Living on the Ragged Edge Workbook
Make Up Your Mind
Man to Man
Moses: A Man of Selfless Dedication
The Mystery of God's Will
Paul: A Man of Grace and Grit
The Quest for Character
Recovery: When Healing Takes Time
The Road to Armageddon
Sanctity of Life
Simple Faith
Simple Trust
So, You Want to Be Like Christ?
So, You Want to Be Like Christ?
    Workbook
Starting Over
Start Where You Are
Strengthening Your Grip
Stress Fractures
Strike the Original Match
The Strong Family
Suddenly One Morning
Swindoll's Ultimate Book of
    Illustrations and Quotes
Three Steps Forward, Two Steps Back
Victory: A Winning Game Plan
    for Life
When God is Silent
Why, God?
Wisdom for the Way
You and Your Child

Dedication

It is with great gratitude
that I dedicate this volume to

The Ramer Brothers—
John, Danny, and Luke

along with three of their sons—
Andrew, Justin, and John.

These men represent a strong work ethic, commitment to excellence,
skill in craftsmanship, attention to detail, and outstanding attitudes . . .
qualities that are virtually unheard of in our day of
hurried and mediocre workmanship.

They not only built our new home, they built it right.
And they took great pleasure in doing so
because they did it for the glory of God.

CONTENTS

Contents

INTRODUCTION

Fascinating Stories of Forgotten Lives

From my earliest years I have admired people who live their lives in the shadows. They often feel the pressure of much responsibility, yet they bear up under it without seeking to be noticed. They do great work, thanks to their God-given skills and seasoned experience. Many fill significant roles and contribute greatly to the accomplishment of important tasks, all the while remaining virtually anonymous. Without applause and usually without public awareness, these faithful men and women press on, knowing that their names will never be in lights. To be honest about it, they would feel uncomfortable if they were. All that attention and acknowledgment makes them nervous. They don't do what they do to be noticed or to call attention to themselves; they do it because it's their role to fill; better stated, it's their calling. Quietly and efficiently, they serve and give of themselves. The world is a better place because of them.

As the song goes, they are the wind beneath our wings. They are the unsung heroes in the battle, the folks who do the work behind the scenes, the people who pick up the pieces, the ones who make sure everything in the project flows freely. As a matter of fact, if you ever take the time to find out, you'll discover that many are downright fascinating individuals with stories to tell that hold you in rapt attention. They may be unknown, but they are not insignificant. They may be overlooked by the public, but in private they fill roles that are invaluable.

While I have been busily engaged in writing this book, my wife and I have been overseeing the construction of our new home. Since it's going to be the last home we will build, we're making it special in many ways. No need to go into all that, except to say that we're taking our time and doing it right. It will be full of reminders of our more than fifty years together as husband and wife—places we have traveled, sights we've seen, books I have collected from all over, people we have met, friends we have cultivated, and memories we have made.

Cynthia and I love things that represent deep roots—old beams, fine architecture, seasoned-looking wood floors, aged bricks, great stone and tile work, stately fireplaces, and of course, splendid woodwork. Those things require close attention to detail, which calls for skilled individuals with a commitment to excellence in craftsmanship. Rare are those who qualify as true, seasoned workmen who know their craft, who take pride in doing their work well, and who do it all to the glory of God. Need I tell you? Those ranks are mighty thin these days. We are fortunate in having chosen a family of brothers to build our home—men who have the unusual blend of skill, experience, taste, and touch. It's doubtful that you know any of them, but they are the ones who deserve the credit for the finished product. Our gratitude for and pleasure in their work are reflected in my dedicating this book to them. I'm convinced they were "called by God" to construct our final house.

Moses certainly felt the same way about Bezalel and Oholiab.

Never heard of them, have you? See what I mean? They stand as classic examples of fascinating people whom everybody has forgotten. Even though they were literally called by the Lord to do a significant work, they represent unknowns in the minds of most people. Who were they? According to the inspired record, they were the lead craftsmen who were called by God to construct the original tabernacle.

Observe God's evaluation of these two men:

> *I have called by name Bazalel, the son of Uri, the son of Hur, of the*
> *tribe of Judah.*
> *I have filled him with the Spirit of God in wisdom, in understanding,*
> *in knowledge, and in all kinds of craftsmanship,*
> *to make artistic designs for work in gold, in silver, and in bronze,*
> *and in the cutting of stones for settings,*
> *and in the carving of wood,*
> *that he may work in all kinds of craftsmanship.*
> *And behold, I Myself have appointed with him Oholiab,*
> *the son of Ahisamach, of the tribe of Dan;*
> *and in the hearts of all who are skillful I have put skill,*
> *that they may make all that I have commanded you.* (EXODUS 31:1–6)

The Bible is full of people like that. The hurried reader will pass over them with hardly a shrug.

Knowing that to be true, I've felt for years that a different kind of biographical work ought to be put into print. I kept thinking that somebody needs to write on some of these *Fascinating Stories of Forgotten Lives.* The longer I thought about that, the more convinced I became that it ought to be next in my biblical biographical series, Great Lives from God's Word. When I brought that to the attention of my longtime friend and publisher, David Moberg of W Publishing Group, I am pleased to say there was instant agreement. The book you hold in your hands is the result. It is my eighth *Profiles in Character* volume that, unlike the others, is designed to acquaint you with many people in the Bible you may have never heard of and, as a result, may otherwise overlook.

Before we meet them, it's appropriate that I mention several significant others who helped me through the lengthy and sometimes tedious process of getting this book written. First, I'm grateful for my son-in-law, Mark Gaither. His splendid assistance as my leading editor has proven invaluable to me, along with his assistance in getting my original work on the manuscript into a much more readable form, Mark has been an insightful sounding board and faithful encourager for me. His fresh ideas and steady discipline mixed with his unwavering excitement over the project helped to keep me motivated from start to finish.

I am also extremely thankful for Mary Hollingsworth with Shady Oaks Studio and her fine team of capable editorial professionals, who not only put the finishing touches on the final copy of the manuscript, they also designed and typeset the interior of the book, as well as researched and secured the rights and approvals for all the quotations and other illustrative material I used in writing this volume. My heartfelt thanks to each one of you for another job very well done.

Finally, I want to mention the support and affirmation I received from my wife, Cynthia, during the months it has taken me to complete this book. She was not only willing to forego any special golden anniversary celebration for our wedding this year in order to give me the time to finish the project, she has remained focused on handling the endless details and decisions that have gone into getting our new home constructed, which we hope to occupy about the time this book is released.

And now, let me introduce to you some fascinating people whose lives have remained in the shadows long enough. Hopefully, you will soon discover why I didn't want them to remain forgotten.

—CHUCK SWINDOLL

Frisco, Texas

(recently moved, and *never* to move again)

CHAPTER ONE

Often-Overlooked Lives of Significance

Let's start with a quiz. Ready? Don't worry; this won't go on your permanent record. See how well you can remember a few details related to some people of significance from the past.

1. Who taught Martin Luther his theology and inspired his translation of the Scriptures from Latin to German?

2. Who spoke to Dwight L. Moody in the shoe store that day—a conversation that ultimately led Moody to Christ, which in turn led to a magnificent life of evangelism.

3. Who served on Harry Ironside's pastoral staff during his meaningful years of ministry at Moody Memorial Church in Chicago?

4. Who was the elderly lady who prayed for Billy Graham every day of her adult life, especially as his ministry reached the zenith of worldwide significance?

5. Who succeeded Hudson Taylor at China Inland Mission, providing remarkable direction and vision for many years?

6. Who was the wife of Charles Haddon Spurgeon, England's "prince of the pulpit" and perhaps that country's most influential Christian voice in the last two hundred years?
7. Who gave Charles Wesley his start as a composer, leaving the church with more than five thousand hymns in its repertoire?

Well, how well did you do? Amazing, isn't it? Just think how much poorer the family of God would be without the richness these significant saints added, yet few today can recall the name of any of these seven people. (I'll admit to you I had to do a fair amount of digging myself.)

Let me turn this around for another perspective. Suppose you have faithfully taught third-grade Sunday school class at your church for a number of years. Or you work in the parking lot wearing a brightly colored vest helping people who are often less than courteous find a place to park. In season and out of season, hot or cold, wet or windy or blazing bright, you're there.

Let's say you're a part of a ministry's staff. The ministry has a few out-in-front people known to the public, but you work behind the scenes. You deal solely with the staff members or people who have complaints and concerns. You copy and distribute information. You greet callers on the phone; you welcome the public. Everybody knows the out-in-front people, but very few would even know your name.

Let's make you the receptionist. You would think everyone would know the receptionist's name! After all, the receptionist probably speaks to more people on a daily basis than anyone in the ministry, but people don't call to talk to you. In fact, they call to speak to someone else and hear your voice instead, which brings its share of mistreatment. Yet, despite how thankless the job, you're there.

Maybe you're responsible for putting together the music for the choir, or helping the children rehearse for their performance in big church. Or you're in charge of the sound system of a well-known singer or musical group—setting mikes, running and taping wires, testing speakers and amps—capturing a flawless recording of this famous individual.

Let me turn this once again for yet another perspective. What about the nurse who assists a famous cardiovascular surgeon while your chest is open and your heart rests in the doctor's hand? What's the name of the trained professional who has the sterile instruments ready at just the right moment? Do you know the person who does the lab work or the x-ray analysis? Don't you hope the blood work is right and the analysis is correct?

How about the airline mechanic who prepares the plane you're going to fly in two hours? Or the person in charge of scanning the luggage at Heathrow International Airport for your El Al flight to Tel Aviv? Don't you hope he's paying attention?

And how about the uniformed soldier who stands watch from midnight to 3:00 a.m. so that his comrades can sleep soundly near the hot zone? Don't you hope he stays awake?

It's amazing, isn't it? Many people would be tempted to call these people of astonishing significance "nobodies." We don't mean to think of them as insignificant, yet it's easy to stay more focused on what we're doing, where we're going, and what we need. And before long, we quite naturally take them and dozens of others like them for granted—we even look right past them as though they were a lamppost or, worse, a tool to be used.

I was reminded of this when I decided it was time to get a new suit and a sport coat. I went to a men's store that advertised a sale. I met a very kind and competent gentleman who greeted me and helped me find what I was looking for. He did a great job, and before long I had exactly what I needed. He asked, "Shall we tailor these?"

"Sure, let's do it," I said.

He disappeared behind a curtain and returned with the tailor—a very skilled man, probably in his fifties. The tailor's accent announced that he was obviously from another country. As he approached, I put out my hand, which he instinctively took. As we shook hands, I could tell he was surprised. I suppose people getting measured for a new suit don't often shake the tailor's hand. I guess it's like greeting the taxi driver and asking for his name. He probably thinks you want it in order to lodge a complaint. As I shook the tailor's hand, I said, "Hi, I'm Chuck. Glad to meet you. Thanks for your good work." He quickly finished measuring and marking, then he walked away. I turned to the salesman and said, "Man, he's terrific. How long has he been at the store?"

"Four years."

"Really," I said. "What's his name?"

The salesman shrugged. "I don't know."

Four years! The tailor alters every suit the store sells, and the salesman didn't even know his name!

I don't know if the following story about President Teddy Roosevelt is true, but it's fun to tell. As the story goes, he's standing in a presidential receiving line one evening, greeting people as they entered a particular function. He always had a man on his left who would whisper the name of each person ahead of time so he could greet each one by name. He looked down the line, turned to his aide, and asked, "Who's this fella?"

He said, "Oh, you know him, Mr. President, he made your pants."

As the man reached the front of the line, the president greeted him, "Oh, yes, Major Pants, we're so glad you're here today. Welcome to the White House."

PEOPLE OF SIGNIFICANCE IN THE BIBLE

Without our realizing it, we were trained to think that the most significant people are star athletes, actors, and musicians—the ones we applaud, those whose autographs others seek. They aren't. Not really. Most often, the people worth noting are the individuals who turn a "nobody" into a "somebody" but never receive credit.

Let me illustrate this by introducing you to a few people in a section of Scripture that's often overlooked. I have a longtime friend who calls these passages in the Old Testament the "pots and pans" section of the Bible. When Hollywood wants to make an epic Bible drama, these are *not* the passages they go to, although these words reveal some very exciting and fascinating history. Because 1 Chronicles 11 and 2 Samuel 23 cover the same time period, we'll examine both to get a complete picture.

Look first at 2 Samuel 23:1–2:

> Now these are the last words of David. David the son of Jesse declares,
> the man who was raised on high declares, the anointed of the God of

Jacob, and the sweet psalmist of Israel, "The Spirit of the LORD spoke by me, and His word was on my tongue."

King David first came to the forefront of history when he slew the giant, and the people of Israel celebrated the victory by singing, "Saul has killed his thousands, and David his ten thousands!" (1 Samuel 18:7). Though David's popularity soared due to his heroic bravery, Saul remained king for more than a decade after David killed Goliath. During those years, Saul's jealousy grew from mild irritation to rage to an insane obsession to see the young hero dead. He eventually declared David an enemy of the state, and Saul dedicated his time and his army to one relentless objective: to exterminate David. But God had other plans for David:

> David became greater and greater, for the LORD of hosts was with him.
>
> Now these are the heads of the mighty men whom David had, who gave him strong support in his kingdom, together with all Israel, to make him king, according to the word of the LORD concerning Israel.
>
> 1 CHRONICLES 11:9–10

During these years, David lived in the wilderness, sleeping in caves and eating off the land, all while attracting large numbers of fighting men—hundreds, in fact (see 1 Samuel 22:1–2). When Saul finally died, David took the throne of Israel at the age of thirty and reigned until he was seventy. Near the end of his life, Israel's historians gathered around David to record the most important facts and preserve the details of the many triumphs that marked his career. You'd think that the old king would want to tell war stories from his glory days or talk about how he turned a tiny, disjointed band of tribes into an empire. He was a brilliant commander, a courageous warrior, a wise statesman, and a master administrator. He could have bragged, and he had the facts to back it up. Instead, he recalled the names of the people he considered to be the true heroes in his rise to power and prominence.

At the beginning, David attracted a group of about four hundred men, and among them was an original "band of brothers" whom the Bible calls "the thirty." This was an elite group of extraordinary fighters, many of whom David commissioned to command the rest of his growing army. Above them all were three remarkable generals. The Bible records these facts about those otherwise-forgotten heroes:

> These are the names of the mighty men whom David had: Josheb-basshebeth a Tahchemonite, chief of the captains, he was called Adino the Eznite, because of eight hundred slain by him at one time; and after him was Eleazar the son of Dodo the Ahohite, one of the three mighty men with David when they defied the Philistines who were gathered there to battle and the men of Israel had withdrawn. He arose and struck the Philistines until his hand was weary and clung to the sword, and the LORD brought about a great victory that day; and the people returned after him only to strip the slain.
>
> Now after him was Shammah the son of Agee a Hararite. And the Philistines were gathered into a troop where there was a plot of ground full of lentils, and the people fled from the Philistines. But he took his stand in the midst of the plot, defended it and struck the Philistines; and the LORD brought about a great victory.
>
> 2 SAMUEL 23:8–12

If we're not careful, it might be easy to overlook the amazing heroism in these few verses. I can tell you from my own experience in the marines, this is Medal of Honor stuff. Killing eight hundred men in battle at one time would be difficult enough with a machine gun. The warrior Adino took out eight hundred armed, skilled, fighting men *with a sword*. Assuming he killed one man every minute, he would have engaged the enemy in hand-to-hand combat, nonstop, for more than thirteen hours!

Notice the guts Eleazar displayed. While most of Israel's men shivered in their foxholes, Eleazar attacked the Philistines—a mean bunch of junkyard dogs armed with state-of-the-art, iron weapons. In fact, he stayed at it so long, his comrades had to pry his sword out of his grip. And Shammah is no wimp. In a fight against these same wicked warriors, his companions ran like scared cats, but he stood his ground—alone.

Three experienced fighting men—Adino, Eleazar, and Shammah—tough and tenacious warriors of uncommon valor and skill on the battlefield. And they were not only strong, they were fiercely loyal to David:

> David had a craving and said, "Oh that someone would give me water to drink from the well of Bethlehem which is by the gate!" So the three mighty men broke through the camp of the Philistines, and drew water from the well of Bethlehem which was by the gate, and took it and brought it to David. Nevertheless he would not drink it, but poured it out to the LORD; and he said, "Be it far from me, O LORD, that I should do this. Shall I drink the blood of the men who went in jeopardy of their lives?" Therefore he would not drink it. These things the three mighty men did.
>
> 2 SAMUEL 23:15–17

This suggests to me that these men didn't fight for David to gain fame, wealth, or even a prominent position in his government. They served him because they loved him. When he expressed an idle wish for a sip of water from his hometown, they risked their lives to get it for him. And David was so humbled by their selfless devotion that he couldn't enjoy the gift. These men shared a bond of loyalty and devotion that far exceeded glory seeking. They were devoted to one another in a God-ordained cause.

Behind these three generals were two commanders, Abishai and Benaiah. Abishai was the brother of Joab, the man who would later become David's secretary of war, as it were. Abishai became famous for killing three hundred enemy soldiers in one battle with a spear, which I'm told is even more difficult than using a sword.

But even meaner than Abishai was Benaiah. This is a guy you want on your side in a street fight:

> Benaiah the son of Jehoiada, the son of a valiant man of Kabzeel, mighty in deeds, struck down the two sons of Ariel of Moab. He also

went down and killed a lion inside a pit on a snowy day. He killed an Egyptian, a man of great stature five cubits tall. Now in the Egyptian's hand was a spear like a weaver's beam, but he went down to him with a club and snatched the spear from the Egyptian's hand and killed him with his own spear.

1 CHRONICLES 11:22–23

How's that for guts? I don't know about you, but if a man standing seven feet, six inches tall threatens me with a megasized spear, I'm looking for an exit—fast. But not Benaiah. The word rendered "club" in most translations suggests that he was armed, but he very likely was not. This Hebrew term is more often rendered "staff," as in a shepherd's rod or a walking staff. So there he stood before the enormous man armed with only a spindly, wooden stick. Can you picture the Egyptian's face when Benaiah snatched the spear from him and ran him through?

Second Samuel 23 goes on to list thirty-seven men in all, but notice that one very prominent name is missing. Where is Joab, David's longstanding top general and secretary of war? His relatives are mentioned, but not Joab. In his song about the faithful heroes he credits for his success, David chose to focus on the lesser-known names. Joab has already gotten plenty of press throughout the telling of David's story. This is David's occasion to praise the "nobodies" who made the dynasty possible. God kept His covenant with David by providing these fighting men and rejecting anyone less worthy (2 Samuel 23:4–6).

PEOPLE OF SIGNIFICANCE MAKE A DIFFERENCE

This section of Scripture reminds me of the rows of white crosses along the wind-swept hills of Normandy. We're free today because, in June 1944, during the three-month battle of Normandy, nearly fifty-three thousand "nobodies" paid the ultimate price to defeat Nazi tyranny. No fewer than 9,387 grave markers overlook Omaha Beach, many of them bearing the names of men who died during the first hours of the invasion called D-day. Beneath every white marker lies a person of significance because each one platform has become a performance stage for musicians—and I mean that in the most ignoble sense. Even when they shout and sing the name of Jesus Christ, somehow the focus of attention is upon them and public praise stays with them.

No, the church doesn't gather for the sake of the out-in-front people—the pastor, the worship leader, the musicians. Church is a gathering of nobodies to worship the only real Somebody: Christ, our Head. The King of creation, raised from the dead, seated with the Father, Commander of heaven, exercising complete authority over all time and space, perfect in His justice, infinite in His mercy, holy in His perfection, the only perfect Somebody who died for nobodies like you and me.

NOBODIES HAVE LASTING SIGNIFICANCE

Nobodies. That's who this book is about. Most are nobodies whose names you probably have never heard. A few are nobodies you have heard about, such as Cain, Abraham, Esau, and Samuel. I don't mean to twist the normal meaning of the term, but at some level, we are all nobodies. A closing scene in Richard Matheson's *The Incredible Shrinking Man* illustrates what I mean.

An accident of science took Scott Carey on a bizarre journey that would have him discover the true nature of his significance in the universe. As he grew smaller and smaller, he felt less and less important—especially as he compared himself to the world around him. As a six-foot scientist of repute, Carey could change his world for the better. But as he shrank, his self-image imploded, pulling into the void any hope of being "somebody." Finally, nearly microscopic in size, he ate a final meal and lay down to sleep, perhaps never to wake up.

Now he lay there quietly on his back, looking at the stars.

How beautiful they were; like blue-white diamonds cast across a sky of inky satin. No moonlight illuminated the sky. There was only total darkness, broken by the flaring pinpoints of stars.

And the nicest thing about them was that they were still the same. He saw them as any man saw them, and that brought a deep contentment to him. Small he might be, but the earth itself was small compared to this.[1]

Staring into the vastness of space, the microscopic man realized something important. Our universe is measured by eons and lightyears, so to the God who created it all, a person standing six feet tall may as well stand six millimeters. From the vantage point of heaven, we are all mere specks. But each one is a speck our great Savior valued enough to die for.

In His universe, we are all little people—nobodies. And yet, because of Christ's sacrifice, there are *no* nobodies living on planet earth. A person isn't significant because fame or stature or publicity makes him or her so. Each is significant because God has said so.

And that includes you.

In God's estimation, you *are* significant. The question, then, is this: are you going to *be* what you are?

FOUR TRAITS THAT CHARACTERIZE PEOPLE OF SIGNIFICANCE

How much impact we have, and whether it's positive or negative, depends largely upon the choices we make. I encourage you to be the significant person you are. I have found that people of significance—a few of them famous, most of them unknown—share similar traits. Here are four that I see most often.

A selfless devotion. High-impact people don't care about who gets the credit, and they never complain about the role they fill. With all the risks and all the heroic effort David's men invested in establishing his monarchy, we do not read about a single complaint, or even one glory hog. Each was selflessly devoted to David and to each other in a great cause that was larger than any one individual.

A mission focus. High-impact people focus on the right objectives and don't waste time pursuing things that don't matter. Many organizations have gotten lost in the weeds because their leaders took their eyes off the objective and majored in minor issues. Organizational charts and clearly defined roles are supposed to support the mission, not the self-interest of people.

A harmonious manner. High-impact people nurture harmony with others to achieve the greater good. They set aside petty differences and choose to overlook offenses because they recognize that the enemy is outside the camp. David's men were unified in their objective to seat David on the throne of Israel. When these heroes reached their goal, they sat for the feast and said, in effect, "David, this is one of the greatest moments of our lives" (see 1 Chronicles 12:38–40).

A contagious joy. High-impact people inspire humility and unity in others, a combination that translates into joy. I am convinced that joy is a choice and can be the most attractive quality in a person. Joyous people have the greatest opportunity to impact others positively, and they rarely leave a room the same way they found it.

WHAT ABOUT YOU?

At the top of this chapter, I asked you several questions you probably couldn't answer. I'd like to ask two more questions that no one but you can answer.

Would you rather be a person of significance or a person of renown? Think carefully. The answer to that question will shape your entire future, including the decisions you make, the manner in which you relate to others, even how you go about fulfilling the roles God has assigned you. Making a positive difference is your responsibility. God will look to issues of credit or fame.

Which is more important to you: the quality of your impact on the world or the size of it? Don't be too quick! That's a probing question that demands some attention. Let's face it: most of us are conditioned by the world to think we can have both when, in reality, you have only one of them. You already know which one it is.

In the chapters that follow, we'll recall the lives of several ancient people. Some of the fascinating lives I have chosen to highlight are typically forgotten and ignored. A few are familiar personalities in the Old Testament, but certain episodes from their lives need to be revisited. The lessons they teach need to be learned by some and relearned by others. Most of these people had a positive impact on the world and the people around them, but a few left tragic legacies in their wake. As we examine each one, we'll try to discover biblical principles and practical applications for living so that we can *be* what we *are* in God's estimation . . . people of significance.

CHAPTER TWO

Cain: The Farmer Who Murdered His Brother

A person can have no greater *negative* impact than when he or she takes the life of another. And to the shame of humanity, our historical paths are littered with acts of murder. Here's a chilling thought: as I write these words, somewhere, someone is planning to kill another. And as you read these words, the intended victim of that insidious scheme will soon die. I am continually amazed by the sheer number of murders, especially mass killing sprees. I'll spare you the bloody details—my desire is to illustrate, not shock—but here is just a small sample:

• On September 6, 1949, in only twelve minutes, thirteen people were fatally shot in Camden, New Jersey. Howard Unruh, the murderer, said later, "I'd have killed a thousand if I had had enough bullets."

• On July 14, 1966, eight student nurses were stabbed and/or strangled in a Chicago dormitory by Richard Speck, age twenty-four.

• Not many days after that, on August 1, 1966, Charles Whitman climbed to the top of a tower on the University of Texas campus with his loaded, high-powered rifle. He ended the lives of sixteen people before the police were able to kill the sniper.

• On Easter Sunday in 1975, eleven people, including eight children, were killed at a family gathering in Hamilton, Ohio. James Ruppert was convicted of two of the murders but found not guilty by reason of insanity for the other nine. *(I have no idea how that works!)*

- On September 25, 1982, George Banks shot and killed thirteen people, including five children, in a township in Pennsylvania.
- On February 19, 1983, Willie Mak and Benjamin Ng shot thirteen people in the head, killing all of them, during the robbery of a gambling club in Seattle.
- On Palm Sunday in 1984, Christopher Thomas ended the lives of ten people, including eight children, in an apartment in Brooklyn, New York. The judge cited "extreme emotional disturbance" in the man.
- On July 18, 1984, James Oliver Huberty entered a McDonald's restaurant in San Ysidro, California, with a gun and randomly killed twenty-one people before a police sharpshooter ended the nightmare.
- On December 7, 1987, David Burke, an airline employee, bypassed security with his credentials—and a pistol—and boarded Pacific Southwest Airlines (PSA) flight 1771. At twenty-nine-thousand feet, he killed the pilots, then himself. The plane crashed, killing all forty-four passengers and crew.
- On January 17, 1989, Patrick Edward Purdy went back to the elementary school he attended as a child and shot thirty-five people, killing five children. Then he killed himself.
- On May 1, 1992, Eric Houston returned to his former high school, shooting fourteen people, killing four. He said it was retribution for the failing grade he received in history class four years earlier.
- On December 7, 1994, Colin Ferguson methodically shot twenty-five people aboard a Long Island train, killing six of them. He had to stop and reload twice.
- On March 24, 1998, two boys, ages thirteen and eleven, shot sixteen people in Jonesboro, Arkansas, killing four girls and a teacher.
- On April 20, 1999, Eric Harris and Dylan Klebold killed twelve fellow students and a teacher at Columbine High School near Littleton, Colorado, before killing themselves.

And, of course, during that same fifty-year period, serial killers stalked and killed hundreds of victims. The FBI claims that during the 1980s alone, roughly thirty-five serial murderers were active.

I could have continued the list to include those after 1999 to the time of this writing, but, frankly, I couldn't stand much more of this research. And I limited my examples to my own country, the United States. Extending the study to include other countries made the task too depressing to handle. As I pushed the research back beyond 1900, I found that the prevalence of multiple murder, mass murder, spree killing, and serial murder was about the same as now. Today, the reporting is more instantaneous and detailed because of modern technology, but not much else has changed.

Chuck Colson's research shows fairly well that even with technology, prosperity, a strong government, and an ethical system of belief, murder has been, and will continue to be a problem:

> We incarcerate more people per capita than any nation on earth, yet our murder rate is 2.6 to 8 times higher than that of other industrialized countries. A comparison of murder rates of other nations reveals that Americans between fifteen and twenty-four years of age are being killed seventy-four times more often than Australians in that age group and seventy-three times more often than Japanese.[1]

Some claim that the problem is getting worse. Others think that the per capita murder rate is going down worldwide. The perspective seems to be skewed one way or the other, depending upon whether the subject is gun control or the value of education and a favorable world economy. A quick search through the Scriptures tells the true story. The Bible is peppered with accounts of one person killing another.

Spend a couple of afternoons studying the history of murder (if you can stand it), and you'll come to one inevitable conclusion: where there are people, there is murder. As proof, all we need to do is trace the crime through the Bible, backward in time, to see where the trail begins. It begins at the very beginning of human history:

> Now the man [Adam] had marital relations with his wife Eve, and she became pregnant and gave birth to Cain. Then she said, "I have created

a man just as the Lord did!" Then she gave birth to his brother Abel. Abel took care of the flocks, while Cain cultivated the ground.

At the designated time Cain brought some of the fruit of the ground for an offering to the LORD. But Abel brought some of the firstborn of his flock—even the fattest of them. And the LORD was pleased with Abel and his offering, but with Cain and his offering he was not pleased. So Cain became very angry, and his expression was downcast.

Then the LORD said to Cain, "Why are you angry, and why is your expression downcast? Is it not true that if you do what is right, you will be fine? But if you do not do what is right, sin is crouching at the door. It desires to dominate you, but you must suppress it."

Cain said to his brother Abel, "Let's go out to the field." While they were in the field, Cain attacked his brother Abel and killed him.

Genesis 4:1–8 NET

A CRIME SCENE INVESTIGATION

My older daughter is a huge fan of what she likes to call "murder shows." *Law & Order* and *CSI* are her favorites. Each episode starts with either the detectives or crime scene investigators getting the initial facts about some act of foul play while the coroner loads up a body. The rest of the program traces the investigation as the investigators unravel all the facts to arrive at the truth. That's why she likes them. Each episode is a quest for the truth . . . and, amazingly, only an hour later, they have it.

That's what I hope to do with this original crime scene. I want to sift through the facts and arrive at the truth—or in our case, truths. The Lord preserved the facts about this incident and strategically placed it early in the biblical record for our benefit. As with any good investigation, this one begins with some simple observations.

Notice that the very first murder took place within the second generation of humanity. This points us to an undeniable theological truth we learn from Genesis 4: humans are murderers, not because we commit murder, but because we are murderers at heart.

Just in case you get hung up on the word *murderer*, let me put it another way. We are not sinners because we have committed sins. We sin because we are sinners. The problem is in the heart. We do wrong because we are wrong. We are wrong all the way to the core, where murder is desired. Murder is merely the fruit of a heart problem we all share. It's not a weapon problem any more than it is a hand problem. Murder is the byproduct of a twisted, selfish nature that came to all humankind as a result of Adam and Eve's fall in Genesis 3.

Another observation: the first homicide occurs in Genesis 4. In Genesis 3 we see innocence. Adam and Eve enjoy unreserved intimacy with each other and with their God. We see no hint of selfishness, shame, or jealousy. Just innocence and beauty. But before chapter 3 ends, the tempter has entered and spun his lies, and the first couple chose his way instead of God's. As a result, they became spiritually polluted. Inwardly corrupt. Murderers at heart.

You might think it would take time for sin to gradually become worse with each successive generation. The children of Adam and Eve telling little fibs, maybe petty theft by the third generation, extortion and racketeering by the fifth, *then* perhaps murder. But the inspired author of Genesis chose to follow the fall of Adam and Eve with this story about their sons. The first murder in Genesis 4—so soon after sin spoiled paradise on earth in chapter 3—demonstrates that corruption doesn't have degrees. It doesn't emerge slowly, like undetected erosion. Humankind had been corrupted entirely, so it should come as no surprise that the first sins were among the most grievous.

Murder is ugly enough, but when it occurs within a family, it takes on an exceptionally horrible dimension. The word *brother* is used six times in verses 8 to 11 of this story as if to punctuate the seriousness of the crime. The first couple had marital relations, and Eve became pregnant, ultimately giving birth to their first son, whom they named Cain, or *Qayin* in the Hebrew. His name is most likely a wordplay on the Hebrew term *Qanah,* because of Eve's statement in verse 1. *Qanah* has two possible meanings: to acquire or to create. Many translations opt for the former, but I think the second meaning makes better sense, which would make Eve's statement, "I have created a man just as the LORD did" (NET). Frankly, that's not a bad way of looking at it from a mother's point of view.

Remember, this was the very first birth of a child ever. Eve took part in a miracle that only God had performed before: the creation of a human life. This had to have been an overwhelming thought, so she gave him a name that would forever remind her of that miracle.

Adam and Eve then produced another son. The biblical text offers a small hint that he might have been a twin. At any rate, he is given the name Abel, which is the Hebrew word for breath, vapor, or futility. Eve didn't comment on his name, so we can only speculate as to why she chose it. Perhaps she meant that he was slight or fragile . . . maybe he was sickly.

We are told that Cain chose to become a farmer like his dad. Abel, on the other hand, was a keeper of the flocks—a shepherd. I find great irony in their names and chosen occupations. Abel's name means "futile," and he cared for sheep. Cain's name is associated with the Hebrew phrase *Qaniti,* "I created," yet he toiled to coax life from sin-cursed ground.

Next, we're told that these adult brothers bought their offerings to the Lord. Notice how Scripture describes the sacrifice each man offered. Give special attention to the comparison:

> At the designated time Cain brought some of the fruit of the ground
> for an offering to the Lord. But Abel brought *some of the firstborn* of
> his flock—*even the fattest of them.* And the LORD was pleased with Abel
> and his offering, but with Cain and his offering he was not pleased.
> Genesis 4:3–5 NET; emphasis added

In the Hebrew, the contrast is even more obviously deliberate. God was displeased with Cain's offering and satisfied with Abel's, which sparked the conflict. Why God was displeased is a subject of debate. Many good scholars hold that Cain's offering should have been a blood sacrifice. An equal number of scholars counter that God's demand for an animal offering wasn't communicated until much later. I see plenty of evidence for both views.

We don't know from the original story how they knew what to bring God, but I am confident that Adam taught Cain and Abel the importance of an offering and how they were to approach God. The consistent message throughout the Scriptures is that sinners are to offer God a sacrifice that requires the shedding of blood. So it's reasonable to assume that God verbally gave this requirement to Adam. He, in turn, taught his sons, who were supposed to teach theirs. Blood sacrifices to God were a part of Hebrew culture long before Moses recorded the detailed requirements as part of Israel's official covenant with the Lord. Before Moses, they probably learned it from the patriarchs. The book of Job confirms this.

Cain's offering could also have been a type of grain offering not unlike what we see in Leviticus 2 and 6. Although, in both of those cases, the grain offering accompanied a blood sacrifice as a peace offering or a guilt offering.

The evidence credibly points us in either direction. We have no way of knowing for sure. But this I do know: the *form* of the sacrifice and the *spirit* in which it is given are both important. Cain's offering had neither the form nor the spirit God desired. Abel's was excellent; Cain's was mediocre. This should serve as a warning to anyone who thinks that God will accept anything we choose to bring as long as we're sincere.

OBEDIENCE IS NOT NEGOTIABLE

"There are many paths to God," some say, "so no particular belief is 'right' or 'wrong,' as long as you sincerely seek Him." And that, according to Scripture, is sincerely wrong! Sincerely place your trust in any means, or any person, other than Jesus Christ who shed His blood for our sins, and God will not receive you . . . sincerely (see John 14:6 and Acts 4:12). If that sounds harsh, let me offer two perspectives for your consideration.

First, *the Lord is loving and kind, but He is also just.* He is a very discriminating heavenly Father who has been specific in how we are to come to Him, but He could not have made that way any less complicated. He provides the free gift of salvation, paid for by the death and resurrection of His Son, Jesus Christ, and has left nothing for us to pay. He's done everything that needs to be done, leaving us no requirement but one: receive the gift. That's about as harsh as a billionaire demanding that you allow him to give you all of his money. Grace abounds.

Second, *faith demands action*. If you really believe God, you will do what He says, when He says it, and how He wants it. Cain came in his own way. Abel came God's way. The manner in which both men approached God revealed the authenticity of their faith. Later in the Bible, the author of Hebrews explains it this way:

> By faith Abel offered God a greater sacrifice than Cain, and through his faith he was commended as righteous, because God commended him for his offerings. And through his faith he still speaks, though he is dead.
>
> 11:4 NET

True faith is marked by obedience. The apostle John explained it this way:

> By this the children of God and the children of the devil are obvious: anyone who does not practice righteousness is not of God, nor the one who does not love his brother.
>
> For this is the message which you have heard from the beginning, that we should love one another; not as Cain, who was of the evil one and slew his brother. And for what reason did he slay him? Because his deeds were evil, and his brother's were righteous.
>
> 1 John 3:10–12

That's God's appraisal of the offerings of Cain and Abel. Abel's offerings, righteous. Cain's offerings, evil.

OUR RELATIONSHIP WITH GOD AFFECTS EVERYTHING

This leads us to another undeniable theological truth, which I'll state here and develop with the remaining facts of this tragic story: the quality of our horizontal relationships depends entirely upon having a good vertical relationship. Put simply, if you're not right with God, you'll find yourself at odds with everyone else . . . including yourself.

I am fascinated by Cain's disposition: "So Cain became very angry, and his expression was downcast" (Genesis 4:5 NET). As a result of doing what was wrong and experiencing God's just response, Cain grew angry and sullen. From a human perspective, I completely understand why, but I find the reaction intriguing. After all, he knew what he was supposed to do, and he chose not to do it. Then, because he didn't receive the favor of God, he grumbled. Probably something about fairness and always getting the short end of things.

The word translated "countenance" is the Hebrew word for "face." We would say his face fell. He became extremely angry, and his face showed it. The Bible doesn't reveal exactly why Cain became so angry, but I can speculate. I suspect that Cain was jealous, plain and simple. He didn't want to be outdone by his younger brother. God's favor on Abel's sacrifice quite probably stirred Cain's jealousy.

This isn't stretching things too far. Jealousy is a common response to one person's receiving something that another feels he deserves. One child gets a toy that's a little nicer than his brother's, and the brother is jealous of him. One has a birthday party at Disney World with his family. The other one has a birthday party where the family has a little cake and ice cream for him after supper. Naturally, he's jealous.

This happens at the office. One fellow gets a nice desk in an office with not just one window but two. Another still sits behind an old desk in a room without windows. Someone who hasn't been with the company as long as most of the others might enjoy a few perks that no one else does. His or her office mates, as we would expect, soon grow jealous and resentful.

I find it strange that this kind of jealousy usually targets the least logical person. Cain was angry and took out his rage on Abel, yet the younger brother did nothing wrong. Cain could reasonably resent the Lord for rejecting his offering. He might be angry with himself for failing to choose sacrifices that he knew God would receive. But why Abel? What had he done except what was right?

Now is a good time to pause and do a little self-analysis as well as firm up an important truth. If you begin to feel jealous, stop for a moment and think. Your anger is likely aimed at the wrong person. On the one hand, you may indeed be the victim of injustice or a situation where someone is getting what should be coming to you. A natural response would be to resent the other fellow, even though he did nothing wrong. What sense was there in Cain's killing Abel when his resentment was against God?

This brings us to another undeniable truth: *choosing to do wrong puts a person at odds with himself.* Don't miss God's counsel to Cain:

> Then the LORD said to Cain, "Why are you angry, and why is your expression downcast? Is it not true that if you do what is right, you will be fine? But if you do not do what is right, sin is crouching at the door. It desires to dominate you, but you must suppress it."
>
> Genesis 4:6–7 NET

The Lord confronted Cain as any good parent would a child. In effect, He said to Cain, "If you do wrong, it is *your* fault. Don't blame anyone else. Once you do what is right, Cain, your face will follow." Obedience comes first; emotions will follow.

One man put it this way:

> Cain began badly by presenting a sinful offering before God. Abel gave God the best, whereas Cain merely brought an offering. When God rejected his offering Cain complicated the problem by responding wrongly to the rejection. The anger and depression were noted by God who observed that this was a wrong response. Instead, God says, do right and you will feel right. Then God warned against failure to repent and offer the right kind of sacrifice. If you continue to complicate the problem with this sinful response (as one version says, "If you misbehave"), you will fall into deeper sin (into the clutches of sin, which is like a wild animal).[2]

Anna Russell wrote a wonderful little satirical song in the 1960s about this blame-shifting habit we have. Her lyrics are funny, but her message is nevertheless convicting. She called it "Jolly Old Sigmund Freud:"

I went to my psychiatrist
To be psychoanalyzed
To find out why I killed the cat
And blacked my husband's eyes.
He laid me on a downy couch
To see what he could find,
So this is what he dredge-ed up
From my subconscious mind:

When I was one, my mommy hid
My dolly in a trunk,
And so it follows naturally
That I am always drunk.
When I was two, I saw my father
Kiss the maid one day,
And that is why I suffer now
From kleptomania.

At three, I had the feeling of
Ambivalence towards my brothers,
And so it follows naturally
I poisoned all my lovers.
But I am happy; now I've learned
The lesson this has taught;
That everything I do that's wrong—
Is someone else's fault.3

Though written nearly four decades ago, those words are an indictment of our failure as a society to take responsibility for the consequences of our own disobedience. And we don't do future generations any favors when we rationalize wrongdoing. Neglected and parentless children are counseled that they are tragic victims of life and therefore not responsible for their poor decisions. Consequently, our prisons are full of self-pitying career criminals. On the surface, the counsel sounds compassionate because it acknowledges that the struggle of the underprivileged is an immense one. But counsel that's long on compassion and short on truth is worse than saying nothing at all. I have long said that truth without love is cruel. At the same time, love without truth is deceptive. We must always speak the truth in love. Anything less robs a person of the very dignity that God gave every human being: the gift of autonomy and, with it, the dignity of living with the consequences.

Better counsel would be, "My friend, you are responsible for each and every choice you make in life. The consequences you reap are yours to own. As painful as it is, as difficult as it is, take full responsibility for all of your own actions. Face the fact that much of your response, revealed in your face, comes from your own choices and the attitude you bring to them."

UNRESOLVED SIN CORRUPTS EVERYTHING

Verse 7 points us to another truth: *leaving a sin unresolved makes us vulnerable to more sin.* Notice again the Lord's counsel to Cain and how He characterized the danger of compounding sin: "Is it not true that if you do what is right, you will be fine? But if you do not do what is right, sin is crouching at the door" (Genesis 4:7). Sin is a snarling beast waiting for us to relax, drop our guard, and forget to stay alert. Sin is a cowardly opportunist, waiting for us to be at our weakest so that it can devour us with the least amount of risk. But if we take responsibility for our error, repent, and obey, we can master sin. The word translated "dominate" or "master" is the same word used of a king having dominion over land and people. We dominate potential sin by repenting of past sin quickly and resolving to do what is right from then on.

This is a loving warning. It's a merciful confrontation. It's a reminder that Cain has the opportunity to turn around; his opportunity to do right isn't over just because he failed to do the right thing earlier. He can repent, obtain the proper offering, and return to the altar with a humble, obedient heart. In other words, *it's never too late to start doing the right thing.* And don't miss the implied benefit: "If you do what is right, you will be fine."

We cannot afford to hesitate or let wrongs linger. That goes for our horizontal relationships too. That's the point of Ephesians 4:26–27: "Be angry, and yet do not sin; do not let the sun go down on your anger, and do not give the devil an opportunity." The general theme of Paul's letter to the church in Ephesus is unity. Great for a church. Perfect for a relationship. Essential for a marriage.

My wife and I have an agreement that we will not go to bed angry. And we'll stay up till two, sometimes three o'clock, talking the issue through. That's helpful on a number of levels. I have found that by three o'clock, you'll agree to almost anything. It's amazing how lack of sleep brings a huge issue down to size. On the other extreme, I have counseled couples in trouble whose anger continually smolders just beneath the surface. This is usually the result of one or both majoring in history. "I remember back in '74, he said this to me in a crowd, and I'll never forget it." These couples spend their days chewing on past grievances, relishing the rush of righteous indignation. Some very small issue becomes, over time, a major point of conflict between the couple, often leading to bitterness, even abuse.

Unfortunately, Cain blew off God's parental advice. Not surprisingly, his resentment grew like a cancer:

> Cain said to his brother Abel, "Let's go out to the field." While they
> were in the field, Cain attacked his brother Abel and killed him.
>
> Genesis 4:8 NET

The Hebrew word translated "killed him" is a term used for murder, judicial execution, and animal sacrifice. I don't want to make too much of the word choice, but I do think it adds a chilling irony to the story. If I were writing a novel with Cain as a character, I would have him hiss the words, "You want a sacrifice? *There's* Your sacrifice, God!"

Abel's blood spilled onto the ground, and his lifeless body sank into Cain's arms. *Qayin*—"I created"—became the first destroyer of life.

RESOLVE NOW TO RESOLVE CONFLICT

Before we cluck our tongues and shake our heads, let us not forget that the same murderous heart that Cain inherited by the Fall beats within each of us. Sin crouches at your door, at my door, just as it did Cain's. I have to admit that I have at times disliked certain people so much that murder would have begun to build up in my heart if I had not forgiven them. Search your past. Be honest. So have you. If you deny it, you are either self-deceived or naive about your own nature.

Thankfully, my murder list is empty. All blank spaces are thanks to the power of Christ, who gave me His grace of forgiveness and demands that I pass it on. But, I've met people who live with murder on their minds. I worked with a young man at a Christian camp several years ago who was extremely disturbed and visibly agitated. He could barely hold back a volatile mix of emotions. He seemed ready to explode at any moment. When I asked him what life was like at home, he described a father who had been very unfair, even brutal. As he spoke of his dad, the boy lost himself in the moment, almost forgetting I was there, and said to me, "I'm just waiting for the right moment, and then I'll kill him." He meant it.

Nurture your resentment; it will sprout into anger. That anger will put down deep, deep roots and grow into hatred. And the fruit of hatred is murder.

Don't be fooled. Very few murderers woke up one day and decided to become a killer. I would venture to say that few of them thought themselves capable of the crime. But by degrees, they nurtured anger until resentment bore its poisonous fruit in their lives.

Unresolved Sin Hardens the Heart

We don't know how much time passed between verses 8 and 9. The Bible doesn't reveal events that occurred in-between, but we can imagine. The sickening silence that follows a murder victim's last sound should reduce anyone with a conscience to tears. A precious human life—a person who once talked and laughed and sang and made others happy—has been snuffed out. It's not a far stretch to imagine that Cain hastily buried his brother's body in the very field where the soil was red with Abel's blood. The very first killing field. Cain walked away with a shrug and washed up for supper.

Eventually the Lord confronted Cain with his sin, but take note of his hardening:

> Then the LORD said to Cain, "Where is your brother Abel?" And he
> replied, "I don't know! Am I my brother's guardian?" But the LORD
> said, "What have you done? The voice of your brother's blood is crying
> out to me from the ground!"
>
> Genesis 4:9–10 NET

A secret sin on earth is open scandal in heaven. Never forget that! Whatever we may hide on this earth is fully known to God. "The voice of your brother's blood is crying out to me." God knew exactly what Cain had done. Go back and study the divine investigation procedure as God questioned Cain. Even after the worst crime ever committed up to that time, the Lord demonstrated grace. The omniscient God asked the murderous Cain a rhetorical question to convict him of his sin. But his heart was too hard for him to comprehend the gravity of his own evil deed. In just two sentences, Cain revealed his impudence, his complete lack of knowledge about God, the absence of remorse, and his utter contempt for Abel.

God then responded with justice:

> So now, you are banished from the ground, which has opened its
> mouth to receive your brother's blood from your hand. When you
> try to cultivate the ground it will no longer yield its best for you. You
> will be a homeless wanderer on the earth.
>
> Genesis 4:11–12 NET

Cain's sin made the cultivation of crops impossible, which ended his livelihood. His destitution would put him on the road . . . permanently. In response, we finally see some emotion from Cain:

> Then Cain said to the LORD, "My punishment is too great to endure!
> Look! You are driving me off the land today, and I must hide from
> your presence. I will be a homeless wanderer on the earth; whoever
> finds me will kill me."
>
> Genesis 4:13–14 NET

God had pressed Cain for a confession and gave him every opportunity to repent in brokenness over his murder of Abel. But Cain's only compassion was for himself. He's been caught, tried, and sentenced, so he begs for mercy. "I'll be homeless. I'll be destitute. I'll be a wanderer. And one of these days, in one of those open, lonely fields, someone will kill me." Interesting, isn't it? He's sure that others will treat him as he has treated his brother.

Let's not be too pious here. Had you or I been in charge of this jury, had you or I been the judge in this case, we would have thrown the book at him. Dropped the gavel with a thud and called for the next case. "Serves you right." But notice God's grace, even for a remorseless murderer like Cain:

> But the LORD said to him, "All right then, if anyone kills Cain, Cain
> will be avenged seven times as much." Then the Lord put a special mark
> on Cain so that no one who found him would strike him down.
>
> Genesis 4:15 NET

I'm sure you are wondering what that special mark was. Frankly, so do I. In my research, I read one idea after another about the "mark" of Cain. I even started a list. Some of the items are downright humorous. Others are plausible. Most of them are intriguing.

- The Lord placed a bright light around Cain so he would appear frightening to others and they'd stay away from him.
- God put leprosy on Cain's forehead so that no one would touch him for fear of disease.
- God gave Cain a dog.
- The Lord changed Cain's personality so others would be intimidated in his presence.
- The Lord gave Cain a brightly colored coat.
- Cain grew horns on his head, which made him look like a kind of animal, so people would stay away from him.

Are you ready for the right answer? No one knows! All we know is that God, in His grace, preserved Cain's life. The only reason I can see for God's doing this was to say, in effect, "Sometime in the remaining years of your life, if you find a place in your hardened heart for repentance, I'm ready to hear you. I'm ready to accept you. I won't even allow your vicious act of murder to keep you from Me . . . not permanently."

I wish stories like this one ended on a happier note. I wish we could wrap up this story with a pleasant epilogue. "And as a result, Cain turned to the Lord, repented, accepted His grace, and lived the rest of his days in humble and worshipful adoration." Unfortunately, that didn't happen.

WRITE YOUR OWN EPILOGUE

Bad for Cain, but maybe better for us. I'll end this chapter gleaning three timeless principles that I hope you will consider. They're uncomplicated. They don't appear to be very profound at first glance; nevertheless, I urge you to ponder each one.

First, *God's way is the only acceptable way. Take it!* The Lord doesn't waste words, so when He gives clear instruction, such as, "I will honor a certain offering," then our response must be obedience. No need to ask why. No need for further explanations or drawn-out answers.

He says, "Come to Me through faith in Jesus Christ." That is both clear and simple. Don't offer God your good deeds; they aren't good enough. Don't come to Him with sincere belief in some religious system that doesn't claim that Jesus is the only way to the Father. He's made the way to Himself plain and simple. Take it!

Second, *jealousy is a sin that cannot be hidden. Release it!* Jealousy is a killer. Jealousy plants seeds in the soul that lead ultimately to anger, resentment, hatred, and yes, perhaps even murder. Be content with doing what is right. Instead of harboring resentment, rejoice with those who receive extra praise or privilege.

Third, *never leave sin or conflict unresolved—especially with God. Address it!* Unaddressed, lingering anger doesn't vanish. On the contrary, it merely goes into remission, multiplies, smolders, and returns stronger. Most wrongs don't correct themselves. They require attention and effort.

A friend of mine was camping in Colorado and watched an eagle hunting for prey, sweeping and soaring. Then, suddenly, the bird swooped down, grabbed an animal in its claws, and took off again. As my friend watched the eagle fly away, he thought it was over. But as the bird flew toward its nest, its wings abruptly flopped down, and the eagle fell into a tailspin all the way to the ground. My friend was understandably curious and examined the animals once he found them. It turns out that the eagle had snatched a weasel for dinner, but during the flight home, the weasel found a vulnerable spot on the bird and bit into an artery in its neck. The eagle bled to death, and the fall finished off the weasel. So there they lay. Both dead.

What an appropriate picture of the danger we face when we hold onto resentment or anger. Anger is not a sin; it's just an emotion. Sometimes resentment is an understandable response when you've been slighted. But if you keep it in your clutches, it will destroy you and quite possibly bring harm to someone else. Today's sportfishing rule is a good one to follow: "Catch and release."

In resolving conflict or sin (no matter who's guilty), the best place to start is in your relationship with God. Whether your contribution is small or great, own it. Own it all. Hold yourself accountable to God, and confess any sinful part. By doing so, you will have the necessary peace to make peace with your brother or sister. Do this, and you will leave a lasting *positive* impact on the people around you, even as a sinner.

CHAPTER THREE

Abraham: The Father Who Released His Son

Shortly before her death, Corrie ten Boom worshiped with us at my former church in Fullerton, California. She had a noticeably peaceful demeanor—so unassuming, so serene in her own way. This gave her worship of God a unique quality. I will admit that her wisdom and intimacy with the Almighty had such a humbling effect on me that I felt a little intimidated in the pulpit with a woman of such stature sitting, of all places, under my teaching. Her gracious spirit always reassured me that she delighted in being among us. She never left the impression that she expected any attention. Wonderful lady!

On occasion, Corrie would speak with me after the service. Her voice—laced with a charming Dutch accent and a tone that I could only describe as tranquil and wise—always caused me to lean in a little, just to be sure I didn't miss a single word. On one occasion, I had spoken on the subject of the family and had mentioned our young children. She took great delight in watching the four of them mature, and she knew how much I loved them. "You know, Pastor Chuck," she said, "I have learned in my years dat ve must alvays hold tings loosely. Da more ve luf dese little vuns, da more ve tend to hold dem too tightly, and then it vill hurt when the Fader pries our fingers from dem and takes dem from us."

Those words, from the lips of one who had lost her own family members yet gained so much, took on more authority than I can describe. I have never forgotten Corrie's face, her eyes, her penetrating words.

Now that all of our children are adults and have their own families, I feel those words even more deeply. In the best possible way, God has taken them from us. They grew to become self-sustaining, responsible servants of Jesus Christ, each in his or her own way. As God intended from the beginning, we released each one to follow the destiny He ordained. Corrie's wise reminder frequently kept their mother and me from clinging.

Some of you reading these words did not release your children in this way. Perhaps you have lost your child through death, a terrible crime, divorce, or some other horrible tragedy. Let me be clear about this. While God is the sovereign ruler of all and nothing is beyond His power or knowledge, a horrible tragedy is *never* a cruel, merciless act on God's part. God did not find delight in making you endure such grief. Yes, as with Job, He *permitted* it, but He is not the author of evil. The evil intent of a world that has been twisted by sin took your child from you.

God hates not only sin, He also hates death. He hates it so much that He sent His Son to destroy death by dying and rising again. Death is called in the Scriptures our "last enemy" (1 Corinthians 15:26). Ultimately, the Lord will have the last word in this fight against evil, and He spoke that word to us through Jesus Christ. Put simply: *Death is the will of a world gone wrong. Resurrection is God's final triumph over evil.*

DON'T HOLD ON TOO TIGHT

Whether we lose our children by tragedy or design, this much is true: Anything we hold dear, we must learn to hold loosely. Let's face it, if we hold anything too tightly, it probably has *us* rather than our having *it*. And God will not allow that for your sake or that of your loved one.

As I ponder this principle, four distinct areas of everyday life come to mind.

Our Possessions. By possessions, I mean anything that has a price tag, material things we purchase, or things that have been passed on to us from others. This doesn't necessarily involve greed. Some of the most treasured items in our home have very little monetary value. These are items that we have received from my wife's parents, and a few from their parents.

And we have treasures from my own family legacy. None of them can be replaced. When we use the words *invaluable* and *priceless,* we can become overly attached to these possessions.

A. W. Tozer communicated profound words on the danger of holding possessions too tightly in what I consider to be his finest work, *The Pursuit of God.* Regarding "The Blessedness of Possessing Nothing," he wrote,

> Before the Lord God made man upon the earth He first prepared for him by creating a world of useful and pleasant things for his sustenance and delight. In the Genesis account of the creation these are called simply "things." They were made for man's uses, but they were meant always to be external to the man and subservient to him. In the deep heart of the man was a shrine where none but God was worthy to come. Within him was God; without, a thousand gifts which God had showered upon him.
>
> But sin has introduced complications and has made those very gifts of God a potential source of ruin to the soul.
>
> Our woes began when God was forced out of His central shrine and "things" were allowed to enter. Within the human heart "things" have taken over. . . .
>
> We must in our hearts live through Abraham's harsh and bitter experiences if we would know the blessedness which follows them. The ancient curse will not go out painlessly; the tough old miser within us will not lie down and die obedient to our command. He must be torn out of our hearts like a plant from the soil; he must be extracted in agony and blood like a tooth from the jaw. He must be expelled from our soul by violence as Christ expelled the money changers from the temple. And we shall need to steel ourselves against his piteous begging, and to recognize it as springing out of self-pity, one of the most reprehensible sins of the human heart.[1]

Tozer wrote so passionately that his words may be too dramatic for you, but you have to admit, they get your attention. If so, then perhaps it's for the best. I don't think God's stance is any less impassioned. Let's not kid ourselves about our desire to clutch "things." And let's not overlook how essential it is that we release them deliberately and consistently. Don't skip over this too quickly. Examine yourself. Be sure. We may *think* we have a proper perspective on material possessions only to find it put to the test unexpectedly—sooner than we think.

I offered this warning in a sermon, which one particular woman heard on tape. She later wrote to me about her experience. She said, "I, in fact, heard your tape that included your mentioning all that, and I thought to myself, *Aw, that will never happen to me.* I was returning to my home late one evening, and as I pulled down the street, to my amazement, I saw everything that we owned in smoldering ruins." She continued, "I later realized that everything that was important to me was not burned up in that fire. The memories, the relationships with my family and my friends, the important things in life had survived just fine." God continues to pry our fingers loose.

Our Positions. Far too many of us identify ourselves by titles and positions. I don't mean the prestige of a title. I mean the sense of identity we have through our occupation, our work. This even shows up in our language. Someone asks me, "What do you do for a living?" I answer, "I am a pastor."

Did you catch that? I *am* a pastor? He didn't ask me what I *was.* He asked what I *did!*

Each and every week, someone somewhere loses his or her job or business. And the financial problems account for only part of the stress. In fact, we can become so enmeshed in our work that the loss of a vocation becomes a loss of identity. If we have a strong sense of who we are, founded upon our relationship with God, then the loss of a job is mainly a change in our schedule and driving patterns. Little more.

Our Dreams. The death of a dream is another difficult loss to accept. Seeing the implosion of a long-awaited desire, or something you planned on and worked for during many years, can leave you reeling, feeling empty—drained of hope and direction. If you are a goal-oriented, driven person, this can feel like a loss of life purpose. Unfortunately, most dreams are either lost or must be set aside before they are fulfilled.

Dream! And I encourage you to dream big. Break out of the box and allow yourself to imagine incredible things. But as you pursue your dreams, hold them loosely.

Our Relationships. The most difficult of all things to hold loosely would be relationships, people. This includes mates, parents, children, extended family members, friends. Romances that are now flourishing may wither. Partnerships that now seem solid may fracture. Friends die. Roommates move out. Neighbors move on. Workmen and women follow callings and offers to work elsewhere. Therefore, we must hold all of our earthly relationships loosely. Yes, *all.*

Ultimately, the decision to hold anything loosely—especially as it applies to relationships—is an act of faith. Human instinct would have us clutch the things we adore most. Releasing them, presenting them to God, requires that we trust Him to do what is right. When we do this for our children, the lasting impact we leave is a practical model of faith. And I can think of no better way to teach our children about the God we worship than by modeling our trust in Him *daily.*

ABRAHAM'S TEST OF FAITH

Probably no one learned this lesson better than Abraham. As the principle patriarch of Judaism, he's hardly a forgotten life. But Genesis 22 describes an episode that many have overlooked—at least in the way we are going to view it. It's another of those fascinating stories worth remembering. This story is not about the loss of possessions, something that could be purchased, or the loss of an occupation or the loss of a dream, a long-awaited desire. This is the loss of a person, the death of a father-son relationship that was closer than words can possibly portray. And unless you are a parent, I fear you won't enter the story quite as fully as if you were. If you are a mom or a dad, you will have no trouble having empathy for Abraham.

This is the story of a father—a very old father—whose lifelong delight is his son, Isaac:

> Now it came about after these things, that God tested Abraham, and said to him, "Abraham!" And he said, "Here I am." He said, "Take now your son, your only son, whom you love, Isaac, and go to the land of Moriah, and offer him there as a burnt offering on one of the mountains of which I will tell you."
>
> GENESIS 22:1–2

By the time of this story, Abraham was well over one hundred years of age with more than a lifetime's share of faith-building experiences. God called him as a younger man to partake in a special relationship and sealed it with a covenant. As a part of that agreement, the Lord promised to build a nation with Abraham and Sarah's offspring.

God's first instruction to Abraham was to leave his native home and all his relatives for a land that He would reveal later. By the time of this episode in Genesis 22, the patriarch had faced pharaohs in Egypt, Philistine kings, invading armies from the East, and the vile depravity of Sodom and Gomorrah. Through every trial and triumph, Abraham and his wife remained childless. They surely must have wondered when God would grant them a son. After all, the covenant depended upon it. Still, no son.

Abraham and Sarah heard her biological clock ticking and decided to give God some help with their own homemade plan. At Sarah's request, Abraham conceived a child with her handmaid, which caused far more harm than good. It was a faithless act. God denounced it as sin. This test, Abraham failed. Still, no son.

THE CHILD OF PROMISE

Then, many years after Sarah had lost her ability to bear children, she conceived. Even in her old age, she found herself pregnant with Abraham's child. Nine months later, she bore a son, whom they named Isaac, which means, "he laughs." When the Lord told Abraham that Sarah would bear him a son in her advanced years, he fell on his face laughing. Later, when the Lord announced that she would give birth at the age of ninety, Sarah couldn't suppress her giggle. I imagine it was a combination of disbelief and delight. Pregnant at ninety? This would take a miracle. The Lord wasn't laughing or kidding as He responded, "Is anything too difficult for the LORD?" (Genesis 18:14).

When Sarah gave birth to her son, she looked upon the fulfillment of her long-awaited promise and said, "God has made laughter for me; everyone who hears will laugh with me" (Genesis 21:6). For Abraham, Isaac became the symbol of everything God had pledged to him in the covenant. The land of Canaan—the Promised Land—would be filled with his descendants, who would grow to become a great nation. All of God's promises, all of the Lord's blessing, would come to Abraham and his descendants through this promised son, Isaac. He adored that boy.

THE TEST

> Now it came about after these things, that God tested Abraham and said to him, "Abraham!" And he said, "Here I am." And He said, "Take now your son, your only son, whom you love, Isaac, and go to the land of Moriah; and offer him there as a burnt offering on one of the mountains of which I will tell you."
>
> GENESIS 22:1–2

As an aged father, Abraham took increasingly more delight in his long-awaited boy. (Older parents seem to enjoy their children so much more than younger ones.) So the words "God tested Abraham" take on a whole new dimension for us as we read the account. Suddenly, the Lord stepped in and commanded this kind, gentle, aging father to put his only son to death on an altar. It was bad enough to hear that Isaac was to die, but it must have seemed beyond belief for the father to hear that he was to do the killing.

Why? Why would a good and loving God ask an obedient and faithful man to do this? The answer can be found in the original language of Moses, the inspired, human author of Genesis. The Hebrew word *nasah*, translated "tested" in Genesis 22:1, has the idea of proving the quality of something, usually by putting it through a trial of some kind. God wanted to prove the validity—the authenticity—of Abraham's faith.

Remember, though, that God is omniscient. He knows all things, including the future. He knew the heart of Abraham better than Abraham did. The purpose of the test was not to satisfy God's curiosity. This was not an experiment. The appointed patch of ground at the top of a lonely mountain in the land of Moriah was to be Abraham's proving ground. This would be the time and place where any question about his faltering faith—so evident in his lying (twice) to save his skin and his pathetic attempt to fulfill the covenant through his wife's handmaid—would be put to rest. His family would see his faith, his friends would see it, we would see it by virtue of this record, and probably most important of all, Isaac would see it. If ever faith would be put on display, this would be the day.

The issue in question: did Abraham love the *gift* of God or God Himself?

Allow me to put Abraham's test on hold and rush into the twenty-first century. This has to be one of the toughest questions any parent has to consider: *Do I adore the gifts God gives me more than I adore the Giver? Have I begun to worship the relationships that God has granted me rather than the One who gave me these delights?*

Don't be too quick to answer.

The word *worship* comes from an Anglo-Saxon term meaning "worthship." When we worship something, we are affirming its value to us. We do that with our actions as well as with our hearts. A parent must ask, *Do I assign more worth to my child than I do my God?* To answer that question, follow the trail of your sacrifices. Tally the results. Be painfully honest now. For whom do you sacrifice more—or more often?

God's instructions to Abraham included the words "burnt offering." This means a *whole* burnt offering. The Hebrew term *olah* refers to putting the entire animal on the altar—hoof, tail, head, ears, horns, carcass—*all of it*. With other types of sacrifice the worshiper was to eat a part of the offering as if to partake in the ceremony with God. But the *olah* offering was to be entirely consumed by the fire before Him. It obviously signifies a complete sacrifice. That's the word used by God. He says, in effect, "I want the entire body of this young man placed on the altar and released back to Me."

Pause. Ponder. Try hard to imagine hearing that command.

I can't help but be impressed with this father's swift obedience. The speed of Abraham's reaction is absolutely remarkable. He offers no argument. There is no delay, no hesitation, no bargaining, not even a question or a hint of reluctance:

> So Abraham rose early in the morning and saddled his donkey, and
> took two of his young men with him and Isaac his son; and he split

wood for the burnt offering, and arose and went to the place of which God had told him.

GENESIS 22:3

This does not suggest that Abraham's response was glib. I am confident that the night was a sleepless one. The anguish he endured must have been overwhelming. Yet we see a certain resignation in his actions. He held nothing back. No hesitation. He rose early, prepared the supplies, got Isaac out of bed before dawn, and started the journey.

I'm also impressed with this dad's simple, trusting faith. Notice what we don't read. We don't see any fanfare or a giant farewell party or even a last-meal meaningful ceremony. Just simple obedience to God's command carried out in silence. Incredible maturity.

> On the third day Abraham raised his eyes and saw the place from a distance. Abraham said to his young men, "Stay here with the donkey, and I and the lad will go over there; and we will worship and return to you."

GENESIS 22:4–5

I had to read this passage several times before I saw Abraham's clearly implied statement of faith. His words and his demeanor are so understated, so matter-of-fact, that it's easy to miss the drama of this scene. If I were about to sacrifice my only son, who embodied all the promises that God had ever made to me, I would have been overcome with emotion. "I don't understand why God is making me do this, but I will do as He says. So I'm going up that mountain to sacrifice my son on that altar, then I'm going home to mourn this terrible loss for the rest of my life!"

But not Abraham. Notice the calm assurance. In this case, the New International Version renders the Hebrew best: *"We* will worship and then *we* will come back to you." See the repeated plural pronoun? In the original language, there is no room for doubt; Abraham clearly expected to return home with Isaac. How could he have known that? Hebrews 11:17–19 gives us the answer:

41

By faith Abraham, when he was tested, offered up Isaac, and he who had received the promises was offering up his only begotten son; it was he to whom it was said, "In Isaac your descendants shall be called." *He considered that God is able to raise people even from the dead,* from which he also received him back as a type. (emphasis added)

GENUINE FAITH

According to the book of Hebrews, Abraham knew three important facts. First, Isaac was to be the vehicle of God's promises; therefore, Isaac must live. Second, God always keeps His promises. Third, God's power is absolute, even over the power of death. The only logical conclusion that remained was that somehow, against all natural reason, after killing Isaac and allowing the fire to completely consume him, God would miraculously restore the life of Isaac—the boy he dearly loved.

Oswald Chambers, in his eminent work *My Utmost for His Highest,* writes about reckless abandonment to the character of God:

Faith is the heroic effort of your life. You fling yourself in reckless confidence on God.

God has ventured all in Jesus Christ to save us, now He wants us to venture our all in abandoned confidence in Him. . . . The real meaning of eternal life is a life that can face anything it has to face without wavering.

Again and again you will get up to what Jesus Christ wants, and every time you will turn back when it comes to the point, until you abandon resolutely. "Yes, but supposing I do obey God in this matter, what about . . . ?" "Yes, I will obey God if He will let me use my common sense, but don't ask me to take a step in the dark." . . . If a man is going to do anything worthwhile, there are times when he has to risk everything on his leap, and in the spiritual domain Jesus Christ demands that you risk everything you hold by common sense and leap into what He says. . . . Trust entirely in God, and when He brings you to the venture, see that you take it. We act like pagans in a crisis, only one out of a crowd is daring enough to bank his faith in the character of God.[2]

This is exactly what Abraham did. What a model of faith he had become! Don't miss his rapid response, his unrestrained follow-through, his simple faith:

> Abraham took the wood of the burnt offering and laid it on Isaac his son, and he took in his hand the fire and the knife. So the two of them walked on together.
>
> GENESIS 22:6

When I was a boy in Sunday school, I remember seeing framed pictures of this story. Invariably, Isaac was a little boy scampering beside his daddy as the old man trudged up the hill. But a little boy wouldn't be able to carry enough wood to burn an offering. Isaac was no little boy. Isaac was half grown, a young adult, old enough to converse with his father, understand the significance of the ritual, and carry the load of heavy firewood.

Read the next verses slowly, and again release your imagination. Try to envision this very touching moment between this elderly father and his nearly adult son. The New English Translation captures the emotion best while preserving the most literal translation of the Hebrew text:

> Isaac said to his father Abraham, "My father?" "What is it, my son?" he replied. "Here is the fire and the wood," Isaac said, "but where is the lamb for the burnt offering?" "God will provide for himself the lamb for the burnt offering, my son," Abraham replied. The two of them continued on together.
>
> GENESIS 22:7–8

Obviously, Abraham didn't tell Isaac everything he knew about what was to happen on the mountain. We can't be sure why he withheld that information. Maybe to spare his son unnecessary fear or dread. We don't know. But I do know that when God does a transforming work in you that involves a trial, He's not testing other people; He's testing you. Because this experience is designed for you, it isn't necessarily required or even appropriate for you to share the whole story with everyone else. Or, for that matter, with anyone else. Occasionally, strength is mustered in keeping it to ourselves . . . completely.

Isaac finally asked the obvious question. They have a knife, wood, and fire for the sacrifice. "Where is the sacrifice?" I love Abraham's answer. "God will provide." The Hebrew uses an idiom that sounds just like something a dad would say today. "The Lord will see to that for Himself, Son. Can you hear his calm, reassuring tone? "God will provide for Himself. That's up to Him. We're doing His will. It's up to Him to work out the details He didn't give to us. Our responsibility is to trust Him. This is a risk we will share together."

FAITH INVOLVES RISK

A life without risk is not much of a life. Eileen Guder writes this observation in her book *God, But I'm Bored:*

> You can live on bland food so as to avoid an ulcer; drink no tea or
> coffee or other stimulants, in the name of health; go to bed early and
> stay away from night life; avoid all controversial subjects so as never to
> give offense; mind your own business and avoid involvement in other
> people's problems; spend money only on necessities and save all you
> can. Yes, and you can break your neck in the bathtub, and it'll serve
> you right.[3]

Some people live so carefully they absolutely refuse to take risks. Everything has to be carefully regulated and kept under control . . . *their* control. Borders defined, guidelines spelled out, every dime accounted for, no surprises. And after having expended so much time and effort trying to live safely, they end life never having accomplished anything of lasting value. They built nothing, tried nothing new, invested in no one.

Not Abraham! His faith had matured to the point that his absolute confidence in God's character gave him the freedom to throw caution to the wind and risk everything to obey. What a perfect lesson in theology for his son.

Now, Abraham didn't raise a fool for a son. Isaac could piece all the clues together. He does that as the story continues. We read that they came to the place of which God had told him. Abraham built the altar there, arranged the wood, and then began to search everywhere for his son for he had run away and hidden from his father.

No! Isaac didn't run or fight or plead or complain or wrestle with his dad to stay off the altar. Look at the remarkable faith and courage of Isaac:

> Then they came to the place of which God had told him; and Abraham
> built the altar there and arranged the wood, and bound his son Isaac
> and laid him on the altar, on top of the wood.
>
> GENESIS 22:9

I've heard this passage preached countless times, and I've never heard anyone talk about the quiet faith of this remarkable young man. He's the sacrifice, yet he allowed himself to be bound up and placed onto that altar! Obviously, this son learned his theology well from his father—a father who released his son because he completely trusted his God. By the way, Isaac didn't learn such faith on his way up the mountain that morning. He'd been cultivating it over the years, thanks to his father who modeled it often.

RELEASE WHAT GRIPS YOU

Some of you parents may find yourselves in a similar situation as you read these pages. Your relationship with your child may have reached a point where you have no other choice but to commit him or her completely to God's care. You would love to work out the details, but you cannot. You know the Lord is good, and you have prayed for a resolution, but nothing has changed. Only God can intervene. And because that is true, you can take your cues from Abraham.

Place your relationship with that son or daughter on the altar today. Surrender him or her to the Lord as an offering. Take this risk. Mentally place your boy or girl on top of the wood and step back from the altar. Trust God. In His time, He will provide.

I write this as a father, so I know from personal experience how difficult this is. Even though my children are grown and are on their own, I still long to protect them. I want to shield them from every difficulty. I don't want my sons and daughters to endure pain. I don't want them to suffer hardship. I don't want them to know mistreatment. I don't want them ever to lose a job or be subject to injustice or get sick or be injured or . . .

I'm still learning. I'm learning, as a father, to give my children to God and trust Him to provide. As Corrie reminded me, I must loosen my grip. I must allow Him to become the Father that they will need when I'm no longer on the earth. After all, they are His children first. I must confess, however, it is much easier to write these words than to carry them out!

Finally, the moment arrived: "Abraham stretched out his hand and took the knife to slay his son" (GENESIS 22:10).

This isn't a movie. As far as Abraham was concerned, the drama didn't have a surprise ending. The knife goes up in order to bring it down into his son's chest or across his throat, and what will happen next is the death of his boy. This is real! This is faith in the wild where the stakes are incredibly high—life and death!

Suddenly, at the last possible moment, God intervened:

> But the angel of the LORD called to him from heaven and said, "Abraham, Abraham!" And he said, "Here I am." He said, "Do not stretch out your hand against the lad, and do nothing to him; for now I know that you fear God, since you have not withheld your son, your only son, from Me."
>
> GENESIS 22:11–12

I believe it is safe to say that Isaac was relieved at this point. But not more than Abraham.

As the Lord stopped Abraham's hand midplunge, He said, in effect, "You've passed the test, my faithful friend. You've proven to Me who is first, My aging son. You have also proven that your faith has reached full maturity. Your willingness to give up your only son has demonstrated that while you love the gift, you love the Giver more."

> Then Abraham raised his eyes and looked, and behold, behind him a ram caught in the thicket by his horns; and Abraham went and took the ram and offered him up for a burnt offering in the place of his son. Abraham called the name of that place The LORD Will Provide, as it is said to this day, "In the mount of the LORD it will be provided."
>
> GENESIS 22:13–14

After this, hundreds of years and ancient sands have covered the site. However, this very mountaintop would one day accommodate a city and a temple. It would become the capital of God's covenant kingdom and His house of worship until, finally, it would be the place where Christ, the King and consummate sacrifice, would die. Moriah, Jerusalem, the place where another Father held His Son loosely, laid Him on an altar, and sacrificed Him for us. On this mountain in the region of Moriah—a place renamed "The Lord will provide"—a lamb became Isaac's substitute and Christ became ours.

ABRAHAM'S FAITH REVEALS GOD

In this fascinating story of faith and sacrifice and trust and surrender, I see the characteristics of a God who asked nothing of Abraham that He didn't demand of Himself. Because it is so significant, I cannot resist sharing with you three powerful truths about our God that I see illustrated here.

First, *God the Father showed us how to live when He released His dear Son to us.* Nine months before that wondrous night in Bethlehem, the Father sent His Son. Christ willingly left His seat of absolute power in heaven, set aside the voluntary use of His divine authority, and became a helpless infant. As a human, subject to all the pains and sorrows and limitations that affect us all, He would mature, learn, minister, suffer . . . and die. If the Father was willing to release His own Son to us, what could be so much more precious to us that we would withhold it from Him?

Second, *God the Son showed us how to die when He released Himself to the Father.* Isaac's quiet obedience to his father illustrates this beautifully. He gave himself over to the will of his father and allowed himself to be placed on an altar without a fight. That's exactly what the Son of God did at Calvary. When our faith is mature, we'll not fear death.

Third, *God the Spirit will show us how to live and die as we learn how to release whatever has us in its grip.* (That last phrase wasn't a mistake.) As long as we're owned by whatever we're clutching, we'll never be given over completely to the Holy Spirit. This would be an excellent moment for you to do some self-analysis. To what, to whom are you clinging? Let it go. Let them go.

A FINAL APPLICATION

Let me press all of this even further. What is it that you are gripping so tightly? A possession? Your vocation? A dream? A consuming relationship?

The Lord may be in the process of taking it from you. He'll gently tug on it at first, giving you the opportunity to release your grip. If you resist, He'll eventually have to pry your fingers away, and I can assure you that it will hurt. My advice? Voluntarily release it. Trust the Lord to provide. He has another ram in the thicket. You can't see it right now, but He has it waiting. Only after you have placed your sacrifice on the altar will you be ready to receive God's provision.

Abraham taught his son well that day so many thousands of years ago. His anguished act of complete faith demonstrated to all—especially to Isaac—that God was his God. I often wonder how the relationship changed after that. I feel sure that Abraham enjoyed his son far more coming down the mountain than he did going up. Not just because he came so close to losing him, but because his releasing Isaac gave Abraham the freedom to love him even more. The impact this had on Isaac must have been equally profound.

The best way to end this chapter is with a prayer. Not mine, but A. W. Tozer's. Read his words slowly and thoughtfully. Pause as each sentence ends and think about what you've just read:

Father, I want to know Thee, but my coward heart fears to give up its toys. I cannot part with them without inward bleeding, and I do not try to hide from Thee the terror of the parting. I come trembling, but I do come. Please root from my heart all those things which I have cherished so long and which have become a very part of my living self, so that Thou mayest enter and dwell there without a rival. Then shalt Thou make the place of Thy feet glorious. Then shall my heart have no need of the sun to shine in it, for Thyself wilt be the light of it, and there shall be no night there. In Jesus' Name, Amen.[4]

Amen, indeed.

CHAPTER FOUR

Esau: the Son Who Couldn't Win

Calling Esau "the son who couldn't win" makes me sad. No matter what, he couldn't pull it off. I have a strong feeling that many who read these words will have little difficulty identifying with Esau and many of his struggles. On the surface, he must have felt like a pawn of fate, who had no luck but bad luck and no choices but bad choices. Everywhere he turned, he got the raw end of the deal. No matter what he did, he simply couldn't make life work.

In truth, life does seem to favor some over others. Babies are born every day into rich families as well as poor ones. Much more significantly, some grow up in the nurturing care of sensitive, loving, involved parents, while others merely hope to survive the horrors of their home life. Even within families, unwise parents will dote on one child, showering her with encouragement and one gift after another, while keeping the other child perpetually under a dark cloud of suspicion and neglect. They see only the successes of one and only the failures of the other.

Let's face it: life is often very unfair. If we accept this at face value, then the question becomes, how should we respond? Is there any justifiable excuse for making poor choices?

Being the son who couldn't win, Esau was born with the deck stacked against him—at least in terms of the role he was to play in history. As we examine his life, we'll see that his response to the sovereign choice of God, plus the actions of those around him, would determine whether the man's destiny would be happy or bitter.

I should openly state from the outset that my purpose is not to look at Esau's life theologically. [I'm aware of Paul's use of Esau as an illustration in his letter to the Romans (9:10–13). And I don't discount the illustration drawn by the author of Hebrews, who characterized the actions of "an immoral godless person" by Esau's choice (12:16). My purpose is broader, more horizontal]. It will help us understand the man as a human being instead of seeing him as a soulless, insignificant puppet dangling from theological strings.

ESAU'S PLACE IN THE GRAND SCHEME

The story in the Bible starts with Esau's genealogy. From this record, we learn that Abraham and Sarah gave birth to Isaac, who married Rebekah. Isaac and Rebekah, in turn, conceived a set of twin boys. Of course, Rebekah had no way of knowing this. All she knew was that the pregnancy had become very difficult. The reason would prove to be a foreshadowing of conflicting things to come:

> Isaac prayed to the LORD on behalf of his wife, because she was barren;
> and the LORD answered him and Rebekah his wife conceived. But the
> children struggled together within her; and she said, "If it is so, why
> then am I this way?" So she went to inquire of the LORD.
>
> GENESIS 25:21–22

Some mysteries can be sensed by a mother when no one else has a clue. Rebekah felt the wrestling in her womb, so she inquired of the Lord. His response was, in effect, "You don't merely have two children; you have the beginnings of two nations in your womb. And they will always be at each others' throats." True to His word, this was the beginning of a struggle that would persist for centuries, even until the time of Christ . . . and far beyond. Herod the Great was Idumean, a descendant of Esau.

The LORD said to her,

> "Two nations are in your womb;
> And two peoples will be separated from your body;
> And one people shall be stronger than the other;
> And the older shall serve the younger."
>
> GENESIS 25:23

Here we find sufficient proof that from the time of conception, a mother has life within her womb. Moreover, God's design and purpose for each individual life begins at conception if not before. God's word to Rebekah: "These will not be simply two children; they will be nations. Each nation, and the child who heads it, has a role in the future I want to create."

In this case, the Lord's plan would have the younger child become the father of His covenant people. *How* that was to come about, easy or difficult, would be determined by the choices and actions of the people involved:

> Now the first came forth red, all over like a hairy garment; and they named him Esau. Afterward his brother came forth with his hand holding on to Esau's heel, so his name was called Jacob; and Isaac was sixty years old when she gave birth to them. When the boys grew up, Esau became a skillful hunter, a man of the field, but Jacob was a peaceful man, living in tents.
>
> GENESIS 25:25–27

PARENTAL FAVORITISM AND DIVIDED DESTINIES

If we look at this only through a narrow theological lens, we'll miss the humanity of this story. Have you ever imagined being sixty years of age and the father of twins? Probably not. Some people pray for twins. I didn't. I was very glad that we had our children one at a time. Some people do very well with twins, demonstrating great patience and unusual strength. Isaac and Rebekah waited and prayed for their children for most of their lives. So you can imagine the hopes they must have had. No doubt, they hoped for harmony, but the boys turned out to be absolute opposites from the day of their birth.

One morning Cynthia and I decided we would take all five of our little grandchildren to breakfast. (That was a few years ago. We have ten now. Needless to say, we'll think carefully before planning that kind of fun again.) So we called both sets of parents the evening before and told them what we wanted to do. Interestingly, they both asked, "Are you sure you know what you're getting yourselves into?" Our response was a quick and casual, "Sure. It'll be great!"

So we picked them up, got them all situated in the car—some in car seats, others in seatbelts—and we drove to the local pancake house, where we began the process of unloading. There we were, two adults and five pint-sized bundles of barely contained energy in constant motion, squeezed into tiny bodies all ready to rock and roll. That restaurant had no idea what they had coming. I'll never forget the face of the gentleman sitting at the table next to us. All he wanted was a lovely, quiet breakfast with his wife. When we asked for three booster chairs and two high chairs, he was frowning, knowing his dream for serenity had been shattered. By the end of breakfast, I think Cynthia ate four bites of food in-between serving the five kids, and every bite was cold.

Something I noticed during our time (we enjoyed every minute of it by the way) was how different each grandchild is. On the one hand, that didn't surprise me. It's been a core principle in our approach to rearing our children that "each should be trained in the way he or she should go" (Proverbs 22:6 NET). On the other hand, I never cease to smile when I see this principle in action.

We could place one of our grandchildren in a high chair, and he was happy to sit there for an hour. Give him crackers to crunch up and shove down his shirt or smear in his hair, and he was completely content. Putting his sister in a highchair was like trying to shampoo a cat in the kitchen sink. One boy couldn't choke down enough food (he wound up eating two orders), while his brother turned his nose up at everything. Same parents, same household, very different little people. That same statement would apply to twins.

Esau was totally different from Jacob. Understand, there is not a thing wrong with that. That's the way God made them. But the next verse reveals a very serious problem that emerged from their parents:

> Now Isaac loved Esau, because he had a taste for game, but Rebekah loved Jacob.
>
> GENESIS 25:28

Each parent chose a favorite, basing the choice on personal affinity. In the language and culture of the Bible, *love* and *hate* are words that have a different connotation than in our Western, English-speaking culture. When someone is said to love something, there is an implied comparison. If you were to say, "Alice loves Peter," an ancient, Eastern listener would be thinking, *More than whom?* Moreover, it also carries the idea of action, showing kindness. So the statement, "Alice loves Peter" to the Eastern mind would suggest that she loves him more than she does anyone else, and she has been showing exclusive, special favor to him.

The same works for the word *hate,* only opposite. If you compare two things and prefer one over the other, you are said to love one and hate the other.

So the phrase "Isaac loved Esau" doesn't mean that Isaac never demonstrated genuine, fatherly love to Jacob. Nor does it imply that Isaac was unkind or abusive. Isaac did, however, play favorites—both parents did. Their dad was probably the manly, outdoors type who shared his love of hunting and the taste of wild game with both boys, and Esau took to it. Naturally, we would say that Esau was a man's man. He was rugged. Isaac liked the way Esau conducted himself. He may have even admired qualities in his favorite boy that he, himself lacked. Rebekah, on the other hand, favored Jacob. He stayed near the tent. Maybe he liked to cook. He'd rather be doing things at home, in comfort, than sleeping in the field.

I've often heard Jacob described as what we used to call a mama's boy. Someone a little on the genteel side, perhaps a little effeminate. That always seemed too extreme to me since it didn't fit with the rest of his story as it unfolds in Scripture. The Hebrew word translated "peaceful" in verse 27 literally means complete, blameless, or innocent. Based on my study of the term, I would choose the word *civilized*. Another word that comes to mind is *cultured*.

Two very different boys grew into manhood. In doing so, two realities emerged. First, the men were very opposite in their temperaments. Second, Jacob was not a sissy, but a normal man by the standards of his day. He was a cultured, even-tempered, civilized man with clean fingernails. Esau was a study in contrast. He was unusually rugged, independent, and passionate. He smelled like the countryside where he preferred to live. Jacob lived by his wits; Esau lived by his gut instinct. Jacob became shrewd; Esau remained gullible. Jacob thought strategically, Esau impulsively. You've got the picture.

CHOICES AND DESTINY

Let's understand that while the brothers were very different, being different doesn't mean one was better than the other. The underlying problem with this situation was parental favoritism, which haunted Esau for the balance of his life. This favoritism put their natural inclinations at odds. As you read the unfolding story, take note of how their personalities influenced their decisions, and how their decisions determined their future:

> When Jacob had cooked stew, Esau came in from the field and he was famished; and Esau said to Jacob, "Please let me have a swallow of that red stuff there, for I am famished." Therefore his name was called Edom. But Jacob said, "First sell me your birthright." Esau said, "Behold, I am about to die; so of what use then is the birthright to me?" And Jacob said, "First swear to me"; so he swore to him, and sold his birthright to Jacob. Then Jacob gave Esau bread and lentil stew; and he ate and drank, and rose and went on his way. Thus Esau despised his birthright.
>
> —GENESIS 25:29–34

The birthright doesn't mean much in our modern, Western, Gentile culture. But in that day, to those people, it involved every aspect of family life. The birthright bore incredible significance. James Hastings, one of the reliable early biographers of biblical characters, makes several statements about the value of a birthright:

> To the birthright belonged pre-eminence over the other branches of the family. To the birthright appertained a double portion of the paternal inheritance. To the birthright was attached the land of Canaan, with all its sacred distinctions. To the birthright was given the promise of being the ancestor of the Messiah—the "firstborn among many brethren"—the Saviour in whom all the families of the earth were to be blessed. And to the birthright was added the honor of receiving first, from the mouth of the father, a peculiar benediction, which proceeding from the spirit of prophecy, was never pronounced in vain. Such were the prospects of Esau.[1]

In a hurried and thoughtless moment of hunger, Esau shrugged off his birthright, including all of the rights and blessings that went with it, for a bowl of soup. Esau's impulsiveness made him susceptible to the allure of instant gratification. In that split-second decision, he sated his immediate hunger at the expense of his entire future. In the deal of a lifetime, he emerged the loser. Horrible decision!

Some would say that Jacob deceived his brother in order to strip him of the birthright. But I don't see much deception here. Later, yes . . . without a doubt. But this was completely up-front and out in the open. Admittedly, Jacob was shrewd. He was manipulative and an opportunist. He took advantage of Esau's weakness, but he didn't lie. This was a straight-up offer for a trade with the terms spelled out clearly. Nothing was hidden from Esau.

The point of this episode is not to show that Jacob was a swindler, but that Esau was of such a mind as to despise something significant for the fleeting satisfaction of his physical needs. Spiritual priorities weren't nearly as important to Esau as physical comforts. Intangibles meant little to him. Stupidly, he saw only the need of the moment, and that was to fill his stomach. Perhaps that's why Hebrews 12:16 (KJV) refers to Esau as a "profane" man.

PARENTAL NEGLECT AND DESTINY

I'm tempted to jump forward to the rest of the story, but we have an opportunity to slow down for a reality check. Rather than simply go through the story, let's pause long enough for this much of the story go through us. God preserved these fascinating stories to provide instruction, so look for similarities between your experience and those of Scripture.

You may have a child with some disquieting traits like those of Esau or Jacob. What we are witnessing at the end of Genesis 25 is fruit of a sinful nature unchecked by parental guidance and constructive confrontation. Both parents were apparently out of touch with how serious the conflict between these two young men had become. We have no evidence from the biblical narrative to suggest that the parents knew anything about the trade. At least not at this point.

The focus of the story shifts back to Isaac and his expanding wealth over a long period of years. The next words about Esau only confirm that the distance between Esau and his parents had grown into a yawning chasm. After the story of Isaac's success and before describing the closing scenes of his life, Moses inserts these sentences:

> When Esau was forty years old he married Judith the daughter of Beeri the Hittite, and Basemath the daughter of Elon the Hittite; and they brought grief to Isaac and Rebekah.
>
> — GENESIS 26:34–35

When Abraham sent servants to find a wife for his son, Isaac, he issued strict instructions to avoid Canaanite women (Genesis 24:3). I cannot imagine why Isaac didn't take as much care to counsel his son. He apparently left Esau on his own to search for his own wife. And with little or no guidance, he searched among forbidden societies; he then shocked his mom and dad by returning with not one, but two Canaanite wives. What was he thinking? Wasn't he aware of how shocking that would be?

Again, Esau just cannot win.

The Sinful Path to God's Plan

Chapter 27 is clearly the most significant chapter in the story of this son who couldn't win. I want to observe carefully four scenes as they unfold and give special attention to Esau's character. We'll revisit them in the order they appear in the biblical text.

Scene 1.

> Now it came about, when Isaac was old and his eyes were too dim to see, that he called his older son Esau and said to him, "My son." And he said to him, "Here I am." Isaac said, "Behold now, I am old and I do not know the day of my death. Now then, please take your gear, your quiver and your bow, and go out to the field and hunt game for me; and prepare a savory dish for me such as I love, and bring it to me that I may eat, so that my soul may bless you before I die."
>
> Genesis 27:1–4

Evidently, the father knows nothing about the earlier trade. It's only natural that Isaac should bless Esau as the elder son and pass the torch to him. Although one has to wonder if he had forgotten the prophecy that God spoke to Rebekah earlier. Remember? "The LORD said to her, 'Two nations are in your womb; and two peoples will be separated from your body; and one people shall be stronger than the other; and the older shall serve the younger'" (Genesis 25:23). Surely she told him about it. Did he forget? Some husbands tend to forget what their wives tell them. After all, it's been more than forty years. Did he choose to ignore it? Impossible to say. But Rebekah didn't forget.

The difficulty with allowing this story to unfold on its own is that we know that God's plan was for Jacob to inherit the blessing and become the father of the covenant people. Yet in all candor, *how* this came about can make one wonder about the goodness and justice of God. Recognizing an important distinction will help. While God ordained the destiny, the people who were involved chose a sinful path to that destiny. And they suffered unnecessarily. They just as easily could have chosen a peaceful, obedient path and enjoyed God's favor along the way.

Unfortunately, they didn't. The consequences dogged their steps. The next scene uncovers a multitude of twisted family relationships.

Scene 2.

> Rebekah was listening while Isaac spoke to his son Esau. So when Esau went to the field to hunt for game to bring home, Rebekah said to her son Jacob, "Behold, I heard your father speak to your brother Esau, saying, 'Bring me some game and prepare a savory dish for me, that I may eat, and bless you in the presence of the LORD before my death.' Now therefore, my son, listen to me as I command you. Go now to the flock and bring me two choice young goats from there, that I may prepare them as a savory dish for your father, such as he loves. Then you shall bring it to your father, that he may eat, so that he may bless you before his death." Jacob answered his mother Rebekah, "Behold, Esau my brother is a hairy man and I am a smooth man. Perhaps my father will feel me, then I will be as a deceiver in his sight, and I will bring upon myself a curse and not a blessing." But his mother said to him, "Your curse be on me, my son; only obey my voice, and go, get them for me." So he went and got them, and brought them to his mother; and his mother made savory food such as his father loved. Then Rebekah took the best garments of Esau her elder son, which were with her in the house, and put them on Jacob her younger son. And she put the skins of the young goats on his hands and on the smooth part of his neck. She also gave the savory food and the bread, which she had made, to her son Jacob.
>
> —GENESIS 27:5–17

Our focus is on Esau, so I will only make a couple of observations here. Take note of the conniving spirit Esau had working against him . . . in his own mother! I can't imagine what it must feel like to have your mother—the person who labored to give you life—deliberately betray you and participate in cheating you out of your future. Observe also Jacob's response. Did his conscience slow him down? Did his integrity have him question the plan? No, only fear. Sheer self-preservation.

Esau was in for the shock of his life. He had no idea what he was up against. The next scene reveals that Jacob mastered the craft of deceit, which he learned from his mother.

Scene 3.

> Then he [Jacob] came to his father and said, "My father." And he said, "Here I am. Who are you, my son?" Jacob said to his father, "I am Esau your firstborn; I have done as you told me. Get up, please, sit and eat of my game, that you may bless me."
>
> GENESIS 27:18–19

Now we see Jacob for the deceiver that he was:

> Isaac said to his son, "How is it that you have it so quickly, my son?" And he said, "Because the LORD your God caused it to happen to me."
>
> GENESIS 27:20

We see now how morally hollow Jacob had become. His complete comfort in telling lies had become such a natural part of his thinking and speech that he thought nothing of involving God in his deception. Additionally, he knew the precise words and phrases to appear genuine in his relationship with the Lord. Obviously, he had plenty of practice pretending to be someone he was not, so posing as Esau didn't present much of a challenge:

> Then Isaac said to Jacob, "Please come close, that I may feel you, my son, whether you are really my son Esau or not." So Jacob came close to Isaac his father, and he felt him and said, "The voice is the voice of Jacob, but the hands are the hands of Esau." He did not recognize him, because his hands were hairy like his brother Esau's hands; so he blessed him. And he said, "Are you really my son Esau?" And he said, "I am."
>
> GENESIS 27:21–24

My, Isaac is a suspicious father, isn't he? He questioned, then felt, then questioned again. Could it be that he knew Jacob's tendency to deceive? It makes you wonder if this wasn't the first time that Rebekah and Jacob had pulled one over on the aging, sightless Isaac.

Never underestimate the impact of your character on your children.

> So he said, "Bring it to me, and I will eat of my son's game, that I may bless you." And he brought it to him, and he ate; he also brought him wine and he drank. Then his father Isaac said to him, "Please come close and kiss me, my son." So he came close and kissed him; and when he smelled the smell of his garments, he blessed him and said,
>
> > "See, the smell of my son
> > Is like the smell of a field which the LORD has blessed."
>
> GENESIS 27:25–27

I'm still amazed by the care Isaac felt he must take to be sure of his son's identity. His ears and hands had been fooled, so he used his nose. But Rebekah had even prepared Jacob for that possibility. Having become the mistress of deceit, she knew all the ropes. And old Isaac, having been completely duped, proceeded with the blessing:

> Now may God give you of the dew of heaven,
> And of the fatness of the earth,
> And an abundance of grain and new wine;
> May peoples serve you,
> And nations bow down to you;
> Be master of your brothers,
> And may your mother's sons bow down to you.
> Cursed be those who curse you,
> And blessed be those who bless you.
>
> GENESIS 27:28–29

Scene 4.

In this final, sad scene, Esau fully comprehends that he cannot escape the Lord's sovereign design. His earlier impulsive choice, his conniving mother and brother, and now his passive father have sealed it for him. This fourth scene is downright tragic:

> Now it came about, as soon as Isaac had finished blessing Jacob, and Jacob had hardly gone out from the presence of Isaac his father, that Esau his brother came in from his hunting. Then he also made savory food, and brought it to his father; and he said to his father, "Let my father arise and eat of his son's game, that you may bless me." Isaac his father said to him, "Who are you?" And he said, "I am your son, your firstborn, Esau." Then Isaac trembled violently, and said, "Who was he then that hunted game and brought it to me, so that I ate of all of it before you came, and blessed him? Yes, and he shall be blessed." When Esau heard the words of his father, he cried out with an exceedingly great and bitter cry, and said to his father, "Bless me, even me also, O my father!" And he said, "Your brother came deceitfully and has taken away your blessing." Then he said, "Is he not rightly named Jacob, for he has supplanted me these two times? He took away my birthright, and behold, now he has taken away my blessing." And he said, "Have you not reserved a blessing for me?" But Isaac replied to Esau, "Behold, I have made him your master, and all his relatives I have given to him as servants; and with grain and new wine I have sustained him. Now as for you then, what can I do, my son?" Esau said to his father, "Do you have only one blessing, my father? Bless me, even me also, O my father." So Esau lifted his voice and wept.
>
>   Then Isaac his father answered and said to him,
> "Behold, away from the fertility of the earth shall be your dwelling,
> And away from the dew of heaven from above.
> By your sword you shall live,
> And your brother you shall serve;
> But it shall come about when you become restless,
> That you will break his yoke from your neck."
>
> GENESIS 27:30–40

OBEDIENCE AND DESTINY

Hold on here! Let's not leave too quickly. Don't overlook this exquisite blend of pathos and tragedy mixed with irresponsibility and deception. Yes, Esau got what he had coming. He had stupidly swapped his birthright for a bowl of soup. But how unjustly it was taken. So his bitter reaction is understandable as he muttered through clenched teeth, "My dad will be dead soon. And when he's gone, I'll repay Jacob for the evil he did me." Anyone who has been deceived and betrayed has no trouble understanding such anger. As I mentioned earlier, it has become murderous.

Remember the prophecy that had been made to the mother before she even gave birth? "Two nations are in your womb; they will be separated from one another . . . and the older shall serve the younger" (Genesis 25:23). With this last scene, the predicted outcome became unavoidable. In the fight for the covenant blessing, once again, Esau couldn't win.

As I read this whole story several times in preparation for this chapter, I couldn't help but ask myself a hard question: was there another way for God's plan to be accomplished without all of this sin and rebellion and deceit and jealousy and tragedy? The answer is obvious. *Of course!* I can see how God's pronouncement to Rebekah could have been a part of His original design. To play that out, let's imagine a few "what ifs."

What if Isaac had been an involved, proactive father who was obedient to God's plan, rather than one who allowed his favoritism to passively resist it?

What if Rebekah and Isaac had prepared the boys to obey early in life, saying something like this: "Now, boys, we have some extremely important information about you two straight from the Lord. Jacob is to receive the birthright and blessing, even though he's the youngest. We don't understand why, but God is good and all His ways are right. Esau, you will be very, very wealthy and you will have a great nation that can be an ally to the covenant people that will come through Jacob. Your descendants can share in all its blessings."

What if Esau had received attention equal to Jacob's and all the approval he craved from his parents? *What if* he had graciously released the birthright to Jacob in humble obedience and surrendered to the Lord's loving, sovereign will? To borrow the idea from Corrie ten Boom shared in the previous chapter, *what if* he had held his birthright loosely?

What if Jacob had humbly received the blessing and offered to share his wealth and privilege with Esau?

How might history have turned out differently? How much happier would everyone have been? How much more glory would God have received through the obedience of His people? It's difficult to say, but the story closes with yet another example of how each person's sinful perspective added further complication. Isaac was passive, uninvolved, and yielding. Rebekah manipulated and spun the truth. Jacob scurried away to avoid owning his responsibility. And, in a move typical of Esau, he reacted with self-destructive impulsiveness to make matters worse.

To save her son from Esau's wrath, Rebekah sent Jacob packing to visit her brother far, far away. But to gain Isaac's support, his wife resorted to manipulation and deceit again. She tricked Isaac into thinking that Jacob should find a wife and that she could be found near her brother:

> Rebekah said to Isaac, "I am tired of living because of the daughters of Heth; if Jacob takes a wife from the daughters of Heth, like these, from the daughters of the land, what good will my life be to me?"
>
> GENESIS 27:46

I ask you, who's she thinking about? Nevertheless, it worked. Note Isaac's advice to Jacob: "You shall not take a wife from the daughters of Canaan" (Genesis 28:1). Then he blessed his younger son and sent him off to find a mate among trusted people. What I find disturbing is that Isaac gave Jacob counsel in how to marry—counsel he never gave Esau. There is no evidence to suggest anything other than Isaac left Esau to strike out on his own and find a wife with no parental guidance at all. The young man, as a result, received only condemnation for what he brought home. Esau couldn't win. No matter what.

All of this forces me to pause once again. As a father of four and a grandfather of more than twice that number, I must write a few words to parents.

My friends, your children need help in knowing how to choose a mate. Best if they see what a good mate looks like by the example you provide. But even if you have made a mess of your marriage (or even a couple of them), take the time to wisely and graciously guide your children. If you feel ill equipped, find resources to assist you. We live in an age where reliable information is very accessible. Use discernment. Go to a name or an organization you trust. As you would expect, I'd suggest your church or Insight for Living. You may also request books or even one-on-one advice. Jacob needed assistance, and he got it. Esau needed it all the more, but he encountered only tight-lipped silence, then condemnation.

If you think I'm making too much of this issue as it relates to this story, read the next few verses. They describe a final scene I want to leave with you. It also illustrates a few points to which I have been building:

> Now Esau saw that Isaac had blessed Jacob and sent him away to Paddan-aram to take to himself a wife from there, and that when he blessed him he charged him, saying, "You shall not take a wife from the daughters of Canaan," and that Jacob had obeyed his father and his mother and had gone to Paddan-aram. So Esau saw that the daughters of Canaan displeased his father Isaac; and Esau went to Ishmael, and married, besides the wives that he had, Mahalath the daughter of Ishmael, Abraham's son, the sister of Nebaioth.
>
> GENESIS 28:6–9

Esau, cut to the heart, made one final attempt to win over the favor of his parents—albeit a pathetic, misguided attempt. This is characteristic of what I have seen defeated, desperate adult children do just before they finally realize that they cannot win. In my forty-plus years in ministry, I've seen this played out more times than I care to count. And it's all I can do to keep from taking uninvolved parents by the shoulders and shaking some sense into them. "Don't you realize that the behavior you are condemning is the result of choices that you have encouraged?" I'll be even more direct. If you fail to guide your children, then please don't blame or turn against them when they lose their way! You have a huge stake in the destiny of your children. Assist them through the maze of their struggles. Help them find their way in obedience and without condemning or exasperating them.

Again, my purpose in this chapter is more horizontal than theological, though my first point involves some sophisticated theology that requires more space than I have. So I'll keep these closing comments simple. I derive each principle or warning from a person in this story.

ESAU

Each of us is born into a set of circumstances that we will never have the power to change. Part of what makes a person great is his or her ability to rise above limitations. But—stay with me here! —when taken to extremes, this same drive can twist an individual's thinking. In the case of Esau, it distorted his values and put him at odds not only with his family but, ultimately, with his destiny. Instead of embracing the role God would have him play, he bucked against it. Over time, Esau became desperate, which fueled his unwise, impulsive tendencies and led to wrong decisions.

If I could shout these next three words to your face, I would: BEWARE INSTANT GRATIFICATION! It's the first sign of desperation and forms a dangerous platform for making decisions. Some are so desperate to escape their loneliness they rush into a quick marriage. Some will flee temporary financial difficulties by entering a business partnership that provides instant financial relief, only to find themselves unequally yoked in business with a partner who doesn't serve the same Lord.

Beware making decisions out of desperation. Take time. Pull back. Listen closely to wise counsel—people who love you enough to tell you what you *don't* want to hear. At least be brave enough to doubt your objectivity.

ISAAC AND REBEKAH

Parental favoritism has a damaging effect on the whole family and will lead to lifelong conflict. Kids rarely outgrow the damage done to them because of prejudiced parents, especially parents who deliberately play favorites. They grow up thinking something is wrong with them rather than recognizing that it's the parent who has the problem. What's interesting is that the children become angry with everyone except the parent, whom they continually try to please . . . until they finally realize that they, like Esau, cannot win. And then *they* get blamed for making wrong decisions, not the parents!

If you have a family with more than one child, you may have a natural affinity, an unconscious connection, with one more than the others. You don't have to work at the relationship with that one. And you may be tempted to put more of your time into him or her because you reap dividends more easily; you feel more successful. You may unwittingly add special favors or go easy on discipline or express less criticism or allow more privileges.

Don't think for a moment that children aren't aware of it. We are more transparent to children than we realize. They can detect the slightest scent of injustice like a bloodhound on the trail.

Determine now to put some extra effort into connecting with the child who seems to make your life difficult. Find what interests him or her, and make that child your hobby. You may endure long moments of silence, but don't give up. It's worth the trouble. He or she will never forget the effort, even if you stumble through much of it.

JACOB

Unconditional acceptance is a longing in the heart of every person, and no one can escape this need. Ironically, Jacob had been guaranteed the covenant blessing before he was born, yet he spent a lifetime conniving to gain it from his father.

Your children may have your unconditional acceptance, but do they sense it? Unless you communicate your love, how will they know? Sure, they can pick up on nonverbal cues, but why not make it plain and simple for them? When was the last time you looked deeply into the eyes of each child and expressed your love, your acceptance, your admiration for his or her qualities? Do your children feel your pleasure? They may never ask for it, but they never forget it when it's given. And may I add, use all three of these words often: "I love you." Say them; don't just think them.

IT'S NOT TOO LATE!

You may be reading this later in life than you wish. Maybe you've blown it. Believe it or not, you still have a chance to give your adult child an unforgettable gift. Take time soon to write a letter or to put your arms around each of your children one by one and express how very much he or she means to you. How about a nice lunch with one of your grown children you haven't been with for a while? The conversation doesn't need to be heavy the whole time, but make sure your time together includes a few moments where you look into those eyes and tell that now-grown child of yours what he or she longs to hear. Don't hesitate to use those three words! You may be very surprised to see how easily it will soften a stony heart.

Then, determine to make it a habit. The impact will be nothing short of profound—I guarantee it.

CHAPTER FIVE

Achan: The Man Whose Sin Brought Calamity

T he subject of sin is never easy to address. Even though the words come easily because there is so much to say, the subject is so unpleasant I always find it difficult. Sin grieves the heart of God, does great damage to the sinner, and as we'll see, almost without exception affects others. A story from the life of a man named Achan offers a classic example of this.

When I was a little boy, we were attending a particular church that was apparently going through a dreadful time. I was too young to know anything about the details, but my mother used an expression that has stuck with me through the years. One Sunday evening, my parents were talking about it, and I overheard her say to my dad, "Earl, I think there's sin in the camp."

I didn't know what it meant then, but that phrase left an indelible impression. Unfortunately, I would hear the expression used again and again throughout my life. I remember on one occasion after a particular ministry had gone belly up, someone lamented, "The problem with that ministry is that there has been sin in the camp far too long." Having become a pastor, the words have taken on a whole new meaning. They sicken me.

While serving as a pastor in Fullerton, California, a few members of our pastoral staff took a trip together. Part our journey included a church that for a number of years was a brightly shining lighthouse to many. This church had been a harbor of hope to other ministries, an example of what God can do through an obedient and unified body of believers. I would even go so far as to call it a pacesetting ministry. It clearly enjoyed God's blessing in terms of effectiveness. But then something happened. Over a period of several months, the church suffered an inexplicable decline in impact. For no apparent reason, the spirit of joy began to erode; morale dropped off. Shadows of discontentment dimmed a place that once glowed with optimism. Laughter was no longer heard in the hallways. Members of the staff began to drift apart from one another. During our visit, we heard the whole story. Again, I heard the sad, sickening words, "There has been sin in the camp."

THE DIFFERENCE BETWEEN FAILING AND WALKING IN DARKNESS

Now, we need to be clear on this. Christians—genuinely redeemed, Spirit-filled, transformed members of Christ's body—will continue to struggle with temptation and moral failure after they receive, by faith, the gift and the assurance of eternal life. I realize that's a mouthful, so take time to read that sentence again. A little more slowly, please. Each word is carefully chosen.

Once we have been brought into the family of God by grace, we must continue to live in grace. At the same time, however, we have no excuse for playing with sin. It's no less damaging, and it speaks volumes about the quality of our relationship with God. That's the point of 1 John 1:5–10. Read the following slowly and thoughtfully:

> This is the message we have heard from Him and announce to you, that God is Light, and in Him there is no darkness at all. If we say that we have fellowship with Him and yet walk in the darkness, we lie and do not practice the truth; but if we walk in the Light as He Himself is in the Light, we have fellowship with one another, and the blood of Jesus His Son cleanses us from all sin. If we say that we have no sin, we are deceiving ourselves and the truth is not in us. If we confess our sins, He is faithful and righteous to forgive us our sins and to cleanse us from all unrighteousness. If we say that we have not sinned, we make Him a liar and His word is not in us.

You will notice that throughout this passage, John strips away any excuse for denial or reason we might use for justifying sin. When someone sins, one of two things is true. Either that person is still following the darkened path to hell, or he is a genuine believer in Christ who is choosing to live in carnality and rebellion. I honestly can't say which is worse, but I lean toward the latter, since the rebellious believer seriously impacts so many others in God's family.

When I refer to carnal rebellion, I don't mean those times when we're walking in the light and fall flat on our faces. That's a natural part of our daily, trial-and-error spiritual growth. As John says later, "Beloved, now we are children of God, and it has not appeared as yet what we will be. We know that when He appears, we will be like Him, because we will see Him just as He is. (1 John 3:2) One day, we will be perfected . . . but not now.

Rebellion is making the conscious choice to continue—even indulge—in sinful behavior. That's what John means by "walking in darkness." It's choosing to live like a nonbeliever. And when that happens, it's time for some constructive, healthy and painfully honest self-examination.

Fortunately, 1 John 1:9 tells us that God has a remedy for both incidental spiritual failure and long-term rebellion. In a word, it's repentance . . . agreeing with God that what we have done is wrong, a reaffirmation of our place in His heart, and our need for an intimate relationship with Him in ours, including a commitment to turn away from that sin. In a practical sense, we may have to pick up and move to the other side of the globe to ensure we don't go back on that commitment. But if we're serious about walking in the Light—with Him—no corrective measure would be too drastic.

In the case of the ministry I mentioned earlier, the "sin in the camp" continued. The leader continued to walk in darkness, resulting in enormous consequences that resonated for many years after. His sin continued to impact the camp.

THE DEADLY EFFECT OF HIDDEN, ONGOING SIN

Joshua 7 tells the story of a victorious community that enjoyed the blessing of God. It wasn't long, however, before it found itself facing inexplicable defeat because one member chose to disobey. The community was the nation of Israel before they had fully conquered and settled down in the Promised Land. The former generation of Hebrews who experienced the first Passover in the land of Egypt and saw the mighty hand of God part the Red Sea had all died by this time. That generation failed to trust the Lord, who promised to give them victory, so He made them live like nomads for forty years in the wilderness.

This new, younger generation needed some encouragement. So the Lord gave them a miraculous victory against the fortress-city, Jericho. That experience sets the stage for the story of Achan, the man whose sin brought calamity. Read Joshua 6:15–21 to help prepare your mind for the shocking contrast:

> Then on the seventh day they rose early at the dawning of the day and marched around the city in the same manner seven times; only on that day they marched around the city seven times. At the seventh time, when the priests blew the trumpets, Joshua said to the people, "Shout! For the LORD has given you the city. The city shall be under the ban, it and all that is in it belongs to the LORD; only Rahab the harlot and all who are with her in the house shall live, because she hid the messengers whom we sent. *But as for you, only keep yourselves from the things under the ban, so that you do not covet them and take some of the things under the ban, and make the camp of Israel accursed and bring trouble on it. But all the silver and gold and articles of bronze and iron are holy to the LORD; they shall go into the treasury of the LORD.*" So the people shouted, and priests blew the trumpets; and when the people heard the sound of the trumpet, the people shouted with a great shout and the wall fell down flat, so that the people went up into the city, every man straight ahead, and they took the city. They utterly destroyed everything in the city, both man and woman, young and old, and ox and sheep and donkey, with the edge of the sword. (emphasis added)

VICTORY TURNS TO DEFEAT

This was an important victory for the younger Hebrews. It was their "Red Sea" experience. God allowed them to participate in a miraculous victory at the very start to assure them that He was leading the campaign to occupy Canaan. It was also a strategic victory. With this fortress out of commission, very little stood between Israel and the conquest of the land promised to Abraham, Isaac, and Jacob.

The conquest of Jericho was very much like the invasion of Normandy during World War II. That victory for the Allies meant the beginning of the end for the Nazi regime. Everyone knew it, including Hitler. But the war was far from over. In a similar way, the victory at Jericho meant that the ultimate conquest of Canaan was only a matter of time, but there were a lot of battles yet to fight. And none of them would be easy, especially with sin in the camp:

> So the Lord was with Joshua, and his fame was in all the land.
>
> But the sons of Israel acted unfaithfully in regard to the things un-der the ban, for Achan, the son of Carmi, the son of Zabdi, the son of Zerah, from the tribe of Judah, took some of the things under the ban, therefore the anger of the LORD burned against the sons of Israel.
>
> JOSHUA 6:27–7:1

"But . . ." Such a powerful word. This tiny, negative particle turns the spirit of celebration in chapter 6 into dismay. This first verse gives us the summary, then verses 2 through 26 provide the details.

We'll come back to what it means for something to be "under the ban," but first, read verses 2 through 5 so that you can appreciate the sudden shock of defeat. This is after the miracle at the fortress-city of Jericho, where those immense, imposing walls fell flat. The town of Ai was nothing by comparison.

> Now Joshua sent men from Jericho to Ai, which is near Beth-aven, east of Bethel, and said to them, "Go up and spy out the land." So the men went up and spied out Ai. They returned to Joshua and said to him, "Do not let all the people go up; only about two or three thousand men need go up to Ai; do not make all the people toil up there, for they are few."
>
> JOSHUA 7:2–3

Observe the report of the spies. "Aw, don't sweat this one, Joshua! Let's give most of the troops a break. They can use it after Jericho. We don't need more than two, maybe three thousand warriors. This is nothing." The report sounded like the Oklahoma Sooners were about to meet a squad of Cub Scouts on the football field. Either the report was accurate, or it reflected gross overconfidence.

Based on how the story unfolds, I believe the report was reasonable. Even the name Ai means "ruin." Just how impressive could this little town have been? Part of being a wise general is knowing how much of your resources to commit to a campaign. Joshua's not so foolish as to throw everything he's got into every battle. So to keep his troops fresh and to protect the camp, he sent only what seemed necessary—about three thousand men to sack Ai. Unfortunately, they were in for the mother of all shocks!

> So about three thousand men from the people went up there, but they fled from the men of Ai. The men of Ai struck down about thirty-six of their men, and pursued them from the gate as far as Shebarim and struck them down on the descent, so the hearts of the people melted and became as water.
>
> JOSHUA 7:4–5

Thirty-six men died in the battle. And, to make it worse, they were shot in the back because they were retreating! Israel was on the run. Why? God handed Jericho to them to demonstrate His power and assure Israel of His presence. But here's this little pipsqueak town of Ai—probably a farming community with minimal protection—and Israel's soldiers run for their lives! There's no logic to it. What on earth had changed?

INEXPLICABLE DEFEAT SHOULD BE A WARNING

When that kind of thing happens—as it happens today in the spiritual realm—we need to perk up our ears. There's always a reason for such illogic. Joshua's exemplary response needs to be our model when faced with similar situations.

Then Joshua tore his clothes and fell to the earth on his face before the ark of the LORD until the evening, both he and the elders of Israel; and they put dust on their heads. Joshua said, "Alas, O Lord GOD, why did You ever bring this people over the Jordan, only to deliver us into the hand of the Amorites, to destroy us? If only we had been willing to dwell beyond the Jordan! O Lord, what can I say since Israel has turned their back before their enemies? For the Canaanites and all the inhabitants of the land will hear of it, and they will surround us and cut off our name from the earth. *And what will You do for Your great name?*"

JOSHUA 7:6–9; emphasis added

What a great leader! His first reaction was grief for the fallen men, then for the nation's future, and ultimately for the integrity of God's name, His reputation. I love that kind of reasoning. His actions and passionate prayer implied: "Lord, I'm not worried about my reputation as a leader. This is Your battle. Your name is at stake."

The man at the top, none other than the commander in chief, poured out his heart before the Lord because he had come upon a mystery. The defeat at Ai was humanly inexplicable, militarily baffling, and from all that Joshua knew, completely illogical from a spiritual perspective. That's why his first question to God was, "Why did You ever bring this people over the Jordan, only to deliver us into the hand of the Amorites, to destroy us?" So this spiritual leader took the only logical course of action when defeat occurs. He took it to the Lord.

There's a lesson for leaders here. This applies to any leader who follows God, whether in business or ministry. In the face of mysterious defeat, put the brakes on, stop everything, and take the time to look up. Ask the Lord God to reveal the reason.

I've gone through periods in my own ministry when back-to-back defeats that made no sense baffled me. This would happen after the team had planned carefully, prayed through the preparation, and moved forward with deliberate, calculated, faithful confidence in the Lord's direction . . . only to suffer an Ai kind of defeat. Occasionally, after prayer and a period of soul-searching analysis, the Lord (some might call it happenstance) uncovered sin in the camp. I cannot adequately describe the chilling disbelief and the utter heartache you suffer upon discovering that a trusted colleague has betrayed the ministry, your friendship, and even the Lord. I'm confident that some of you reading this know the horror of betrayal all too well. It leaves you reeling.

Since this dreadful experience still occurs, we'd be wise to take our time and watch the following events transpire. What occurred on Joshua's watch is worth careful analysis.

SIN IN THE CAMP MUST BE CONFRONTED

Joshua prayed in earnest and the Lord was faithful to respond—in his case, verbally:

> So the LORD said to Joshua, "Rise up! Why is it that you have fallen on your face? Israel has sinned, and they have also transgressed My covenant which I commanded them. And they have even taken some of the things under the ban and have both stolen and deceived. Moreover, they have also put them among their own things. Therefore the sons of Israel cannot stand before their enemies; they turn their backs before their enemies, for they have become accursed. I will not be with you anymore unless you destroy the things under the ban from your midst. Rise up! Consecrate the people and say, 'Consecrate yourselves for tomorrow, for thus the LORD, the God of Israel, has said, "There are things under the ban in your midst, O Israel. You cannot stand before your enemies until you have removed the things under the ban from your midst." In the morning then you shall come near by your tribes. And it shall be that the tribe which the LORD takes by lot shall come near by families, and the family which the LORD takes shall come near by households, and the household which the LORD takes shall come near man by man. It shall be that the one who is taken with the things under the ban shall be burned with fire, he and all that belongs to him, because he has transgressed

the covenant of the LORD, and because he has committed a disgraceful thing in Israel.'"

JOSHUA 7:10–15

The defeat at Ai finally made complete sense. Important facts had been revealed. God had promised Israel victory and delivered them a huge triumph at Jericho. But, like many of God's promises, this one was conditional; it required obedience. The town called "ruin" put Israel to flight for one reason: there was sin in the camp. Someone had taken items "under the ban."

In ancient times, a soldier was compensated by the plunder he took after victory. Normally, after a city had been taken, the soldiers were encouraged to grab all the valuables they could carry and add the spoils to their wealth. That was considered the warrior's pay. But not in this case. Remember God's instructions for the destruction of Jericho?

> The city shall be under the ban, it and all that is in it belongs to the LORD; only Rahab the harlot and all who are with her in the house shall live, because she hid the messengers whom we sent. But as for you, only keep yourselves from the things under the ban, so that you do not covet them and take some of the things under the ban, and make the camp of Israel accursed and bring trouble on it. But all the silver and gold and articles of bronze and iron are holy to the LORD; they shall go into the treasury of the LORD.

JOSHUA 6:17–19

The *cherem*, translated "the ban," was not a complicated concept. Rather than hoard the spoils of victory for themselves, the soldiers were to take nothing home. Everything living was to have been put to death. Everything valuable was to have been put in the treasury of the Lord. Everything was set apart for Him. Simple.

Ushers receiving an offering in a church have a similar code. The ushers don't say, "Well, if I were being paid to do this very important job for the church, I think thus-and-such amount would be fair compensation. I'll take out a little less than that so, in the end, the church is coming out ahead. After all, if no one did this job, the church would receive no money at all."

That looks stupid just reading it, doesn't it? No one in his right mind would expect that logic to work. In fact, the integrity of most people carrying out this function in church is so high that none of them even wants to be alone with the money. That way the whole process remains above reproach and every penny is tallied, accounted for, and given to the Lord.

Unfortunately for Israel, someone after the battle of Jericho had emptied a full offering plate into his own pockets. Joshua was innocent. The vast majority of Israel was blameless. Still, the entire nation suffered. J. Sidlow Baxter describes the effect this way: "The electric wire of fellowship between God and Israel had been cut and the current of power therefore ceased to flow." That's precisely the consequence of sin in the camp. That's also why I think the intelligence report on the strength of Ai was a reasonable one. This should have been an easy victory, even without the Lord's involvement. No miracle needed there, but the presence of sin interrupted God's desire to bless the nation with another victory.

Let's face it: we often stand in the way of our own blessings. The Lord is a God of grace, so I certainly don't mean to suggest that He only blesses us when we're good. I have received far more goodness than I will ever merit. As a sinner, I deserve only punishment. But if the short-term blessing will cause us long-term harm, it cannot be called grace. God will never bless us at the expense of our holiness.

The effect of concealed sin in the camp is one of the most perplexing experiences of leadership. Things that should work don't, and you can't understand why. Then, later—sometimes years later—after enough time has passed and all of the facts come to light, you're able to see those events with crystal clarity. But at the time it's happening, you are pulling your hair out, wondering, *What in the world?* In the case if Israel, the sin had been buried . . . literally.

PRIVATE SIN HAS PUBLIC CONSEQUENCES

One of the soldiers who had stormed the flattened walls of Jericho had disobeyed the command of God and taken treasure that was supposed to be consecrated to the Lord. Not long afterward, the crime had been discovered and the search was on for the guilty party. And what a search it was!

> So Joshua arose early in the morning and brought Israel near by tribes, and the tribe of Judah was taken. He brought the family of Judah near, and he took the family of the Zerahites; and he brought the family of the Zerahites near man by man, and Zabdi was taken.
>
> JOSHUA 7:16–17

Imagine the racing heart and pulsing blood pressure of the thief as, tribe by tribe, family by family, household by household, Joshua's dragnet closed in on him. What could the thief have been thinking? Had he ignored the ban, he at least heard of the defeat, and he doubtless saw the funerals for those thirty-six men. He knew the penalty. "It shall be that the one who is taken with the things under the ban shall be burned with fire, he and all that belongs to him" (7:15). The pressure mounting within the thief must have been overwhelming.

It occurs to me that God simply could have given the name of the thief to Joshua instead of orchestrating this very elaborate, very public search. Perhaps in His grace, He was giving the man every opportunity to step up, confess, repent, spare the community any further suffering, and take his punishment. Still, through it all, the guilty man said nothing. His sin remained buried.

Before we go on, allow me to point out, once again, the public nature of the thief's sin. Some sins become a very public scandal, the kind that ruins ministries forever. Even when the personalities are gone, a dark cloud shrouds the reputation of the organization in suspicion and cynicism. But let's admit that most sins are private in the sense that no one knows about them but you and God—no one but *me* and God. In this case, God wanted it handled publicly.

The manhunt continued in progressively smaller concentric circles as the Lord had Joshua cast lots to fine-tune his search. In the Old Testament, before the Holy Spirit took up permanent residence in the hearts of believers, this was the process for determining God's will. Not unlike rolling dice, the priest played a game of chance, as it were, except that God controlled the outcome, and the stakes made it anything but a gamble. With each round, the noose tightened around the thief's neck. First by tribe, then by family, then by household, then man by man.

Finally, the elimination search left only one man, naked in his sin before the whole camp. The thief was discovered. The finger of undisputed accusation finally pointed at Achan:

> [Joshua] brought [Zabdi's] household near man by man; and Achan, son of Carmi, son of Zabdi, son of Zerah, from the tribe of Judah, was taken. Then Joshua said to Achan, "My son, I implore you, give glory to the LORD, the God of Israel, and give praise to Him; and tell me now what you have done. Do not hide it from me."
>
> JOSHUA 7:18–19

My heart is heavy for Joshua as I read again this account of a leader having to confront sin in the camp. As I read, I find myself reliving those few, awful occasions in ministry when I had to sit face to face with someone who had buried a secret sin and told a lie that damaged a ministry and destroyed a family. Each confrontation was different. Sometimes it takes a person hours to come out with the truth. With others, the confession gushes out immediately with a rush of tears, as in Achan's case:

> So Achan answered Joshua and said, "Truly, I have sinned against the LORD, the God of Israel, and this is what I did: when I saw among the spoil a beautiful mantle from Shinar and two hundred shekels of silver and a bar of gold fifty shekels in weight, then I coveted them and took them; and behold, they are concealed in the earth inside my tent with the silver underneath it." So Joshua sent messengers, and they ran to the tent; and behold, it was concealed in his tent with the silver underneath it.
>
> JOSHUA 7:20–22

Do not miss the downward spiral of Achan's sin.

"I saw . . .
    I coveted . . .
        I took . . .
            I hid."

That's the way it happens. But he failed to see the final phase of the progression: "I got caught." We rarely think of that one before we sin. Only after, when the paranoia sets in.

At the time of his sin, Achan probably thought something along these lines of rationalization. "My family and I have been deprived of many good things during our years of wilderness living. Here is this beautiful, new, stylish garment, a little bit of silver, and a handful of gold. This is no big deal. God will never miss this in light of all the treasury that we'll haul back from Jericho. I fought hard, so I'm entitled to a few enjoyable things in life, after all."

I realize that I'm speculating, but that's how the human mind works. Carnality can be incredibly inventive when it comes to rationalizing sin. In the heat of the moment, the excitement of hidden sin, the adventure, the forbidden pleasure drives away all reason. We see, we covet, we take, and we hide.

Alexander Whyte's eloquent words on Achan bear repeating:

> Everybody who reads the best books will have long had by heart Thomas à Kempis's famous description of the successive steps of a successful temptation. There is first the bare thought of the sin. Then, upon that, there is a picture of the sin formed and hung up on the secret screen of the imagination. A strange sweetness from that picture is then let down drop by drop into the heart; and then that secret sweetness soon secures the consent of the whole soul, and the thing is done. That is true, and it is powerful enough. But Achan's confession to Joshua is much simpler, and much closer to the truth. "I saw the goodly Babylonish garment, I coveted it, I took it, and I hid it in my tent." Had Joshua happened to post the ensign of Judah opposite the poor men's part of the city, this sad story would never have been told. But even as it was, had Achan only happened to stand a little to the

one side, or a little to the other side of where he did stand, in that case he would not have seen that beautiful piece, and not seeing it he would not have coveted it, and would have gone home to his tent that night a good soldier and an honest man. But when once Achan's eyes lighted on that rich garment he never could get his eyes off it again. As à Kempis says, the seductive thing got into Achan's imagination, and the devil's work was done.

O sons and daughters of discovered Achan! O guilty and dissembling sinners! It is all in vain. It is all utterly and absolutely in vain. Be sure as God is in heaven, that He has His eyes upon you, and that your sin will find you out. You think that the darkness will cover you. Wait till you see! Go on sowing as you have begun, and come and tell us when the harvest is reaped how it threshes out and how it tastes.

The eagle that stole a piece of sacred flesh from the altar brought home a smoldering coal with it that kindled up afterwards and burned up both her whole nest and all her young ones. . . . Once a son, always a son, even when a prodigal son. Every son has his father's grey hairs and his mother's anxious heart in his hands, and no possible power can alter that. Drop that stolen flesh! There is a coal in it that shall never be quenched.[2]

CONFRONTATION MUST BE SWIFT, DECISIVE, AND THOROUGH

Achan brought home more than he thought; and, for sure, his sin would not stay buried:

> They took [the stolen items] from inside the tent and brought them to Joshua and to all the sons of Israel, and they poured them out before the LORD. Then Joshua and all Israel with him, took Achan the son of Zerah, the silver, the mantle, the bar of gold, his sons, his daughters, his oxen, his donkeys, his sheep, his tent and all that belonged to him; and they brought them up to the valley of Achor. Joshua said, "Why have you troubled us? The LORD will trouble you this day." And all

Israel stoned them with stones; and they burned them with fire after
they had stoned them with stones.

JOSHUA 7:23–25

Joshua used an interesting play on words with Achan's name, which in
Hebrew, interestingly, means "trouble." "Why have you lived up to your
name, Achan?" Then they took him to a place called Achor, which comes
from the same root, meaning "place of trouble," and Israel executed justice.
After executing Achan and all the people who helped him conceal his sin,
their possessions were burned in accordance with God's command, and
their graves marked by memorial stones so that no one would forget.

Shocking, isn't it? Such harshness offends our modern sensibilities,
softened by compromise. Our reaction is either to minimize the severity
by glossing over the details or to recoil in fear from a God who could be so
severe. How different it would be in our politically correct day. Attorneys
would defend Achan by declaring him temporarily insane or by finding a
technical loophole. ("Joshua failed to read the man his rights!") Or they
might have him plead guilty to petty theft and plea bargain a lighter sentence
rather than involve the whole camp in a lengthy, expensive trial. Public
opinion might come to the rescue. "He apologized and returned the goods.
What purpose does an execution serve? It would be inhumane. Furthermore,
will it restore the thirty-six fallen soldiers to their families?"

We live in the age of grace, but some would twist that concept into
a license to sin. Many others would redefine sin to exclude any act that
doesn't hurt someone else. In their words, sin isn't something that defies
God; sin is something that harms others. Yet, I can find nowhere in Scripture anything to suggest that an action has to hurt someone else in order
for God to consider it a sin.

For that matter, I cannot find any indication, either in Scripture or in
my experience, that sin is *ever* isolated. Not really. Private perhaps, but
never isolated. Sin, to some degree, *always* affects others. Just because we
can't build a logical, cause-and-effect case every time, doesn't make that
any less true. As a pastor, I have seen one person's "private" sin break the
hearts of family members as well as hinder the work of an entire church.

As a nation we have seen more than one president's "private" sin corrupt an administration. Sin in the camp is a powerful enemy to a fruitful ministry. Satan would love nothing more than to keep that sin buried, convince us that our choices are nobody's business but our own, and let it rot our lives from the inside out. The Adversary's logic feeds on such deception.

One individual who continues to walk in darkness—contrary to the mind of God—can erode the effectiveness of an entire organization and steal any hope of victory. One Judas can affect an entire group of disciples. One Achan can stop a nation in its tracks. One person with unconfessed, unrepentant, unresolved sin buried in his or her tent can have untold negative impact on everything and everyone he or she touches. Sin in the camp is deadly, even in this age of grace.

SERIOUS PRINCIPLES WORTH REMEMBERING

As I observe the story of the man whose sin brought calamity, and compare it to my own experience in ministry leadership, I want to leave you with three serious principles to consider. Because we live in a fallen, broken, twisted world, you are likely in one of three situations. You may be the leader of an organization with sin in the camp. (Don't become suspicious, but please do remain alert.) You may be a member of an organization with sin in the camp. Or you may be the one nurturing sin. You have it buried in your tent, and when no one is looking, you dig it up to caress it. Whatever your position, consider these three principles.

First, *sin in the camp stinks, and others can detect its unique stench.* I've chosen those words carefully. I realize they are somewhat crude, but they're appropriate. There is a unique stench, there's a smell about suspicion. Interestingly, the closer we walk with God, the more quickly we catch the nauseating odor. A tender heart that is intimate with God is particularly sensitive to the presence of sin. This can easily become twisted into fear and habitual suspicion. Let's not go there. No one is immune to Satan's deception, and we can't go about jumping at every shadow. But trust your gut instincts. Intuition is rarely wrong.

Don't be thickheaded as a spiritual leader. If inexplicable defeat and decline begins to plague your ministry with no logical explanation, pay attention. Wake up and smell the roses . . . or better, the rubbish. It may or may not be the result of sin in the camp, but don't be naive. Do what Joshua did. Take it before the Lord with complete candor and humility. Lean hard upon Him. Ask Him to open a window from His heavenly perspective. Remember that this is His battle, and that He will protect what belongs to Him, including His reputation.

If you, my friend, are the Achan of your family or ministry or company or (you fill in the blank) . . . if you are nurturing a secret sin, don't think others can't smell the stench. They may not be able to place the source—not yet, anyway—but the pungent odor of your sin hangs in the air. And it quite likely keeps the people around you from experiencing victory.

Repent. Today! Don't delay. Decide *now* that this sin must go. Remember our opening section of Scripture?

> This is the message we have heard from Him and announce to you,
> that God is Light, and in Him there is no darkness at all. If we say that
> we have fellowship with Him and yet walk in the darkness, we lie and
> do not practice the truth; but if we walk in the Light as He Himself is
> in the Light, we have fellowship with one another, and the blood of
> Jesus His Son cleanses us from all sin. If we say that we have no sin,
> we are deceiving ourselves and the truth is not in us. If we confess our
> sins, He is faithful and righteous to forgive us our sins and to cleanse
> us from all unrighteousness.
>
> 1 JOHN 1:5–9

Come out of the darkness and walk in the Light. Let your repentance be the first step in the right direction. It is never too late to start doing what is right.

I need to add here: ministry leaders, prepare to receive the penitent ones in grace. Deal in mercy. Make it your goal to restore them to a right relationship with God and with the community you lead.

Second, *uneasiness is the companion of hidden sin.* Try coping all you like, but the heart isn't equipped to remain comfortable with hidden sin.

God designed the human heart to beat in rhythm with His. When it does, we experience a deep and satisfying peace. Nurturing sin, something God hates most, will replace that peace with a nagging uneasiness. While no one can live completely free of interruption by sin, we can teach ourselves to hate it. Sin in the camp becomes a problem for everyone when we leave it buried in our tents to keep it close—not because we fear discovery as much as we fear losing the sin we secretly love.

Third, *when wrong is uncovered, God honors swift, decisive, and thorough action.* This is one of the most unpleasant life principles to consider, but we must. Personally, I would just as soon brush aside sinful behavior and enjoy a nice dinner. I hate confronting sin. I dislike with a passion wading through the muck and mire. Yet I cannot remember a time when I chose to delay a necessary confrontation that I didn't later regret it. In fact, when I forced myself to deal with a person guilty of nurturing a hidden sin, I was always grateful when I did it without delay. I wish I could say that it always turned out well; that the guilty man or woman always surrendered and sobbed a heartbreaking confession in complete brokenness; that our community of redeemed sinners could restore him or her, in love, to a joyous relationship with God and the community again. Sometimes it did happen that way, and I am astounded by the healing power of Christ's forgiveness and grace. Usually it doesn't, but at least the integrity of the ministry is preserved, God's name is glorified, and we can look forward to future victories, although stained with sadness at the loss of a friend.

Achan's story turned out that way. He rejected every opportunity to repent as the swift, decisive hand of God closed in on him by degrees. When he forced the Lord's hand and Israel dealt with his sin without delay, sin was gone from the camp. Not surprisingly, the very next chapter tells the story of the nation's victory over Ai.

A FINAL PLEA

Scripture tells us that if we would judge ourselves we would not be judged (1 Corinthians 11:31). If we hold ourselves accountable for sin, no one else needs to. The simplest, most direct way to handle personal sin is to deal with it personally. If you find yourself arguing with yourself over behavior, trying to rationalize something that haunts your conscience, that should be sufficient warning to you. It may be the first step in the Lord's bringing you to account. If you don't make the choice to deal with it swiftly and decisively, your sin will begin closing in on you.

If you feel you can't do it alone, get some help. Begin with a person you feel sure you can trust to take your sin seriously yet graciously, someone who will guide you on what is likely to be a difficult journey. Whatever you do, don't wait. Do *something*, anything to get out of the situation that is compromising your walk and the health of your church or ministry or family or marriage . . . in fact, all of the above. Don't force someone else to go through the painstaking search, having to narrow it down to tribes and families and households and then, finally, to you. Through it all, the stench of hidden sin will be in the nostrils of those around you, and the fallout from your sin will continue to drag them down.

For the sake of those you love, for the sake of God's good name, and for the sake of your own relationship with Him . . . deal with it.

Do it *now*.

CHAPTER SIX

Samuel: The Boy Who Heard God's Voice

I magine for the next few moments that you are a child again, a child in Sunday school. You're about seven years old and, as usual, your mind is drifting and wandering from one thing to another. You're busy. You're fidgety. You're not thinking much about what the teacher has on her mind. And then, suddenly, something catches your eye. The teacher brings in a series of posters, large pictures, each one depicting a story out of the Scriptures. She asks you to name the story by just looking at the picture.

Got it? OK. Play along with me as I hold up the pictures, and let's see how well you do in a class of seven- to eight-year-old children in Sunday school.

The first large poster shows a young man standing beside a fresh grave. He has blood on his clothing, a knife in his hand, and a guilty look on his face. He's speaking toward the sky with a shrug. What story is this?

Cain and Abel? Good. One for one.

Second, a series of black clouds darkens the top of the poster; the sea is turbulent with no hint of land anywhere in the distance. In the center of the picture you see a very large, crudely constructed bargelike boat. Through the window of the vessel, you see a monkey sitting on a giraffe's head.

Yeah, I know. That one is easy. You immediately said Noah and the ark. You're right. Very good.

Here's a third. A mother is standing waist deep in a muddy river. She's placing her baby into a little handmade, reed basket. A small girl looks on with a worried face.

That's not much to go on, but you might have recognized the story of how the mother of Moses saved him from certain death. With the help of her daughter, she floated him down the Nile so that the daughter of Pharaoh would discover and adopt him. Another magnificent story out of the Scriptures.

I have one more. It's a young boy in bed, sitting up like something has just pulled him from his dreams. He is trying to wake up. His face reflects a mixture of confusion and concentration. He has his head slightly tilted as though he's trying to hear something.

I love stories. Especially those about humble beginnings. Stories that tell you what a lowly, unknown person was like before he or she became great or how an underdog got the best of some bully or how a huge company started in someone's garage. And every story has a setting—or at least it should. A story without context is like a diamond without a mounting. The stone may be beautiful lying loose on a table, but when it's carefully mounted in the right setting it can dazzle you with its brilliance and sparkling beauty.

We need to understand the setting of the little boy who was awakened from his sleep. When we do, the significance of the story takes on a deeper meaning.

ISRAEL'S DARK SETTING

The setting is Israel before the glory days of King David. There has been a long period—a couple hundred years—of intermittent warfare, cycles of events during which Israel would suffer invasion followed by famine; then a judge would emerge and win a temporary peace. During the peace, the people would sin, and the cycle would kick in again. Another invasion followed by defeat, resulting in yet another famine, growing more severe each time. This story takes place during a lull in the violence, a restful season of relative peace. Days were unusually quiet and uneventful.

My grandfather used to take me fishing down near Palacios, in the South Texas area not too many miles from Matagorda Bay, which led into the Gulf of Mexico. Every once in a while, we'd find ourselves in the middle of what he called a "slick." If you fish, you know what that's like. It's a patch of water so glassy smooth you can flip a penny into the water and count the ripples. It's quiet, calm, and windless. Politically and socially, this time in Hebrew history is like a "slick" after a long stretch of recurring turbulence.

The people of Israel have settled back into a lax lifestyle that could be described as downright complacent. Their attitude toward God and His vision for them as a nation has become indifferent, a little ho-hum, boring. Their leader, the high priest, is Eli, an old man whose eyesight has begun to grow dim. Unless something changes, he will turn the reins of leadership over to his two rebellious sons, Hophni and Phinehas, who helped him minister in the tabernacle, which was the place of worship during this period of Israel's history.

There's more to the setting, so bear with me. A few years earlier, a woman named Hannah was a regular visitor to the temple. She spent most of her time in prayer, begging God for the gift of a son. She vowed to the Lord that if He would grant her request, she would give the boy back to Him. The Lord finally gave her a son, whom she named him Samuel. Appropriately, the name means "asked of God." Soon after he was weaned, she fulfilled her promise and placed Samuel in the care of Eli, the aging, almost blind, high priest of Israel. Eli was responsible for Samuel's welfare and education. He was tutoring him in spiritual things, preparing him for a lifetime of service to God.

> Now the boy Samuel was ministering to the LORD before Eli. And word
> from the LORD was rare in those days, visions were infrequent.
>
> 1 SAMUEL 3:1

The whole land of Israel, stuck in a political and spiritual "slick," was half asleep, yawning its way from one day to the next. God is silent. No one has visions, except maybe a few charlatans (sounds a little like today, doesn't it?). Meanwhile Samuel, still a young lad, carries out his duties for the Lord under the watchful eye of Eli, a preoccupied, doting, grandfather type who's very kind and gentle with him. So much for the setting.

A CHILD CONVICTS THE JUDGE

Whenever a story begins with a very placid, ultra-calm setting, you can usually expect something to change soon:

> It happened at that time as Eli was lying down in his place (now his eyesight had begun to grow dim and he could not see well), and the lamp of God had not yet gone out, and Samuel was lying down in the temple of the LORD where the ark of God was, that the LORD called Samuel; and he said, "Here I am."
>
> 1 SAMUEL 3:2–4

Everything in the tabernacle revolved around the Most Holy Place. This was where the sacred, laserlike brilliance of God's presence hovered over the ark of the covenant—a place so holy it was dangerous to mere humans. So a thick curtain divided it from the rest of the inner chamber where the implements of worship were located. One of the special fixtures of this holy area was a menorah, which, according to the Law of Moses, was never to go out. To keep the lamp supplied with oil around the clock, the priests would take turns sleeping near the Most Holy Place to be sure it burned perpetually.

Eli and Samuel were probably taking their turn sleeping in the tabernacle to keep the lamp lit. They slept in little rooms or closets near that special area of God's presence. It was when Samuel heard a voice call his name that he sat up in his little pallet and called back, "Yes?" No one answered, so . . .

> He ran to Eli and said, "Here I am, for you called me." But he said, "I did not call, lie down again." So he went and lay down.
>
> 1 SAMUEL 3:5

You can't always tell from Scripture whether God's voice is audible or "heard" by some other means. When Saul (later Paul) was on the road to Damascus, he heard the voice of the resurrected Jesus talking to him in a vision, and the sound could be heard by his entourage. It was audible. In Genesis 6, God spoke to Noah and gave him specific instructions. We might assume that the voice was audible—that is, he heard spoken words with his ears—but the Lord may have "spoken" to him mind to mind. We don't know for sure. God's voice to Daniel sounded like thunder, but centuries earlier to Elijah, He spoke with "a noiseless sound." In Samuel's case, God spoke in such a way that Samuel literally heard His voice. He spoke with the voice of a normal, Hebrew man so that the boy thought it was Eli calling to him from the other room.

Back in the late 1970s, my aging father lived in our home and needed help on occasion. Our bedroom was upstairs, his was downstairs, and I remember hearing the sound of his voice winding its way through the darkness, penetrating my dreams, pulling me out of my sleep. As I awoke, I went to see what he needed. If you're a parent, you've experienced that with a child. So it makes sense that Samuel would scamper off to Eli's room to see what the old man needed. "Here I am."

Eli probably thought Samuel had been dreaming, so he sent him back to bed.

> The LORD called yet again, "Samuel!" So Samuel arose and went to Eli
> and said, "Here I am, for you called me." But he answered, "I did not
> call, my son, lie down again." *Now Samuel did not yet know the LORD,*
> *nor had the word of the LORD yet been revealed to him.*
>
> 1 SAMUEL 3:6–7; emphasis added

The last sentence represents the storyteller's clarifying comment to the reader, who already knew of Samuel as a powerful prophet of God. It's the author's way of saying that this occurred before the Lord had initiated a personal relationship with the boy. Keep this in mind, as it will become an important part of the story as it unfolds.

By the way, in the Old Testament, having a personal relationship with the Lord in the way we have come to know it by the new covenant and the indwelling Holy Spirit was a rare and truly awesome privilege. I think we take this privilege *far* too lightly!

Remember the opening verse of chapter 3 said, "And word from the Lord was rare in those days, visions were infrequent." Because Samuel and God weren't yet on speaking terms, everything the boy knew of the Lord came through Eli, not by personal experience. Before people had the Scriptures, the Lord would break the silence and speak audibly to a prophet or give direction from some supernatural source. But it had never happened to Samuel. He was not only inexperienced, he was confused. He did the only thing a little, confused boy knew to do; he ran to Eli:

> So the Lord called Samuel again for the third time. And he arose and went to Eli and said, "Here I am, for you called me." Then Eli discerned that the Lord was calling the boy.
>
> 1 Samuel 3:8

I'm intrigued by the word "discerned" here. The Hebrew word involves a heavy element of skill—wisdom by experience. You can't take a course in college to learn discernment. It comes only through the passage of time as you apply yourself to discovery by trial and error. Eli had never heard the voice of the Lord himself, and God's revelation in this way hadn't occurred for a very long time; yet he was discerning of the Lord's ways. He had come to know God well. By the third time around, it became clear to him that this had to be the Lord's voice. I appreciate his counsel to Samuel:

> And Eli said to Samuel, "Go lie down, and it shall be if He calls you, that you shall say, 'Speak, Lord, for Your servant is listening.'" So Samuel went and lay down in his place.
>
> 1 Samuel 3:9

Just imagine. You're a young person working for someone who has years of experience in the ways of God and that person you greatly respect says, "That's God's voice. If you hear it again, you listen. Stay sensitive to what God has to say." This must have been strange for a small boy to hear, but he obeyed without hesitation.

Then the LORD came and stood and called as at other times, "Samuel!
Samuel!" And Samuel said, "Speak, for Your servant is listening."

I SAMUEL 3:10

As a child in Sunday school, I remember seeing Bible story posters on
the walls of the classroom. Invariably, one of them was Samuel, lying in
bed, propped up on one elbow, tilting his head slightly as he strained to
hear something. The artist had drawn everything so perfectly I could almost
hear the voice of God . . . but the story for me ended there.

I used to wonder, well, what did He say? Why did He wake him three times?
What was so important? Unfortunately, the message God gave to Samuel was
one of the most severe warnings He had ever issued—so severe that my Sunday
school teachers probably felt like a child ought not hear it. In the silence of his
bedchamber, Samuel heard these frightening words of warning:

The LORD said to Samuel, "Behold, I am about to do a thing in Israel
at which both ears of everyone who hears it will tingle. In that day I
will carry out against Eli all that I have spoken concerning his house,
from beginning to end. For I have told him that I am about to judge
his house forever for the iniquity which he knew, because his sons
brought a curse on themselves and he did not rebuke them. Therefore
I have sworn to the house of Eli that the iniquity of Eli's house shall
not be atoned for by sacrifice or offering forever."

I SAMUEL 3:11–14

The message was a huge burden for little Samuel, but, tragically, it
was not something Eli hadn't already heard. God had pulled Eli aside on
previous occasions and told him about his wayward sons. In the previous
chapter, we read:

Then a man of God came to Eli and said to him, "Thus says the LORD,
'Did I not indeed reveal Myself to the house of your father when they
were in Egypt in bondage to Pharaoh's house? Did I not choose them
from all the tribes of Israel to be My priests, to go up to My altar, to

burn incense, to carry an ephod before Me; and did I not give to the house of your father all the fire offerings of the sons of Israel? Why do you kick at My sacrifice and at My offering which I have commanded in My dwelling, and honor your sons above Me, by making yourselves fat with the choicest of every offering of My people Israel?' Therefore the LORD God of Israel declares, 'I did indeed say that your house and the house of your father should walk before Me forever'; but now the LORD declares, 'Far be it from Me—for those who honor Me I will honor, and those who despise Me will be lightly esteemed. Behold, the days are coming when I will break your strength and the strength of your father's house so that there will not be an old man in your house. You will see the distress of My dwelling, in spite of all the good that I do for Israel; and an old man will not be in your house forever.'"

1 SAMUEL 2:27–32

THE SIN OF ELI

If you're not familiar with the backstory, you may be wondering, what is this all about? The short answer is this: two extremely wicked sons, Hophni and Phinehas.

Eli was a great preacher, a fine priest. As the high priest, he was responsible, once each year, to enter the Most Holy Place and offer an atoning sacrifice on behalf of the nation. No one else had that privilege. He judged, he instructed the people in matters of worship, he gave counsel, he devoted his entire life to serving in the tabernacle of God and ministering to the needs of His people. But he was a passive, inactive father who indulged his sons. Those boys of his were a piece of work!

> Now the sons of Eli were worthless men; *they did not know the LORD and the custom of the priests with the people.*
>
> 1 SAMUEL 2:12–13; emphasis added

The author used similar words with little Samuel, but with a very different emphasis. The word translated "know" *(yada)* is the same, but the context makes an enormous difference. Samuel didn't know the Lord due to youthful ignorance. Hophni and Phinehas didn't know the Lord because they were willful, carnal reprobates. Morally, they were hollow, spiritual losers! Yet they had been anointed priests. The following is one example of how they would abuse their positions:

> Also, before they burned the fat, the priest's servant would come and say to the man who was sacrificing, "Give the priest meat for roasting, as he will not take boiled meat from you, only raw." If the man said to him, "They must surely burn the fat first, and then take as much as you desire," then he would say, "No, but you shall give it to me now; and if not, I will take it by force." Thus the sin of the young men was very great before the LORD, for the men despised the offering of the LORD.
>
> I SAMUEL 2:15–17

According to the Law of Moses, they were to burn the fat as an offering and take whatever didn't burn from the altar. In this way, they were to receive only what the Lord provided. Eli's worthless sons defied God's instructions and reserved the choicest cuts of meat for their dinner table. That's bad . . . but it only gets worse. Much worse.

> Now Eli was very old; and he heard all that his sons were doing to all Israel, and how they lay with the women who served at the doorway of the tent of meeting.
>
> I SAMUEL 2:22

Along with their audacious disrespect for the sacrifices of God, they were perverse men who took sexual advantage of the women who came to worship. And they did so without shame, right there in the house of God. And Eli knew it! You would think that a genuine man of God like Eli would be outraged. Remember, he also served as Israel's judge, meaning that his responsibility was to carry out justice on behalf of God. These sons of shameless lust should have been carried to the edge of town and stoned to death. Instead, they receive a mild scolding. How pathetic is *that*?

He said to them, "Why do you do such things, the evil things that I hear from all these people? No, my sons; for the report is not good which I hear the LORD's people circulating. If one man sins against another, God will mediate for him; but if a man sins against the LORD, who can intercede for him?" But they would not listen to the voice of their father, for the LORD desired to put them to death.

I SAMUEL 2:23–25

Meanwhile . . . "Now the boy Samuel was growing in stature and in favor both with the LORD and with men" (I Samuel 2:26).

As difficult as it is to imagine, Samuel was raised in this environment, but apparently knew little about it. While Hophni and Phinehas turned the tabernacle into a chamber of unbridled lust, Eli kept one hand over Samuel's eyes and the other over his own. God's patience finally reached its end. He was through talking to Eli about it. Instead He would place His final word of judgment on the lips of an innocent little boy:

In that day I will carry out against Eli all that I have spoken concerning his house, from beginning to end. For I have told him that I am about to judge his house forever for the iniquity which he knew, because his sons brought a curse on themselves *and he did not rebuke them.*Therefore I have sworn to the house of Eli that the iniquity of Eli's house shall not be atoned for by sacrifice or offering forever.

I SAMUEL 3:12–14; emphasis added

COMPLACENCY IS THE ENEMY OF OBEDIENCE

Eli's behavior reflected his times. Politically, socially, and spiritually, the nation existed in a sluggish, lazy complacency. He folded his arms and thought, *Well, I just can't do a thing with these boys of mine. Hophni and Phinehas have been rebellious all their lives, and I'm so busy. I've got so many things to take care of, surely God will understand.*

No, God *won't* understand! His anger has risen to such a level that He awakens this young boy in the tender years of childhood to tell him, "This warning I am giving you so you will know what is going to happen."

> So Samuel lay down until morning. Then he opened the doors of the house of the LORD. But Samuel was afraid to tell the vision to Eli. Then Eli called Samuel and said, "Samuel, my son." And he said, "Here I am." He said, "What is the word that He spoke to you? Please do not hide it from me. May God do so to you, and more also, if you hide anything from me of all the words that He spoke to you." So Samuel told him everything and hid nothing from him. And he said, "It is the LORD; let Him do what seems good to Him."
>
> 1 SAMUEL 3:15–18

Just as Eli requested, Samuel told him *everything* that the Lord had said. He hid nothing from him. I am amazed by Eli's response. He says, in effect, "Well, that's the way it goes. The Lord knows what He's doing." How much better if he had finally taken the Lord's warning seriously. How much better if he had stood to his feet and said, "That's it. I've heard enough. I'm doing exactly what God says in the Law. I'm taking these boys to the elders of the city so justice might be carried out! The years of my own negligence and the years of evil in the tabernacle end *now*. When I die, I will die in obedience."

That's not Eli's style. He did the same on this day as he had been doing throughout the years. *Nothing*.

ANY FAMILY CAN DISINTEGRATE; NONE IS IMMUNE

God has preserved for us fascinating stories to leave us with enduring lessons. Fathers in particular need to take heed. It has been my observation that Eli's paralysis of leadership is not uncommon . . . even among those in ministry. As a father whose vocation is service to the Lord, I have made it my intentional mission to avoid the failure of Eli. While I have been far from perfect, I've worked hard not to be passive.

To avoid his fate, each one of us today must recognize that our family could very easily end up like Eli's. We must recognize that any family can come unraveled—an elder's family, a pastor's family, a missionary family whose father walks with God and pours his heart into a church, rich, poor, healthy, strained . . . any family. The warning signs are often evident. From Eli's family we can detect no less than four.

First, *disintegrating families have parents who are preoccupied with an occupation to the exclusion of family needs.* Eli was a busy priest. He was a respected judge. He was engaged in serving the public. We can be reasonably sure that if he weren't, God would have mentioned it in His warning. Public ministry wasn't his weakness. The problem was that he failed to give his boys the kind of attention he gave Samuel. His sons were slowly eroding into a lifestyle of cynicism and skepticism and Eli not only overlooked it, but he failed to discipline them. Yet he did his job well.

Alexander Whyte, one of Scotland's most insightful writers of yesteryear, points out his observations with eloquence:

> Now the sons of Eli were sons of Belial; they knew not the Lord. Impossible! you would protest, if it were not in the Bible. But just because it is in the Bible, we are compelled to ask ourselves how it could possibly come about that the sons of such a sacred man as Eli was could ever become sons of Belial.
>
> What! not know the Lord, and they born and brought up within the very precincts of the Lord's house! Were not the first sounds they heard the praises of God in His sanctuary? Were not the first sights they saw their father in his robes beside the altar with all the tables, and the bread, and the sacrifices, and the incense round about him?[1]

That causes me to stop and think about my now-adult children. They have seen me serving communion, they have seen me preaching for years in a pulpit, they have seen me studying Scripture at home, they have seen me singing hymns with great passion and volume! Sunday after Sunday they observed me involved in tasks of ministry. And throughout the week they heard the stories. They were with us in prayer around the table. While all of that is good, it would grieve me if that's all they knew of their father.

If they didn't know any part of my personal life like they know of my involvement in ministry, I would be crushed. And to make matters worse, they would not imbibe my love for Christ. That's exactly the way it was with Hophni and Phinehas. Oh, I can't prove it from a Bible verse, but the signs are everywhere to anyone paying attention.

Whyte continues this way:

And yet, there it is in black and white; there it is in blood and tears—"The sons of Eli knew not the Lord."

Let me think. Let me consider well how, conceivably, it could come about that Hophni and Phinehas could be born and brought up at Shiloh and not know the Lord. Well, for one thing, their father was never at home. What with judging all Israel, Eli never saw his children till they were in their beds. "What mean ye by this ordinance?" all the other children in Israel asked at their fathers as they came up to the temple. And all the way up and all the way down again those fathers took their inquiring children by the hand and told them all about Abraham, and Isaac, and Jacob, and Joseph, and Moses, and Aaron, and the exodus, and the wilderness, and the conquest, and the yearly Passover. Hophni and Phinehas were the only children in all Israel who saw the temple every day and paid no attention to it.

And, then, every father and mother knows this, how the years run away, and how their children grow up, till all of a sudden they are as tall as themselves. And very much faster than our tallest children did Eli's children grow up. All things, indeed, were banded against Eli; the very early ripeness of his sons was against Eli. He thought he would one day have time but it was his lifelong regret that he had never had time. And, what with one thing, and what with another; what with their father's preoccupation and their own evil hearts; the two young men were already sons of Belial when they should still have been little children.[2]

The temptation of any child of vocational Christian ministers is to see the work of the ministry as just another thing, just another religious occupation. Breaking through the wall of "public religion" must be the intense responsibility of the parent-minister if his or her children are to understand that this isn't a business, a slick profession, or an entertainment arena where Mommy or Daddy puts on a performance.

The key word is authenticity. Not perfection, understand, for no one gets it right all the time. But *being real*. Admit your faults, own them completely, ask for forgiveness, be quick to give it, allow children plenty of room to fail, and let them see you live your life behind the scenes with love, grace, and humor. All of that takes time and effort, both of which will cost you productivity on the job. Consider it a priceless, permanent investment.

Second, *disintegrating families have parents who refuse to face the severity of their children's actions.* Eli knew how horrible his sons had become, yet he did nothing! I've seen parents in such denial that they cannot bring themselves to admit that their child has a serious problem with drugs or pornography or sexual promiscuity or stealing—behavior that most any other normal person would consider a red flag. Yet they act as though the crisis will resolve itself if given a little patience.

I've seen too many disintegrating families miss the warning signs, so I have even less reason to doubt the wisdom of Proverbs 19:18. Read these words in several different translations:

> Discipline your children while there is hope. If you don't, you will ruin their lives. (NLT)

> Discipline your children while they are young enough to learn. If you don't, you are helping them to destroy themselves. (TEV)

> Discipline your children while you still have the chance; indulging them destroys them. (MSG)

If you have children who are young, you have children who are impressionable. That's the time to make your most important investment in them. To wait until they're as tall as you, you will have already allowed them to self-destruct.

If your children are nearly adults, take responsibility for your part in their poor choices, then do whatever is necessary to save them. Because you've waited so long, there are few options that don't have grave consequences in the short term. So consider the long term, and do what you must. I repeat: It is never too late to start doing what is right.

Third, *disintegrating families fail to respond quickly and thoroughly to the warnings of others.* Listen to their teachers. They may seem biased against your child, but they rarely are. Take the early reports seriously, and get involved soon. Listen to your pastor or your youth leader. Listen to the uniformed officer with a badge who comes to your door.

Don't be so quick to jump to your child's defense. At least take time to hear the report in full. Ask direct, hard questions to be sure you have the whole picture. Then take time to reflect on what you have heard. If it resonates, causing you to think that it might be accurate, then dig deeper and go to whatever measure is necessary to make certain you have it resolved. Without being impulsive in your reaction, don't be like Eli. He didn't listen to the man of God who came to him (see 1 Samuel 2:27), and he later paid dearly for his negligence.

Fourth, *disintegrating families rationalize wrong behavior, and thereby become part of the problem.* Eli participated in his sons' behavior. We know this because Eli got fat on the food his boys had stolen from the altar. Read again 1 Samuel 2:29 and try to imagine the scene God paints for Eli:

> Why do you kick at My sacrifice and My offering which I have commanded in My dwelling place, *and honor your sons more than Me,* to make *yourselves* fat with the best of all the offerings of Israel My people? (emphasis added)

Eli rationalized and excused the sins of his sons while eating meat that had been stolen from the altar.

As for Samuel, the boy who heard God's voice, the closing words of this episode tell us that the sleepy, spiritual indifference that had lulled Israel into complacency was about to come to a screeching halt. Samuel would rouse the nation from its slumber and call it to action:

Thus Samuel grew and the LORD was with him and let none of his words fail. All Israel from Dan even to Beersheba knew that Samuel was confirmed as a prophet of the LORD. And the LORD appeared again at Shiloh, because the LORD revealed Himself to Samuel at Shiloh by the word of the LORD.

1 SAMUEL 3:19–21

A man of action was on the scene, and Israel's spiritual drift was about to end. Even as a little boy, he not only heard the Lord, but he obeyed His voice.

DO SOMETHING . . . GET INVOLVED

As you ponder all of this, especially as you evaluate the condition of your family, remember that hearing the truth isn't enough. Action is essential. Only on the rarest occasions does the Lord bless someone for merely listening to Him. Faith is an action. That means His blessings almost always lie on the other side of obedience. According to Scripture, knowledge alone merely puffs up, but with action comes humility (1 Corinthians 8:1). Besides, problems like those of Eli do not solve themselves. They multiply and intensify with the passing of time. If the willful acts of rebellion and carnal conflicts that you permit in your family are never resolved, they become unwelcome wedding gifts when your children choose to marry.

If you have reached the conclusion that your family is in danger, choose to do something rather than nothing. Refuse to be like Eli. In the end, after achieving public success in ministry, God considered Eli a failure at home . . . and judged him for it.

Don't go there.

CHAPTER SEVEN

Saul: The King Who Refused to Bow

People never fail to fascinate us. Probably like you, I'm continually engaged in the study of people. No two lives are identical; every person's story is different. However, I've noticed that the plot lines for their stories can be identified by just a few general types. Let's consider four.

Some lives are like racecars on a speedway. They move at blinding speed. They're active; they're highly motivated; they seldom pause except for the occasional pit stop to eat, get the bare minimum of rest, and let their heart slow down before they're peeling out again. Yet for all their speed and fury, they accomplish very little of anything meaningful. They pursue lots of activities and they pour every ounce of energy into them, but when the race is over, their lives are like their tanks—empty. They accomplished very little with the years God granted them. No impact.

Then there are those like meteors, hurtling through space until they hit the world with a blinding flash. They rise to fame because of some achievement or because they're engaged in some notable enterprise. Not long after they catch the public eye, though, they crash and burn. The very world that fueled their fire, causing them to burn brightly, consumed them. Again, no lasting impact. We're left to wonder, *whatever happened to . . . ?*

Others remind us of deep, quiet rivers. These are faithful people who are consistent, giving, supportive, quietly powerful, and profoundly mysterious. They delight in using their silent, almost limitless strength to carry others.

Content to allow other people to skim their surface, restful in the knowledge that they'll never make the headlines, they just keep moving toward their destiny. And when they arrive, they empty themselves—and anyone who cared to float along—into something much, much greater.

Finally, some are like a roofline. For this person, life begins on a pleasant slope upward and ascends with time. God has gifted this person with multiple talents, superior intellect, striking good looks, inner confidence, and every advantage for success. This is the youngster about whom older people say, "Keep your eye on him; he's going places." Sure enough, as soon as he moves into leadership, he begins making a significant contribution. Then . . . something happens. Maybe several things back to back. At a peak, he abruptly pivots downward and the rest of his life moves in the opposite, descending direction. A life of great promise begins to come unglued. Surprisingly, the one who started well becomes characterized by rebellion, scandal, disappointment, embarrassment, and finally complete failure.

The Bible has them all—the intense racecar, the screaming meteor, the enigmatic river, but most common of all, to my sad surprise, the life that resembles the rise-and-fall roofline. How well they begin, yet how dismal their long, miserable decline.

Such was the life of Saul, the king who refused to bow.

The tragic story of Saul reminds me that the impact of any one life—whether positive or negative, large or small—cannot be measured with accuracy until it has run its full course. Beware the temptation to form early opinions about certain individuals, especially those greatly gifted. Assume the best and be willing to give every benefit of doubt, but remember that the end of a life reveals more than the beginning. I often say to university or seminary graduates when I have the privilege of bringing a commencement message, "Don't show me your honors today. Come back in thirty years, and then we'll talk. Today, I'll congratulate you for the four, five, maybe six years of work it took to graduate. But show me thirty years of faithful consistency; then I will applaud."

A nineteenth-century woodsman's proverb says it well: "A tree is best measured when it's down." God has preserved the record of Israel's first king, Saul, who is now "down," and He invites us to count his rings and measure his spiritual stature.

J. Sidlow Baxter, in his book *Mark These Men,* describes Saul this way:

> Saul, the first king of Israel, is one of the most striking and tragic figures in the Old Testament. . . . In some ways he is very big and in others very little. In some ways he is commandingly handsome, and in others decidedly ugly. All in one he is a giant and a dwarf, a hero and a renegade, a king and a slave, a prophet and a reprobate, a man God-anointed and a man Satan-possessed. He began so promisingly, yet deteriorated so dismally, and ended so ignominiously as to make the downgrade process which ruined him monumental for ever afterward to all who would read, mark, and learn.[1]

When interviewing someone for a position on our staff at Stonebriar Community Church or at Insight for Living, I often ask the candidate to give me his or her desired epitaph. "How would you like your stone to read?" The answer tells me a lot about that individual's values, vision, and self-image. At one point, Saul uttered his own epitaph, which the Lord preserved for all of us to remember. The king said, "Behold, I have played the fool and have committed a serious error" (1 Samuel 26:21).

In those five words we read the etching on Saul's tombstone: *I have played the fool.*

As I sit to write this chapter—many months, perhaps even years before anyone holds the finished book—I wonder who might be reading these words. Is your life potentially that roofline type? Could it be that I was led by God to write this chapter just for you as you're approaching that critical pivotal point? Perhaps you are close to making a crucial decision that could very well lead into decline. You may be approaching a crucial intersection where the choices you make will set you on a path that turns you either toward God or away from Him. How you choose to view the truth will make all the difference.

If you face a significant moral dilemma and you know the Lord's take on the matter, but you still find yourself wrestling, then this chapter is for you. Read slowly. Stop frequently for reflection. Ask the Lord to reveal everything you need to see—about Saul, first, then about yourself and your own future. As you read, keep the words of Jesus in the forefront of your mind: "If you continue in My word, then you are truly disciples of Mine; and you will know the truth, and *the truth will make you free*" (John 8:31–32; emphasis added).

THE POWER OF A SINGLE DECISION

From the time that Joshua died until Saul took the throne of Israel, the Hebrew government was not a monarchy like most surrounding nations. Theologians refer to it as a theocracy—"God-rule." The Lord ruled over Israel, issuing His decrees and governing through prophets and priests. Each major region looked to a judge for what most other cultures would expect from a king. He (occasionally, she) led the people in battle, decided civil cases, and enforced God's law.

Samuel judged all Israel with God reigning as king over the Hebrew people. In this way, the Israelites were like no other nation on earth in that they could claim God as their leader, the invisible Creator, the God of Abraham, Isaac, and Jacob, the Almighty One who crushed Egypt, parted the Red Sea, and conquered Canaan. But, much in the same way that the wandering generation tired of manna, the people grew tired of the theocracy. First Samuel 8:1 tells us why:

> And it came about when Samuel was old that he appointed his sons judges over Israel. Now the name of his firstborn was Joel, and the name of his second, Abijah; they were judging in Beersheba. His sons, however, did not walk in his ways, but turned aside after dishonest gain and took bribes and perverted justice.
>
> Then all the elders of Israel gathered together and came to Samuel at Ramah; and they said to him, "Behold, you have grown old, and your sons do not walk in your ways. Now appoint a king for us to judge us like all the nations."
>
> 1 SAMUEL 8:1–5

Those words offer three reasons the people wanted a king. First, Samuel was old and no longer able to keep pace with the demands of the nation. Second, his sons had disqualified themselves by losing the respect of the people. And third, "we want to be like all the nations."

Before we move on, let's not bypass an important point of interest. In the last chapter, we observed the failure of Eli to guide his sons. Now we see little evidence to suggest that Samuel did any better. Scripture doesn't offer as detailed information about his parenting, but the remarkable similarity between Samuel's sons and those of Eli leaves us with little else to conclude. Eli was a great priest and a faithful judge but a lousy father. Samuel, sadly, followed in his footsteps. His sons became unfit as leaders like those of Eli.

According to verse 6, the request displeased Samuel, who took the matter before the Lord:

> The LORD said to Samuel, "Listen to the voice of the people in regard to all that they say to you, for they have not rejected you, but they have rejected Me from being king over them. Like all the deeds which they have done since the day that I brought them up from Egypt even to this day—in that they have forsaken Me and served other gods—so they are doing to you also. Now then, listen to their voice; however, you shall solemnly warn them and tell them of the procedure of the king who will reign over them."
>
> 1 SAMUEL 8:7–9

This was a pivotal moment in the life of Israel. Take special note of the Lord's assessment of their decision. "They have not rejected you, but they have rejected Me from being king over them."

This is extremely significant. Rejecting God's rule for what seems to be a better plan led to a widespread problem in Israel and a series of complications in this story. Nevertheless, the warning that follows comes from the heart of a compassionate Father. Like the dad who sees that his son is doggedly determined to pursue a course of action that will cause great heartache later, the fatherlike God of Israel spell outs the consequences of submitting themselves to a human king.

So Samuel spoke all the words of the LORD to the people who had asked of him a king. He said, "This will be the procedure of the king who will reign over you: *he will take* your sons and place them for himself in his chariots and among his horsemen and they will run before his chariots. *He will appoint for himself* commanders of thousands and of fifties, and some to do his plowing and to reap his harvest and to make his weapons of war and equipment for his chariots. *He will also take* your daughters for perfumers and cooks and bakers. *He will take* the best of your fields and your vineyards and your olive groves and give them to his servants. *He will take* a tenth of your seed and of your vineyards and give to his officers and to his servants. *He will also take* your male servants and your female servants and your best young men and your donkeys and use them for his work. *He will take* a tenth of your flocks, and you yourselves will become his servants.

1 SAMUEL 8:10–17, emphasis added

Observe how many times Samuel said, "He will take . . ." More often than not, earthly kings are takers, not givers. A kingdom revolves around the king, and the nation winds up serving him, not the other way around. When a mere man is on the throne, he becomes the focus of attention, and when that kingdom belongs to God, as in Israel's case, that presents an enormous conflict of interest. Nevertheless, the Hebrew people were determined to have a king, just as the Lord had predicted through Moses back in Deuteronomy 17:14–20. To leave the people with no room to claim ignorance later, He issued this final warning through Samuel. "Then you will cry out in that day because of your king whom you have chosen for yourselves, but the LORD will not answer you in that day" (1 Samuel 8:18).

In effect, the Lord (sounding like a parent) said, "You are determined to go down this path—one that will certainly cause you sorrow—and I will not stop you. You have rejected My way for your own. Therefore, you will lie in the bed you have made."

Nevertheless, the people refused to listen to the voice of Samuel, and they said, "No, but there shall be a king over us, that we also may be like all the nations, that our king may judge us and go out before us and fight our battles."

1 SAMUEL 8:19–20

Does this sound like an exchange between a father and a teenager? After all of the explanation, after all of the warning . . . "nevertheless." And don't miss the basis of their reasoning. "That we also may be like all the nations." To be like someone else, they were willing to lose. Lose their distinctiveness. Lose their possessions and security. Lose their direction, their identity, their God-ordained purpose and destiny. The Lord called Abraham and perfected his faith so that he would give birth to a faithful nation whose king is God. But Israel, the headstrong teenager, wouldn't listen. So the fatherlike God gave the people of Israel their desire.

Sometimes the Lord will let us have our way, knowing we will be hurt. Because He's good, we know that if there were a better way to teach us, He would use it. Unfortunately, painful experience is usually the only way we will learn. Painful consequences play a major role in maturing us.

THE START OF SOMETHING GOOD

Now that we have established the social, political, and theological background, we're ready to meet Saul, Israel's first king—the king who refused to bow. Take note of how God's Word introduces him. Talk about great first impressions!

Now there was a man of Benjamin whose name was Kish the son of Abiel, the son of Zeror, the son of Becorath, the son of Aphiah, the son of a Benjamite, a mighty man of valor. He had a son whose name was Saul, a choice and handsome man, and there was not a more handsome person than he among the sons of Israel; from his shoulders and up he was taller than any of the people.

—1 SAMUEL 9:1–2

What a candidate! Could any choice be more obvious? He came from good stock. He was the son of a valiant, honorable warrior with an excellent family name. He was a big man, impressive, strikingly handsome. The term translated "choice," when used of a young man, means in the prime of manhood, virile, young, strong.

If you're tempted to think that our generation is more superficial than those before us, here's proof that nothing much has changed. For some reason, looks, image, mystique, and style have an influence on success. When Israel wanted a king, they found a fine-looking specimen in Saul. On top of that, he was genuinely modest. When told that he was to be the king of Israel, he replied, "Am I not a Benjamite, of the smallest of the tribes of Israel, and my family the least of all the families of the tribe of Benjamin? Why then do you speak to me in this way?" (1 Samuel 9:21).

Chapters 9 and 10 reveal Saul to be a man of discretion, a man who was interested in trusting God, a man with a generous spirit, a man who spoke for God, energized and inspired. And because he was a man of such quality and promise, Samuel empowered him with these words:

> Then the Spirit of the LORD will come upon you mightily, and you
> shall prophesy with them and be changed into another man. It shall
> be when these signs come to you, do for yourself what the occasion
> requires, for God is with you.
>
> 1 SAMUEL 10:6–7

The old prophet was ready to present Saul to the nation as the king, but to be sure that everyone saw that God had done the choosing, not him, he used a procedure that's very familiar to us by now. Remember when Israel became the victim of "sin in the camp"? Remember how Joshua found the guilty man? Samuel gathered the nation at a traditional meeting site and said, "Present yourselves before the LORD by your tribes and by your clans" (1 Samuel 10:19).

> Thus Samuel brought all the tribes of Israel near, and the tribe of
> Benjamin was taken by lot. Then he brought the tribe of Benjamin

near by its families, and the Matrite family was taken. And Saul the son of Kish was taken; but when they looked for him, he could not be found.

—I SAMUEL 10:20–21

When the God-directed casting of lots established Saul as the new king and the people were ready to crown him, he couldn't be found. Why?

Therefore they inquired further of the LORD, "Has the man come here yet?" So the LORD said, "Behold, he is hiding himself by the baggage."

I SAMUEL 10:22

One of the chief qualities I look for in a prospective staff member or employee is modesty. I want a confident man or woman, but one who finds the job a little daunting. That tells me that he or she has a healthy view of the role we're looking to fill. It *is* daunting! A modest person will be more likely to rely upon the Lord to succeed, and will be much less likely to fail. I am always leery of people who seek the limelight.

Truthfully, Saul behaved like a man I'd consider hiring. He was genuinely modest. And rather than confidently strutting to the front of the crowd, boldly claiming Israel's crown and throne, expecting every knee and head to bow, he stood in the back surrounded by the luggage.

Samuel said to all the people, "Do you see him whom the LORD has chosen? Surely there is no one like him among all the people." So all the people shouted and said, "Long live the king!"

I SAMUEL 10:24

When the people located their new king, they celebrated. And why not? This was a glorious day. Saul was tall, strong, modest, and had the full support of his nation. From a human point of view, this was a beautiful start to a new era—from a *human* point of view. At last, the Israelites let out a heavy, contented sigh and said, in effect, "Finally, we have what we have longed for and needed. We are equipped with strong, centralized leadership like other nations, so now we're safe. Now we're ready to mix it up with the empires." There must have been dancing in the streets.

But from God's point of view, this was a sad day. His people had rejected Him as king, replacing Him with a handsome film star. Unlike all those cheering people, God knew that this was not the beginning of Israel's glory days. A disaster would soon begin to happen.

The Turning Point

Almost overnight Saul's popularity index was off the chart. He had demonstrated himself to be a brave and capable warrior, an able general, and a strong leader. When the Ammonites attacked, he acted decisively and firmly, and he did so with honor. This won the confidence of the people and earned him a great endorsement speech by Samuel. But don't forget that this story is a tragedy. This is a roofline life, and Saul has reached his peak.

Following his burst of glory, Saul's life began to unravel. He became a victim of himself: full of pride, impatience, rebellion, jealousy and attempted murder. Over a long and painful stretch of years, he shriveled into a twisted, maniacal, pathetic figure. Eventually, he would commit suicide. Evil had begun to pour into his life like sewage flowing into a harbor, deep beneath the surface, under cover of night. No one could see it. In fact, for a long time, no one could even smell it, but slowly and ever so surely it polluted the waters of his soul. Scripture reveals Saul's descent with three brief yet illuminating scenes: his arrogance at Gilgal, his obsession with winning, and his insubordination at Amelek.

Saul's Arrogance at Gilgal

The first occurs in 1 Samuel 13 where we see a subtle display of irreverence in a single presumptuous act. Verses 1 through 4 tell us that Saul had picked a fight with the Philistines. Nothing wrong with that. These people lived on land promised to Israel, and they were anything but peaceful neighbors.

Mean as junkyard dogs, the Philistines had been a thorn in the side of the Hebrew people for generations. After Saul provoked them, he had to rally Israel to prepare for all-out war, so he summoned his army to Gilgal. His orders from God, given through Samuel, were simple:

> And you shall go down before me to Gilgal; and behold, I will come down to you to offer burnt offerings and sacrifice peace offerings. You shall wait seven days until I come to you and show you what you should do.
>
> 1 SAMUEL 10:8

This was no small test for the nation and for the new king. Let's not forget why the people wanted a king:

> There shall be a king over us, that we also may be like all the nations, that our king may judge us *and go out before us and fight our battles.*
>
> 1 SAMUEL 8:19–20; emphasis added

The king was doing exactly what everyone hoped he would do. Saul issued the call and waited in Gilgal for the men of Israel to put feet to their faith, so he could lead them against their most troublesome enemy. This was a test for Saul. Would he follow the Lord into battle as Joshua had done? Or would he take matters into his own hands and conscript the Lord?

While waiting for troops to arrive, the odds of winning began to decrease. The Philistines had perfected the process for making iron weapons, which could slice bronze into ribbons. They also had chariots . . . *lots* of chariots, the modern-day equivalent of a tank. They not only had superior numbers, but they were seasoned soldiers, tough veterans of combat. So it's no surprise that Saul's army suffered a high rate of desertion. Those who didn't disappear trembled in their boots.

> When the men of Israel saw that they were in a strait (for the people were hard-pressed), then the people hid themselves in caves, in thickets, in cliffs, in cellars, and in pits. Also some of the Hebrews crossed the

Jordan into the land of Gad and Gilead. But as for Saul, he was still
in Gilgal, and all the people followed him trembling.

1 SAMUEL 13:6–7

Saul waited impatiently for Samuel to arrive, all the while watching his
army drift away. He was to wait seven days, after which the prophet would
arrive, offer sacrifices, and deliver the Lord's battle plans.

Five days, hundreds vanish into the bushes.

Six days, the Philistine camp grows.

Seven days, widespread murmuring in Hebrew turns into talk of mutiny.

Seven days, and Samuel hadn't arrived. Eight days, and the Hebrew army
would be down to nothing. Saul felt sure he had to do something, anything.
Panic replaced patience. So he took matters into his own hands:

> Now he waited seven days, according to the appointed time set by
> Samuel, but Samuel did not come to Gilgal; and the people were scat-
> tering from him. So Saul said, "Bring to me the burnt offering and
> the peace offerings." And he offered the burnt offering.
>
> 1 SAMUEL 13:8–9

Saul's actions involved at least three major errors.

First, *kings weren't supposed to offer sacrifices on behalf of the community.*
Kings could offer sacrifices for themselves, but never for the nation. That
was done only by priests.

Second, *it was Samuel who was to convey the Lord's battle plans.* Saul was to
wait for him. However, since Saul kept his eye on the sundial and his dwindling
army, he rushed ahead on his own. This reduced the sacrifice to a pointless
ritual that looked more pagan than Hebrew. Gentile generals decided where,
when, and whom to attack, mobilized their troops, *then* sacrificed to their gods
to gain favor. The Hebrew sacrifice was an act of submission, not bribery.

Third, and most important to our study, *Saul made the decision to trust
himself at the crisis point.* His decision to sacrifice and attack was based on
good, common sense (from an earthly perspective). Just like Israel's desire
to have a human king and their ready acceptance of Saul based on his out-

ward appearance, the new king was ready to advance on the enemy with a human strategy. Probably a good one, but human, nonetheless.

Remember the victory at Jericho? Who could have guessed God's battle plan? Imagine the disaster that might have happened if Joshua had been thinking in merely human terms. But he followed the Lord's very strange instructions to the letter, and the walls of that great fortress fell down flat.

We serve a God who has limitless power and creativity. Why would we want to rely on our own resources to win a victory that He has promised by His? When we think only in terms of our own abilities, our own strength, or our own ingenuity, we invariably rush ahead and forfeit untold joy and blessing. He *longs* to give us more than we desire, but we limit Him by preempting His plans with our own hasty and clumsy solutions.

Saul's faith failed. He saw his army evaporating like water and the town of Michmash teeming with his enemy. He saw that the appointed seven days had passed and that Samuel was late. So he tossed aside any pretense of decorum and protocol. He, in effect, put on the priestly garb along with his crown and signet and tried to make the altar his instrument of power. Something he had no right to do.

When a person has come to this place in life, when he or she is living on the down-sloping side of pride and arrogance, roles get blurred and responsibilities become meaningless. He or she assumes command of everything and everyone, even going so far as to feel noble and righteous in the process. Observe Saul's response when confronted by Samuel. Pay close attention to the telltale mixture of rationalization, mischaracterization, and blame shifting:

> As soon as he finished offering the burnt offering, behold, Samuel came; and Saul went out to meet him and to greet him. But Samuel said, "What have you done?" And Saul said, "Because I saw that the people were scattering from me, and that you did not come within the appointed days, and that the Philistines were assembling at Michmash, therefore I said, 'Now the Philistines will come down against me at Gilgal, and I have not asked the favor of the LORD.' So I forced myself and offered the burnt offering."
>
> 1 SAMUEL 13:10–12

He said, as it were, "I mean, I . . . I just couldn't help myself. I looked down and my hands were doing it. I mean, it . . . it just kind of happened. In fact, I had to make myself do it. I didn't want to, but you were late, the enemy was enlarging its ranks, and time was running out, so it's really your fault, not mine." Wrong. This was deliberate disobedience based upon presumption and arrogance. And Samuel called him on it. "Samuel said to Saul, 'You have acted foolishly; you have not kept the commandment of the LORD your God, which He commanded you'" (1 Samuel 13:13).

Confrontation is rarely pleasant but frequently necessary. We all need a Samuel, someone who cares more about our character than our comfort. Often, that kind of loving honesty calls for sharp words. "You have played the fool" is never easy to hear, but when it comes from the mouth of a trusted, godly friend, we *must* take heed. In this case, the situation was far more grievous than Saul realized. Don't miss the rest of Samuel's rebuke:

> Samuel said to Saul, "You have acted foolishly; you have not kept the commandment of the LORD your God, which He commanded you, for now the LORD would have established your kingdom over Israel forever. But now your kingdom shall not endure. The LORD has sought out for Himself a man after His own heart, and the LORD has appointed him as ruler over His people, because you have not kept what the LORD commanded you."
>
> 1 SAMUEL 13:13–14

For the king of Israel, obedience is nonnegotiable. If Saul were overly secure in his position, this set him straight. Likewise, we would do well to take this principle to heart: no one is irreplaceable. There is no person so powerful that he or she cannot be removed and replaced quicker than the bat of an eyelid. Positions having authority quite naturally come with a fair amount of power. Generally the more authority, the greater the power. And if we're not careful, we might become deluded into thinking that our power and authority buys us security. Again, wrong! The Lord demands responsibility in exchange for authority, and I have seen more than a few stunned by how quickly the Lord can take everything away.

Saul hit his peak just before this incident, and the Lord's rebuke through Samuel marked a significant turning point. The king has been told that God no longer wants him on the throne and that the position now belongs to his replacement. What happens next proves that Saul's perspective on his position had been skewed all along:

> Then Samuel arose and went up from Gilgal to Gibeah of Benjamin.
> And Saul numbered the people who were present with him, about
> six hundred men.
>
> 1 SAMUEL 13:15

This astounds me. If I had been given news like this, I would have fallen to my knees and begged for forgiveness. But not Saul. He acted like Samuel had said nothing. He continued his plans, proving that he didn't take God seriously. He took his circumstances seriously, but not his God.

When a person has peaked and is now headed downward, he or she will become so caught up in self-serving activities and preoccupied with image that obedience to God takes a backseat to looking good in front of others. Beware! This can be a powerfully self-deluding problem. The events that follow demonstrate that Saul came away from this confrontation feeling justified, misunderstood, and probably a little indignant. He had become so blinded by his own rebellion that, in his mind, his actions were honoring to God, even if the Almighty didn't agree.

SAUL'S OBSESSION WITH WINNING

While Saul's turning point was almost imperceptible to those around him, the second step in his decline would gain considerable attention. If he thought little of God, he thought less of people. I've always said that the depth of your vertical relationship dictates the quality of your horizontal relationships. This next scene occurs at the beginning of Saul's long demise, and it hints of things to come.

After Samuel rebuked Saul and left him at Gilgal, Israel defeated the Philistines. Not because of Saul's great faith, but because of the faith of his son, Jonathan. The king's son took his armor bearer on a secret raid of the enemy camp, saying, "Come and let us cross over to the garrison of these uncircumcised; perhaps the LORD will work for us, for the LORD is not restrained to save by many or by few" (1 Samuel 14:6). While the two men killed several of the enemy, God caused an earthquake under the Philistine camp, which sent them into a panic. This put the invaders to flight back home with the Israelite army in hot pursuit. Defectors and deserters rejoined Saul as he chased the enemy into the wilderness.

However, before Jonathan saved the day, Saul had issued a very rash order, which nearly cost Israel the victory:

> Now the men of Israel were hard-pressed on that day, for Saul had put the people under oath, saying, "Cursed be the man who eats food before evening, and until I have avenged myself on my enemies." So none of the people tasted food. All the people of the land entered the forest, and there was honey on the ground. When the people entered the forest, behold, there was a flow of honey; but no man put his hand to his mouth, for the people feared the oath.
>
> 1 SAMUEL 14:24–26

Now, from any reasonable viewpoint, no one can figure why the king would declare such a ridiculous vow. But when someone is on the downward slope of the roofline, he or she will often make decisions or give orders that are foolish, irresponsible, and occasionally dangerous. This was likely during Saul's seven-day wait. He obviously didn't care about his men as much as he cared about winning the battle. The mere fact that men who are weak from fasting die quicker in combat didn't faze Saul. They were just numbers to him, not comrades. Even his own son could see that:

> But Jonathan had not heard when his father put the people under oath; therefore, he put out the end of the staff that was in his hand and dipped it in the honeycomb, and put his hand to his mouth, and his eyes brightened. Then one of the people said, "Your father strictly put the people under oath, saying, 'Cursed be the man who eats food today.'" And the people were weary. Then Jonathan said, "My father

has troubled the land. See now, how my eyes have brightened because I tasted a little of this honey. How much more, if only the people had eaten freely today of the spoil of their enemies which they found! For now the slaughter among the Philistines has not been great."

1 SAMUEL 14:27–30

In other words, "What an unwise vow for my dad to make. Why would he say such a thing? Look, I'm an example. If we were cursed, God would kill me! But I'm strengthened!" Jonathan was the voice of reason on this day. Clearly, Saul had already started to lose it mentally:

> Saul said, "May God do this to me and more also, for you shall surely die, Jonathan."

1 SAMUEL 14:44

I suspect that he was reaching for his sword with these words. Try to imagine the insanity. Rather than admit that his order was impulsive and idiotic and repent before God, he was about to execute his son just to save face. Fortunately, his subjects intervened with some common sense:

> But the people said to Saul, "Must Jonathan die, who has brought about this great deliverance in Israel? Far from it! As the LORD lives, not one hair of his head shall fall to the ground, for he has worked with God this day." So the people rescued Jonathan and he did not die.

1 SAMUEL 14:45

Stop. Let this scene soak in. Observe how blinded by obsession Saul had become. So bent on winning the war at any cost, so determined to preserve his image, he was willing take the life of his son to avoid retracting a foolish decision. This tendency will factor heavily in his demise.

SAUL'S INSUBORDINATION AT AMELEK

The third episode marks the beginning of Saul's end and seals his fate. As God rejects him as the anointed king of Israel, Saul's true colors begin to bleed through his phony mask. By this point, he was so deluded by his own twisted desires that he was able to behave one way and to talk another with no crisis of conscience at all.

In the time since Saul's very foolish order, the Lord left him to lead Israel on his own, which he did well. Israel was surrounded by enemies, and the king was able to put each in its place so that the nation began to enjoy reasonable security. After a period of time—months, perhaps years—Samuel came to Saul with words that might be confusing at first. Samuel had already told Saul that the Lord no longer wanted him as king and had found another— "a man after God's own heart" —to rule in his place.

> Then Samuel said to Saul, "The LORD sent me to anoint you as king over His people, over Israel; now therefore, listen to the words of the LORD.
>
> 1 SAMUEL 15:1

On the one hand, that may seem like a contradiction. But we shouldn't be surprised. After all, we've come to know the Lord as a God of second chances . . . and third, and fourth, and many more chances. In the end, if we continue down the same path, each time rejecting His offer to bow the knee, submit, obey, and follow, then we have no one to blame but ourselves.

The Lord, as always, saw the future with crystal clarity; and He knew exactly what Saul would do. Yet, as a matter of integrity, He gave the king every chance to bow before Him and recognize God as the true king of Israel. Saul's rebellion would publicly vindicate the Lord, who knew well in advance that he would fail, and leave the insubordinate king without excuse.

The Lord's final test will remind us of a previous chapter:

> Thus says the LORD of hosts, "I will punish Amalek for what he did to Israel, how he set himself against him on the way while he was coming up from Egypt. Now go and strike Amalek and *utterly destroy all that he has*, and do not spare him; but put to death both man and woman, child and infant, ox and sheep, camel and donkey."
>
> 1 SAMUEL 15:2–3; emphasis added

How clear is that? "Utterly destroy all that he has." If a Hebrew soldier heard this from his Hebrew commander, he would know instantly that everything in the enemy camp is "under the ban." Furthermore, this is the Lord issuing the order, not Samuel. Saul was given his orders with absolute clarity straight from God: kill everything and everyone. Period.

> So Saul defeated the Amalekites, from Havilah as you go to Shur, which is east of Egypt.
>
> 1 Samuel 15:7

Good. But then we read,

> He captured Agag the king of the Amalekites alive.
>
> 1 Samuel 15:8

Wait. He *captured* Agag? I don't read "captured" in the original orders. I read "put to death, destroy, utterly destroy, strike, do not spare." And it gets worse!

> But Saul and the people spared Agag and the best of the sheep, the oxen, the fatlings, the lambs, and all that was good, and were *not willing* to destroy them utterly; but everything despised and worthless, that they utterly destroyed.
>
> 1 Samuel 15:9, emphasis added

Just to be certain, go back to 1 Samuel 15:2–3 and see if you can find any loopholes in the language. Did Saul misunderstand? Did he miss the mark by a small margin? What part of "utterly destroy" did he not understand? Who gave Saul and his men the right to divide the spoils into "good" and "worthless"? They were to leave only corpses on the land in obedience to God. But they didn't. So Samuel arrived to find Saul reclining in the tent, pondering which pasture would best feed his new sheep:

> Then the word of the LORD came to Samuel, saying, "I regret that I have made Saul king, for he has turned back from following Me and

has not carried out My commands." And Samuel was distressed and cried out to the LORD all night.

1 SAMUEL 15:10–11

The Hebrew word translated "distressed" here means to burn with anger. Samuel was incensed with Saul and sat up all night stewing in his righteous rage. The Lord gave the rebellious king yet another chance to do what was right, to bow in submission to Israel's true King, but, again, he blew it.

> Samuel rose early in the morning to meet Saul; and it was told Samuel, saying, "Saul came to Carmel, and behold, he set up a monument for himself, then turned and proceeded on down to Gilgal." Samuel came to Saul, and Saul said to him, "Blessed are you of the LORD! I have carried out the command of the LORD."

1 SAMUEL 15:12–13

Even though I have known people like this, still, I cannot fathom Saul's perspective. How can anyone be so clueless? He disobeyed the Lord's direct command by keeping not just a few things under the ban, but keeping everything having any value. On top of having no sense, Saul had no shame. Instead of being humiliated by his own guilt, he erected a monument to himself to commemorate the day. At least Achan had the good sense to be ashamed of his sin. But not Saul! Somehow he managed to twist events and rearrange facts to portray himself as God's champion.

Samuel's response is priceless: "What then is this bleating of the sheep in my ears, and the lowing of the oxen which I hear?" (1 Samuel 15:14).

Amazing how simple facts can so easily prick a deceiving heart. The fog of Saul's self-delusion seems to have lifted. Observe his change in tactics:

> Saul said, "They have brought them from the Amalekites, for the people spared the best of the sheep and oxen, to sacrifice to the LORD your God; but the rest we have utterly destroyed."

1 SAMUEL 15:15

Take note of the pronouns Saul used. "*They* have brought them . . . to sacrifice to the Lord *your* God . . . but *we* have destroyed." In Washington, D.C., they call it spinning. I call it rationalizing. A quick glance in my dictionary turns up this definition: "to attribute (one's actions) to rational and creditable motives without analysis of true and especially unconscious motives."[2]

Rationalization is a thin veneer that covers deceit. I don't think anyone missed Saul's motives. His claim that the spoils were preserved for sacrifice was meant to stroke Samuel's priestly emotions. But this, too, was a symptom of Saul's disease: a twisted mind. Just as he underestimated Samuel, Saul had no sense of the gravity of his situation—the importance of his position, the place he was to occupy in history, the significance of obedience, and most of all, the immensity of the God he served.

Samuel wasn't buying it. The following dialogue dispels any notion that Saul had merely bumbled his way into disobedience. He stretched his preposterous lie to the limit, perhaps hoping that his defense would have Samuel questioning himself. Don't miss Saul's brash impudence:

> Then Samuel said to Saul, "Wait, and let me tell you what the LORD said to me last night." And he said to him, "Speak!" Samuel said, "Is it not true, though you were little in your own eyes, you were made the head of the tribes of Israel? And the LORD anointed you king over Israel, and the LORD sent you on a mission, and said, 'Go and utterly destroy the sinners, the Amalekites, and fight against them until they are exterminated.' Why then did you not obey the voice of the LORD, but rushed upon the spoil and did what was evil in the sight of the LORD?" Then Saul said to Samuel, "I did obey the voice of the LORD, and went on the mission on which the LORD sent me, and have brought back Agag the king of Amalek, and have utterly destroyed the Amalekites. But the people took some of the spoil, sheep and oxen, the choicest of the things devoted to destruction, to sacrifice to the LORD your God at Gilgal."
>
> 1 SAMUEL 15:16–21

The word translated "wait" uses a particular part of speech and nuance that is rare in Hebrew. It was not unlike saying, "Shut up!" The best contemporary rendering would be something like, "give it up" or "come off it." Samuel said, in effect, "Just drop that pathetic line of reasoning, Saul. Let me convey to you what God had to say about it last night."

Saul's response tells me that he felt like he was calling Samuel's bluff, that he doubted the prophet's relationship with God. Furthermore, Saul's convoluted sense of right and wrong actually had him thinking that he was doing right. Self-delusion writes its own tragic script.

So Samuel ran down the facts for him again, ending with a clear statement of where Saul stood with respect to right and wrong. "Why then did you not obey the voice of the LORD, but rushed upon the spoil and did what was evil in the sight of the LORD?" To which Saul responded with more detailed excuses, more emphatic blame shifting, and more deceptive rationalization than before.

OBEDIENCE IS NOT AN OPTION

Samuel's next words cut to the heart of the matter, and they lead us to an important principle—one that may preserve your life if you ever find yourself nearing a crucial juncture. Read his words slowly. I imagine that his voice suddenly grew quiet. I hear compassion in these next lines, a man pleading for his younger friend to see the truth:

> Samuel said,
> "Has the LORD as much delight in burnt offerings and sacrifices
> As in obeying the voice of the LORD?
> Behold, to obey is better than sacrifice,
> And to heed than the fat of rams.
> For rebellion is as the sin of divination,
> And insubordination is as iniquity and idolatry.
> Because you have rejected the word of the LORD,
> He has also rejected you from being king."
>
> 1 SAMUEL 15:22–23

Samuel was no longer trying to save Saul's crown; that was already lost. The old prophet was trying to do for Saul what he could never do for his own sons: save him from further rebellion and inevitable self-destruction. Unfortunately, he couldn't. This marks only the beginning of Saul's long, miserable decline.

The man whose epitaph was "I have played the fool" didn't start out that way. He was once tall, handsome, modest, generous, a valiant warrior, and a humble servant-leader. But because he refused to bow, Saul's heart hardened, he became greater in his own eyes than his God, and he resisted everything that he had been chosen to represent.

TIMELESS PRINCIPLES . . . ESSENTIAL STRATEGIES

I see two timeless principles at work in the story of Saul that deserve our attention.

First, *how you finish is far more important than how you start.*

No one graduates from college thinking, *OK, now how can I fail?* No bride or groom tells the wedding guests, "Enjoy the party; this thing won't last more than a couple of years." Only when a woman or man finishes well can we call that life a success. A good beginning does nothing to guarantee a good ending. Happy endings are the result of good choices and consistent discipline put in sequence over a lifetime and faithfully maintained.

Second, *rationalization is disobedience because it refuses to accept the truth.* I've heard it said that the most destructive lie is the one you tell yourself. Rationalizing is an insidious form of self-delusion. It starts small—usually with something innocent—and quietly twists the mind to define truth in convenient ways. In the end, the self-deluded mind rationalizes everything so conveniently, so automatically, that the person has no concept of how preposterous his or her thinking and behavior have become. And—never forget this—no one is immune.

To avoid this pitfall, consider these three essential strategies:

Remain accountable. Listen to the counsel of those who love you and have your good at heart. They may be desperately trying to help you see a particular truth about yourself. Give reproof a hearing.

Reject pride. Pride would have you defend foolish decisions when it's best simply to admit that you blew it. If you're in a position of leadership, your followers will respect you more, not less, when you accept responsibility for failure, ask for forgiveness, and make the most of future opportunities. Rationalization fools no one and makes you look stupid.

Pursue truth. I've lived my life by those two words. Follow the truth wherever it leads, and you'll find God's blessing every time. I need to warn you; the road will be disquieting and risky and will make you feel vulnerable. Your relationship with truth will cause you to face some unpleasant things and will often leave you isolated . . . in the short term. Remember that you are never really alone. Furthermore, the honor God gives you will be far greater than what you could have given yourself.

Strict obedience is better than good intentions. This isn't complicated. When you hear a clear command, don't analyze or interpret it. Just obey it. When God says, "Don't marry a nonbeliever," no amount of love or hope will make the marriage any more acceptable to God. When the Lord says, "Abstain from sexual immorality," obey that command. Do not look for ways to get around it or try to justify compromising your purity. None of that will make your sin any less destructive.

Rationalizations are usually based on good intentions, but they always lead to trouble.

You may have already chosen poorly. You may be, even now, continuing to rationalize your decision. To use the words of Samuel, stop . . . give it up . . . drop the rationalization. You're fooling no one but yourself. You have only one choice now. It's not easy, but neither is it complicated.

Unlike Saul, turn back. Admit your error. Seek the Lord's mercy. Bow humbly before your God. Put an end to your rebellion. You will find Him quick to hear, willing to forgive, and overflowing with grace.

CHAPTER EIGHT

Abigail: The Woman Who Saved Her Husband's Neck

Almost every husband I know has a story about how his wife rescued him. I don't mean a dramatic feat of strength and cunning where she swoops in at the last moment to save him from some life-threatening disaster. Usually, she rescues him from himself. By her wisdom and tact, she keeps him from doing or saying something that he would later regret. In fact, I recall two particular situations that could have turned very ugly were it not for Cynthia's kind, understated but firm counsel.

Back when our youngest son, Chuck, was about to become a teenager, my involvement in preaching, publishing, teaching on the radio, being on the road, and church ministry was becoming more than I could handle. I hadn't learned the discipline of saying no, so I had days that kept me busy from very early in the morning to long past Chuck's bedtime. I say to my shame that my wife and children—the most important people in the world to me—were left with the crumbs of my time and energy.

Cynthia saw it long before I did and had been growing more concerned about one particular aspect of my neglect: our youngest, Chuck. Being the wise partner she is, she carefully selected the right moment to correct my perspective. When offering a reproof, remember that the goal is to be heard, not to prove that you're right and the other person is wrong. She knew my moods and when I would be able to hear her counsel without feeling attacked. And she presented it in a way that would give no reason for me to feel defensive.

"Are you aware of how much time you spent with Curt [our oldest son] and how little you're spending with Chuck?" she asked, "I remember looking out the front door several years ago and seeing you and Curt playing catch or touch football or batting practice until it was dark. And you were at most of his practices, all his games, and any special occasion that came along. But," she continued, "you very seldom do any of that with Chuck."

Even though she was right, I became defensive. I wasn't really open as I should have been . . . until I got alone and thought about it. Fortunately, the result of that rescuing experience was wonderful. She spoke at just the right time, which became a pivotal moment for me as a father and as a husband. That conversation led to a much closer relationship with Chuck than I would have had otherwise. She rescued me. Or, as we sometimes say, she saved my neck.

More recently, I found myself increasingly at odds with a brother in the Lord who lives in another state. The offense started small, but then a number of other events added to my agitated feelings. Even though we were close enough for me to bring it to his attention, I hadn't said anything. Then, something more significant happened that prompted me to sit down one Saturday afternoon and write a letter. I wanted it to be firm and fair, while leaving sufficient room for grace, so I edited it and then rewrote it. I did that more than a few times until it was just right. I spent well over two hours preparing my written reproof. I had other things to do, but this was important.

When I finished, I decided to sit down Saturday night and read it to Cynthia. We share almost everything, so this was par for the course. I read the letter with all the passion and feeling that had gone into my writing it. She listened and nodded her agreement with much of it as she affirmed my perspective. Clearly, she understood.

When I finished, she didn't say much, but she offered this advice: "You know, honey, if I were you, I would sleep on that letter before I mailed it. Everything you say is true, and I don't think it's exaggerated, but it's awfully strong. And I think you may regret it if you mail it."

Well, I didn't sleep on it. I lay awake on it—all night. It churned in my stomach as I turned in the bed. Early the next morning, I unfolded the letter and read it again. And before Sunday passed, I tore it up. I'm so glad

I did. He didn't need my letter, and little of what I had to say would have been helpful in the long run. In fact, the issues were resolved through a set of circumstances that never would have happened if I had sent that written missile.

Once again, Cynthia saved her husband's neck. That's one of the great benefits to having a solid marriage, where the communication lines stay open. You can face the challenges of life with a partner who loves you unconditionally, who will look out for your very best, even when you can't . . . or won't.

THE WOMAN NAMED ABIGAIL AND THE MAN NAMED FOOL

This is the story of Abigail, the woman who saved her husband's neck. And I don't mean figuratively; I mean literally. She rescued him from a violent death, a peril he brought upon himself by his own foolishness. First Samuel 25 unfolds this account of passion, danger, irony, and intrigue. It reminds me of a classic Western movie, with wide-open country; gritty heroes on horses; a tough, beautiful heroine; and a crusty, hard-hearted villain who complicates life for everyone. Only this story is not fiction, and it revolves around three very complex, conflicted characters who wound up on a collision course. Allow me to introduce each of them.

THE HERO

Think of this as a movie. As the overture concludes, the camera pans across a vast, rugged wilderness, where might makes right and rough-hewn people survive without the help of government and laws. The camera slowly zooms in on a handsome, young warrior standing in front of several hundred battle-hardened soldiers. The warrior's name is David.

> Then Samuel died; and all Israel gathered together and mourned for him, and buried him at his house in Ramah. And David arose and went down to the wilderness of Paran.
>
> 1 SAMUEL 25:1

By this time, David had killed Goliath, received his anointing as the king of Israel, and taken to living in the wilderness to avoid jealous King Saul, whose heart was set on murder. We read of Saul's long, slow decent into evil in the previous chapter. Part of that downfall was his utter contempt for David, who had served him faithfully. Instead of showing gratitude, Saul turned on the young man and wound up trying to murder him. For years, David lived in the most rugged places in Israel, places that were too difficult for an army to survive long enough to track him down.

As I wrote in the first chapter, David attracted a band of four hundred fighting men, whom he trained in the cave of Adullum.By the time of this story, that number has grown to six hundred. These were sharp, seasoned warriors living on the edge of trouble; but under David's leadership, the random collection of malcontents had become a disciplined fighting force. After moving to the wilderness of Paran, they became the self-appointed peacekeepers and lawmen of the region. Their services were both needed and appreciated.

The wilderness of Paran lay to the very far south of Israel, down below the Dead Sea, just above Sinai. We would call it no man's land. It was too far from anything to be influenced by government, so anyone living there had to fend for themselves. Any flocks or herds that grazed in the wilderness of Paran would become victims of thievery or wild beasts were it not for David and his troops. Fortunately for the businessmen who owned herds and flocks, these men had taken it upon themselves to police the southern frontier.

This arrangement was not without tradition, and the custom was that the peacekeepers would not demand payment for their services. However, as a matter of integrity, the businessmen would voluntarily offer compensation out of gratitude. To withhold payment would be like failing to tip a waitress for the service she provides. If she does a fair job, the tip would be modest. If she does a great job, the tip should be generous. In this case, the protection that David provided was superb. None of the herds or flocks were harmed. None of them were taken by thieves. Since sheep-shearing time was payday, it was the right time to gently remind the businessmen of the protection they enjoyed.

THE ANTAGONIST

Now imagine that the scene shifts from the wilderness to the trading center of Carmel, where businessmen gather to buy and trade. Bales of wool are being loaded onto beasts of burden in the background, while a shrewd entrepreneur, wearing the very finest clothes and a satisfied smile, fondles a silver coin—one of the many he made that day. His eyes are hard. He's savvy in the ways of making money, but in every other respect, he's boorish and smug. Despite his condescending manner, he's very popular . . . because he's very rich.

> Now there was a man in Maon whose business was in Carmel; and the man was very rich, and he had three thousand sheep and a thousand goats. And it came about while he was shearing his sheep in Carmel (now the man's name was Nabal, and his wife's name was Abigail. And the woman was intelligent and beautiful in appearance, but the man was harsh and evil in his dealings, and he was a Calebite.)
>
> 1 SAMUEL 25:2–3

The name Nabal is the Hebrew word for "fool." It's the same word used throughout the proverbs and other wisdom literature to refer to churlish, rude, ignorant, dishonest, belligerent, obstinate, stupid people. It's unlikely that this was the name given to him by his mother. The biblical writer may have used this as a nickname for the man, but it also could have been the name people used behind his back. Verse 3 is a parenthetical aside to the reader, in which the writer says, "Oh, by the way, the man's name is Fool."

Regardless of how he came by his name, Nabal lived up to it. He was a bigoted, stubborn, rigid, prejudiced, and underhanded businessman. On top of it all, the man was a tightwad. Aside from all that, I suppose we could say that Nabal was a fine gentleman.

THE HEROINE

Finally, the scene fades from the bustling trade center in Carmel to a homestead just a few miles south in Maon. The music softens, and a stunningly beautiful woman steps into the picture. Her dark hair and exquisite features frame a pair of eyes that only hint at the wisdom at work behind them. She is as industrious and ingenious as she is beautiful. Her name is Abigail, which means "my father is joy."

Though the woman was intelligent and beautiful, her husband was harsh and dishonest in his dealings. From our modern perspective, we wonder how a woman like Abigail could end up married to a klutz like Nabal. The irony here is painful. A woman having noticeable wisdom, married to a loser named Fool. But in those days, marriage was a business arrangement between fathers, not the culmination of courtship and love like today. Now, don't believe what the revisionists of history would tell you. Most of the time, the marriage worked out beautifully. Fathers loved their daughters and took great care to choose a man who would not only provide for and care for his daughter, but love her and treat her tenderly. And almost always, a genuine love grew between the couple very quickly.

However, people then, just as today, could be fooled. Abigail sounds like she came from a good home, but her father didn't see the obvious character flaws in his future son-in-law. This was a terrible marriage and, as a result, Abigail suffered. But you wouldn't know it to see her.

THE CRISIS

As the story unfolds, we can see and admire Abigail's display of remarkable poise and keen judgment:

> And it came about while he was shearing his sheep in Carmel . . . that David heard in the wilderness that Nabal was shearing his sheep. So David sent ten young men; and David said to the young men, "Go up to Carmel, visit Nabal and greet him in my name; and thus you shall say, 'Have a long life, peace be to you, and peace be to your house, and peace be to all that you have. Now I have heard that you have shearers; now your shepherds have been with us and we have not insulted them, nor have they missed anything all the days they were in Carmel. Ask

your young men and they will tell you. Therefore let my young men find favor in your eyes, for we have come on a festive day. Please give whatever you find at hand to your servants and to your son David.'"

When David's young men came, they spoke to Nabal according to all these words in David's name; then they waited.

1 Samuel 25:2, 4–9

I appreciate the tactful way David went about this. First, he didn't gallop at full tilt to Carmel with all six hundred men on stallions, demanding payment. This is a quiet reminder that Nabal's profit at the market would not have been nearly as high were it not for David's protection. Furthermore, David extended remarkable honor to the man, recognizing his station as a nobleman. And he did it with incredible humility, considering that the throne of Israel would one day be his. Don't miss the fact that he didn't expect a specific amount. The request was, in essence, "Give whatever you think is fair."

If this were a bill, I would call it a very gracious, considerate statement. I don't remember ever getting anything like this from the people who manage the electric company.

Dear Mr. Swindoll,
Peace be upon your home and to your family. You have enjoyed electricity in your home, lo, these many weeks. Since we have expenses we must pay, do you think you might be able to help us with those? Please return the enclosed envelope with anything you care to send.

May God bless you,
Your humble servants at the power company

I think I'd faint. Normally it says, "Pay now! Put it in here! Send it by this date, or we'll shut your power off and charge you an extra heap to turn it back on!" David didn't do that. He said, in effect, "Send whatever you think is fair and we will receive it with gratitude. Shalom."

Nabal's response could not have been more insulting:

But Nabal answered David's servants and said, "Who is David? And who is the son of Jesse? There are many servants today who are each breaking away from his master. Shall I then take my bread and my water and my meat that I have slaughtered for my shearers, and give it to men whose origin I do not know?" So David's young men retraced their way and went back; and they came and told him according to all these words.

1 SAMUEL 25:10–12

Take note of Nabal's response. Look for clues to his character. Don't be fooled by his first question. He knew very well who David was. This was meant to disparage David as having no pedigree. Nabal, on the other hand, was a direct descendant and heir of the great Caleb, something akin to having George Washington as your ancestor with the deed to Mount Vernon in your name. Caleb stood with Joshua during the Exodus and urged Israel to take Canaan as the Lord promised. Later, after the wilderness wandering, at the age of eighty-five, he stood in the southern frontier of the land and said, "Give me that hill country!"

Asking, "Who is David?" and "Who is the son of Jesse?" was a calculated slap in the face—both for David and his lineage. Of course, we know that David was destined to become Israel's king, but very few people knew that at the time. So, this was like saying, "You're a nobody! You come from nothing. Who are you to be talking to someone as important as I?"

Nabal's next comment takes aim at David and his followers. It was a very clever jab insinuating that they were all no better than slaves (the lowest people in society), and that they were a ragtag rabble who were disloyal to both Saul and Israel.

Then he completed the insult with a final flourish. "Shall I then take my bread and my water and my meat that I have slaughtered for my shearers, and give it to men whose origin I do not know?" In other words, "I prefer to give the reward of labor to those who earned it, not a bunch of hooligans trying to extort a living from real producers like me."

Notice the response of David's men. No fighting. No arguing. They simply leave.

Nabal went back to trading, socializing, and reveling in the success earned in part by David. Being habitually oblivious, he probably thought everything would carry on as usual. While the festival in Carmel continued, an emotional earthquake shook the desert, and David was its epicenter. He was not yet the mature man of God that he would become. It would take many more years in the desert to temper his steel. He was still rough and uneven. In 1 Samuel 24, he showed supernatural restraint in sparing the life of Saul, whom he still regarded as "the Lord's anointed." But in chapter 25, we see a different David. The heart of a passionate man of war beats his chest. And the impudent response from the thankless Nabal brought out the worst in him.

This was not David's best moment. His reaction was a rash act of the flesh, not a prompting by the Spirit of God. The Lord may act severely and His judgment may be swift, but He is never rash.

Let me offer this as a quick aside. Be careful to test what you may think to be a prompting from the Lord. He doesn't speak to us audibly as He did in those days, and what may feel like a compelling unction from the Holy Spirit may just as well be your own hidden desire. It is true that you have living within you the Holy Spirit of Almighty God, and He always gives good guidance. But you also carry with you many pounds of carnal flesh that makes wrong seem right. A transformed mind will tell the difference, but that doesn't take place overnight. Maturity comes with time and experience; it's a product of a growing intimacy with the Almighty.

So I urge you to put your promptings to the test. The Lord will honor His truth by confirming it for you. Refuse to act impulsively. Instead, weigh your words carefully, sleep on decisions having significant consequences, and remain open to reproof. Does Scripture affirm the wisdom and morality of your choice? Do the wise, godly people in your life have any objections? What has your own past experience taught you? Have you asked the Lord to examine your heart over the matter and then prayed quietly?

David did none of that. Instead he issued the order, "Each of you gird on his sword." He left two hundred troops to guard the camp, while four hundred and one took off in a cloud of dust for the shearing festival in

Carmel. Soon the ground outside Nabal's tent would be soaked with his blue blood. And not only his, but that of his sons too. This was a massacre in the making.

THE PLOT DEEPENS

Meanwhile, an unnamed servant who overheard Nabal's insults slipped silently out of Carmel to alert Abigail. Notice that he didn't talk to Nabal. You get nowhere talking to a man named Fool. But he knew that Abigail would listen because that's what intelligent people do. They listen—especially to servants:

> But one of the young men told Abigail, Nabal's wife, saying, "Behold, David sent messengers from the wilderness to greet our master, and he scorned them. Yet the men were very good to us, and we were not insulted, nor did we miss anything as long as we went about with them, while we were in the fields. They were a wall to us both by night and by day, all the time we were with them tending the sheep. Now therefore, know and consider what you should do, for evil is plotted against our master and against all his household; and he is such a worthless man that no one can speak to him."
>
> 1 SAMUEL 25:14–17

That last statement is telling, isn't it? I'm taken back by how casually the servant speaks of Nabal's worthlessness to his wife. Yet, in Hebrew culture, she must show him honor and respect, both in private and with his servants. What an awful existence. How tragic it is to live under the authority of a person who won't listen and doesn't even have his servants' respect.

Do you live with someone like that? Were you reared by a mother or father who simply could not be wrong? Do you have a grown child, now an adult, who will not listen? Do you have a spouse who is completely out of touch with how he or she affects others? If so, then you understand why that is one of the most difficult situations in life to endure. You can't get through to them. You know before you begin to communicate that they're going to shut out your words. And they have a dozen reasons why what you say is wrong. Nabals still exist.

Allow me an extra measure of imagination with this next comment, OK? Abigail could have thought, *Oh, my. David's on his way to kill Fool? God moves in mysterious ways, His wonders to perform!* But she didn't go there. And I'm impressed with her integrity. She chose to protect her husband, not because he deserved it, not because he was good, but because *she* was good. Despite how bad a husband he had been, she chose to remain honorable in her role as his partner . . . even when he was not present.

If you're in a situation similar to Abigail's, you know how hard that is to do. And you may be growing weary, wondering, *How long, Lord?* You may have periodically given up and behaved poorly—reacting with hostility or subtly getting revenge here and there. I don't mean to judge your reaction as I convey what Scripture teaches by Abigail's model. She could very easily have done nothing, and we would have little cause to blame her. But her incredible response is worthy of study and emulation. Amazingly, she immediately put a plan in motion that would protect her husband from harm. This is one remarkable lady!

> Then Abigail hurried and took two hundred loaves of bread and two jugs of wine and five sheep already prepared and five measures of roasted grain and a hundred clusters of raisins and two hundred cakes of figs, and loaded them on donkeys. She said to her young men, "Go on before me; behold, I am coming after you." But she did not tell her husband Nabal.
>
> 1 Samuel 25:18–19

She put together a meal big enough to feed an army . . . literally! No one prompted her; no one suggested she intercede for her husband. In fact, she never told him what she was doing. Of course, he probably would have stopped her if she had. This intelligent, beautiful, unselfish woman moved to save her husband's neck because that's what a good mate does. And all the while, she was mentally preparing her speech for David.

THE CLIMAX

It came about as she was riding on her donkey and coming down by
the hidden part of the mountain, that behold, David and his men
were coming down toward her; so she met them. Now David had
said, "Surely in vain I have guarded all that this man has in the wilderness, so that nothing was missed of all that belonged to him; and
he has returned me evil for good. May God do so to the enemies of
David, and more also, if by morning I leave as much as one male of
any who belong to him." When Abigail saw David, she hurried and
dismounted from her donkey, and fell on her face before David and
bowed herself to the ground.

1 SAMUEL 25:20–23

All of the tension in the story has been building to this moment. The
two men were about as opposite as men can be, yet they have behaved in
similar ways. Both were obstinate, proud men. Each believed the other
to be a fool. Both allowed anger to rule their judgment. Each shot off his
mouth about the other. Both acted rashly, led by impulse rather than good
sense. But here, at the climax of the story, who did Abigail approach to
resolve the conflict?

Her only hope was to appeal to David. She knew that speaking to Nabal would change nothing. Her speech is a classic example of a persuasive
address in the Near East, and it drips with wisdom. Her primary goal is to
remind David of his identity as the Lord's anointed, then she urges him to
behave accordingly. Read the following slowly, thoughtfully:

She fell at his feet and said, "On me alone, my lord, be the blame.
And please let your maidservant speak to you, and listen to the words
of your maidservant. Please do not let my lord pay attention to this
worthless man, Nabal, for as his name is, so is he. Nabal is his name
and folly is with him; but I your maidservant did not see the young
men of my lord whom you sent.

"Now therefore, my lord, as the LORD lives, and as your soul lives, since the LORD has restrained you from shedding blood, and from avenging yourself by your own hand, now then let your enemies and those who seek evil against my lord, be as Nabal. Now let this gift which your maidservant has brought to my lord be given to the young men who accompany my lord. Please forgive the transgression of your maidservant; for the LORD will certainly make for my lord an enduring house, because my lord is fighting the battles of the LORD, and evil will not be found in you all your days. Should anyone rise up to pursue you and to seek your life, then the life of my lord shall be bound in the bundle of the living with the LORD your God; but the lives of your enemies He will sling out as from the hollow of a sling. And when the LORD does for my lord according to all the good that He has spoken concerning you, *and appoints you ruler over Israel,* this will not cause grief or a troubled heart to my lord, both by having shed blood without cause and by my lord having avenged himself. When the LORD deals well with my lord, then remember your maidservant."

1 SAMUEL 25:24–31, emphasis added

In effect, she said, "David, look ahead! You're not even thirty! You can afford to return good for evil because you are God's choice to become the king of Israel. Don't stain your reputation before you take the throne. Our God will bless you if you behave like the king you are. Besides, the battle is the Lord's. Let Him deal with Nabal."

Now observe David's response:

Then David said to Abigail, "Blessed be the LORD God of Israel, who sent you this day to meet me, and blessed be your discernment, and blessed be you, who have kept me this day from bloodshed and from avenging myself by my own hand. Nevertheless, as the LORD God of Israel lives, who has restrained me from harming you, unless you had come quickly to meet me, surely there would not have been left to Nabal until the morning light as much as one male."

1 SAMUEL 25:32–34

Two bullheaded men were about to clash over what was essentially a common courtesy, and David was ready to murder a man because he wounded his pride. In this story, we don't see much of a difference in character between David and Nabal . . . until the climax. The difference is small, but it makes all the difference. Whereas Nabal wouldn't listen to reproof, David did. Don't miss the profound gratitude he expressed to Abigail. She not only saved her husband's neck, but she also saved David's. F. B. Meyer, in his chapter on David, appropriately calls this episode in David's Life, "A Cool Hand on a Hot Head."[1]

Scripture calls David "a man after God's heart." Obviously that can't mean that he was perfect, as this story clearly illustrates. He was impatient. He was rash. He was passionate. He was a man who had many women before his death. Far from being perfect, being a man after God's heart means that whatever touches the heart of God also touches the heart of David. Whatever moves God to acts of compassion or judgment also moves David. The heart of David beat in sync with God's. Abigail reminded the future king of this relationship with the Lord, and as she spoke, his anger melted away.

> So David received from her hand what she had brought him and said
> to her, "Go up to your house in peace. See, I have listened to you and
> granted your request."
>
> 1 SAMUEL 25:35

Catastrophe averted. Nabal lives to insult again, and David avoids gaining a reputation for being a capricious tyrant before taking the throne. And both men have the wisdom and tact of Abigail to thank.

The end.

Wait. That's a wonderful story as it is. But there's more. Obedience usually requires us to sacrifice something we want in favor of what God desires. And when we obey, He delights to surprise us with a far greater blessing than the one we gave up. This story is no exception:

> Then Abigail came to Nabal, and behold, he was holding a feast in
> his house, like the feast of a king. And Nabal's heart was merry within

him, for he was very drunk; so she did not tell him anything at all
until the morning light.

1 SAMUEL 25:36

After this courageous act of wisdom and grace, wouldn't it have been
wonderful if Abigail could have come home to tell Nabal what she had
done for him? Even better, wouldn't it have been great if he had put his
arms around her and thanked her for saving his neck? Instead she came
home to a beer party and a drunk husband. He had no idea that death was
breathing down his collar just a few hours before. He had no idea how great
a prize he had in the person of Abigail. In fact, considering her situation,
she would have been much better off to allow Nabal's foolishness to catch
up to him and take his life.

My heart goes out to mismatched mates, who struggle to make it through
the week, craving the slightest affirmation. If that's where you are, you're still
waiting for kind words to come your way. I've dealt with married couples
in which one partner or the other is all-consuming in his or her selfishness.
So self-centered, self-contained, self-concerned, not even gracious enough
to recognize the everyday blessing of a faithful mate.

Let me go a step further. I've buried some people only to have their
mates whisper to me, "I don't know why it just now dawns on me all the
things she meant to me." In light of that, allow me to offer this simple advice: don't wait until your husband or wife is gone before you say, "Thank
you for all you do. I don't even want to think about what life would be
without you. I love you." In fact, be specific. Name the reasons you appreciate your partner.

Poor Abigail didn't receive any of that. Seeing her husband's condition, she decided to let him sleep it off. It's probable that after the hours
of preparation, riding, pleading, and after the sudden release of emotions,
this wonderful woman fell into her bed, exhausted, and cried herself to
sleep. The music and the drunken howls of Nabal and his cohorts no doubt
drowned out the sensible voice in her head telling her that she did the right
thing. She saved her vile husband's neck by appealing to the honor of the
man—a real man—who would have freed her from future heartache.

But in the morning, when the wine had gone out of Nabal, his wife told him these things, and his heart died within him so that he became as a stone. About ten days later, the Lord struck Nabal and he died.

1 Samuel 25:37–38

I want to proceed with caution and avoid misapplying Scripture. We have to accept that this story, like many in the Bible, describes extraordinary events in order to teach us important principles. The death of any human being is not something to be taken lightly; but frankly, if this were a movie, the audience would be cheering.

The Resolution

David left justice in the hands of God. Abigail entrusted her future to Him. Both sacrificed a foreseeable future that looked attractive to them, yet they chose to do what was right. After the Lord brought justice down on the man named Fool, His plan could be seen clearly. It was there all the while, standing just behind the door of obedience.

If you're a fan of fairytale endings, you'll love this story. If this were the last few minutes of a movie, you don't want the credits to roll with Abigail wasting away in front of her tent, watching sheep graze in the distance. Where's the "happily ever after" in that? Take note of David's reaction to the news:

> When David heard that Nabal was dead, he said, "Blessed be the Lord, who has pleaded the cause of my reproach from the hand of Nabal and has kept back His servant from evil. The Lord has also returned the evildoing of Nabal on his own head." Then David sent a proposal to Abigail, to take her as his wife. When the servants of David came to Abigail at Carmel, they spoke to her, saying, "David has sent us to you to take you as his wife." She arose and bowed with her face to the ground and said, "Behold, your maidservant is a maid to wash the feet of my lord's servants." Then Abigail quickly arose, and rode on a donkey, with her five maidens who attended her; and she followed the messengers of David and became his wife.

1 Samuel 25:39–42

Once David stepped through the door of obedience, he saw the Lord's plan and pursued the blessing that lay before him. Abigail wasted no time either. I can't blame either of them! Abigail's actions demonstrated that she was an extraordinary woman, a wife that a king would be a fool to overlook. David's actions demonstrated that he was a real man—a man strong enough to realize he was wrong to take a wise rebuke to heart, examine his choices, trust the Lord, and do what is right in God's eyes.

Some might question the timing. Nabal's funeral is barely over and these two have known each other for only minutes. But don't forget that these are not twenty-first-century, urbanite lovers. Marriage in those days was motivated more by honor and duty than love. Ancient Near Eastern society was not kind to widows, even rich ones. And life on the southern frontier of Israel was a dangerous place for anyone not equipped to fight.

David saw a widow in need, who also happened to be an uncommonly good and insightful woman. Abigail saw a protector to preserve her estate, who also happened to be a man after God's heart. This was a match made in heaven.

Over the years, I have learned that, when making big decisions, tradition and conventional wisdom should be taken seriously. Grieving the loss of a mate takes time, usually about three years (some suggest five) before a person can even begin to think and function normally, much less contribute to a new relationship. I have seen far too many jump out there too quickly, and someone's heart winds up getting crushed. My advice: listen! Listen to those wise people who love you and have demonstrated that they have your best interest in first place. If they say wait, then wait.

On the other hand, let's be careful about etching those hard-and-fast rules in stone. Tradition and conventional wisdom should be taken seriously, but let's leave room for God to do the unusual. Miracles are, by their very nature, precious and rare enough without our trying to quash them. David and Abigail demonstrated uncommon faith, choosing to set aside a future they would make for themselves. Consequently, God moved quickly to bless both of them rather than make them wait.

THE MORALS OF THE STORY

Each character points us to a lasting lesson. After all, God's stories are not merely for entertainment, though the entertainment value is high. He preserved these narratives for our spiritual development.

From David, we learn that *rash reactions never pay off.* David's quick-tempered reaction almost led him to murder. Just think, if David had killed Nabal in a fit of passion, his proposal and marriage to Abigail would have tainted his reputation. I can only imagine how differently Israel's history might have played out if David had failed this test of self-control. Thanks be to God that he was the kind of man who would listen to others.

For all I know, even as you read this, you have a plan that you are ready to put into operation. It's a passionate act. I warn you, if it's rash, it's wrong. Stop! Rash actions never pay off. Think through the consequences. Sleep on it. Seek wise counsel . . . and then listen. You've spent your time only on one side of the dilemma. Force yourself to look at it through another set of eyes. If you find yourself frequently on the defensive, and you're feeling all alone in your perspective, recognize that your perspective is the one that should be doubted. Act on raw and shallow emotions, and you are going to bring pain on yourself that will hurt for years to come.

From Nabal we learn that *insensitive mates leave untold heartache all around them.* This applies to wives who rob their husbands of dignity and respect with their continual criticism and generally dismissive attitude. Don't fool yourself into thinking that because you love him, he doesn't need to feel your respect and admiration. To him, love and respect are the same. When you criticize him, or insult him, or fail to trust him, it causes untold heartache. The tragedy is that you may never know it. (Don't ask him. He won't tell you.)

This applies to husbands who strip their wives of self-worth and value by dismissing their counsel and failing to see their positive qualities. Communication is to a woman what physical intimacy is to a man. To dismiss her when she talks is no less demoralizing to her than when she rejects your advances. Do that over a long enough period of time, and she will eventually get the message and stop trying, just like Abigail. And, trust me, men, when a woman stops trying to talk to you, your marriage is in deep trouble. The tragedy is that some of you may never know it. Your own insensitivity is keeping you in the dark.

Let me take this a step further. Your insensitivity not only crushes your wife, but it could also lead to your own destruction. Nabal remained insensitive to those who protected his flock. And the earthquake that shook the hills of Paran could have led to his own demise. He was also insensitive to his wife so that when he was in danger, she could not even come to him with the warning.

If you happen to be a Nabal, please . . . *wake up!* God has given you a gift beyond compare in that wife of yours. He's given her a gift for insight, which I have learned to heed from my wife in our fifty years of marriage. I became much more successful once I began giving my wife's perspective equal weight with my own.

From Abigail we learn that *wise partners make the best use of timing and tact.* When Abigail sensed danger, no one had to tell her to move swiftly. Wisdom knows when to slow down and evaluate all angles of a situation, and also when to seize a moment before it slips away. She hurried to put that meal together. She acted swiftly to catch the moment before it was gone. Almost without exception, timing is everything.

And when she saw murder in David's eyes, she spoke courageously, though calmly. She carefully chose her words, not to win the argument, but to put David in the very best position to hear and heed her counsel. And when she finished her task, she returned home without speaking a word to Nabal. It wasn't the right time. First light was better.

As you turn the last page of this chapter, do yourself a favor. Bookmark this place, put the book down, and ask your married partner several pointed questions. I'll suggest a few to get you started, or you can come up with your own, then simply listen. *Listen.* Don't defend, don't try to explain how he or she came by that opinion. Listen.

Start with these questions:

- When do I make you feel good about yourself and us? When do I make you feel the worst?

- If you could change one thing about yourself, what would it be?
  What would you want changed about me?
- If I am about to make a terrible mistake, how likely are you to
  tell me? What would keep you from doing that?
- Do you feel like I value your judgment? Please be honest with
  me. I want to know.

One more time, let me urge you to listen to the mate God has given
you. Who knows? One day he or she may save your neck. Literally!

CHAPTER NINE

Absalom: The Rebel Prince Charming

The Bible never flatters its heroes. The handsome, young warrior who swept wise and beautiful Abigail off her feet was, in fact, a polygamist. Apparently one woman was not enough. So David compromised God's sacred institution of marriage—one woman, one man, together for life—and chose to marry not just one, but many women.

I must admit that this part of David's character has always disturbed and perplexed me. He was a man after God's heart, a valiant warrior who learned to trust the Lord for everything. He was also a tender and talented worshiper with the soul of a poet and a talent for music. His integrity outdistanced that of his peers, yet . . .

We can only wonder what it must have been like for Abigail to find out that she was just another in his harem once the honeymoon was over. David married her while he was king of nothing, learning obedience on the rugged frontier of Judea. Some time after, he became king over part of Israel and moved his wives into the palace in Hebron. Then, after another seven and one-half years, his enemies died, leaving no resistance to his becoming the unrivaled monarch of the twelve tribes. That's when he and his wives moved to Jerusalem.

Despite the Lord's express command against Israel's kings building harems (Deuteronomy 17:17), Abigail shared the palace in Jerusalem with Michal, Ahinoam, Maacah, along with a number of other wives and concubines. The practice was socially acceptable—almost expected of royalty in those days. However, as we'll see, it kept David's dynasty from becoming everything God would have wanted.

The inspired human author of 2 Samuel tells us in his opening remarks that David fathered a number of sons by these women. Alexander Whyte paints a vivid word picture of David and his household:

> Polygamy is just Greek for a dunghill. David trampled down the first and best law of nature in his palace in Jerusalem, and for his trouble he spent all his after-days in a hell on earth. David's palace was a perfect pandemonium of suspicion, and intrigue, and jealousy, and hatred—all breaking out, now into incest and now into murder. And it was in such a household, if such a cesspool could be called a household, that Absalom, David's third son by his third living wife, was born and brought up.[1]

In this seething cauldron of intrigue and deceit, Maacah (which means "oppressed" in Hebrew) reared her son, Absalom. His name means "Father of peace," which will become more ironic as the story unfolds. Even without their association with David, Maacah and her son had royal blood running through their veins. She was the daughter of Talmai, the king of an important city up near the Sea of Galilee.

ABSALOM'S CHILDHOOD INFLUENCE

Twenty years transpired between 2 Samuel 3 and 13. David's kingdom grew, and the friends who remained loyal to him during his humble days in the wilderness began to reap the rewards of their devotion. The Bible calls them "the thirty," as you may remember from our first chapter. Eliam gave his beautiful daughter in marriage to Uriah, a fellow member of this elite "band of brothers." And David gave Uriah an estate just behind the palace. He also gave Eliam's father an important role as one of his chief advisors—secretary of state in his royal cabinet, if you will. His name was Ahithophel. (Another name to remember.)

During these twenty years, David remained exceptionally busy. He defeated the Philistines, conquering Moab, Edom, Ammon, and Aram. He also wiped out a number of massive invading armies. And when David wasn't conquering or building, he was lost in the endless affairs of state. Much of his time was spent in secret council chambers making decisions concerning war, diplomacy, building, taxation, administration. The remainder was spent in travel, on parades, giving speeches, and making appearances in one venue after another. He had too many wives and too many children to have much of an influence on any of them—except by accident. He helped conceive lots of children, but he helped rear none of them.

To give you a more specific idea of how many wives and children we're talking about, I've developed a chart, which is located on the following page. I count eight wives who are named, a number of unnamed wives who bore him children, and no fewer than ten concubines. Then each of the named wives has at least one child, though Michal had none. She had her father's (King Saul) temperament, which may explain her remaining barren (2 Samuel 6:20–23).

During an uncharacteristic lull in David's life, when the king was supposed to be at war, he saw Bathsheba, the beautiful wife of Uriah, bathing in the backyard of the estate he had given his longtime friend. His idleness and lust made for a bad combination. While Uriah fought the enemy, David committed adultery with his wife. And when she became pregnant, David wound up having his steadfast friend murdered to cover his sin. As soon as Bathsheba ended her time of mourning, he made her his wife. Scripture says, "the thing that David had done was evil in the sight of the LORD" (2 Samuel 11:27). The Lord ultimately broke open the scandal and pronounced this judgment on David:

> Behold, I will raise up evil against you from your own household; I will even take your wives before your eyes and give them to your companion, and he will lie with your wives in broad daylight. Indeed you did it secretly, but I will do this thing before all Israel, and under the sun.
>
> 2 SAMUEL 12:11–12

Although David repented—genuinely and completely—and the Lord restored him to complete favor, the palace was never the same place again. The sins he had committed took an awful toll. The king became a timid judge of right and wrong, reluctant to rule with kingly authority.

THE FAMILY OF DAVID

1 Samuel 18:27; 1 Samuel 25:42–43; 2 Samuel 3:3–5; 1 Chronicles 3:1–9; 14:3–4

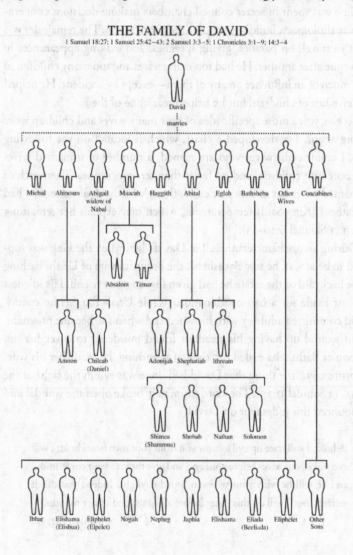

During all of this, Absalom entered adulthood encircled by his father's bickering, jealous wives. He already had resentments built up against his absentee father. But after discovering that his dad was an adulterer and murderer, his struggling respect slowly sank into utter disgust.

ABSALOM'S DEFINING MOMENT

In tragic homes like this, the siblings must depend upon one another for emotional strength and survival. Absalom and his sister Tamar became very close. In fact, Absalom loved her so much that later he would name his own daughter after her.

As chapter 13 opens, we find Absalom a bitter, angry man. What happened next would cause him to snap:

> Now it was after this that Absalom the son of David had a beautiful sister whose name was Tamar, and Amnon the son of David loved her. Amnon was so frustrated because of his sister Tamar that he made himself ill, for she was a virgin, and it seemed hard to Amnon to do anything to her.
>
> 2 SAMUEL 13:1–2

Amnon, David's oldest son fell in love with Tamar, his half sister. His incestuous affections were all wrong. The Old Testament called both his desire and what he did next an "abomination" (Leviticus 18:6–18, particularly verse 9; Leviticus 20:17; Deuteronomy 27:22). Jonadab was an evil influence on Amnon as he encouraged him to act on his lust:

> So Amnon lay down and pretended to be ill; when the king came to see him, Amnon said to the king, "Please let my sister Tamar come and make me a couple of cakes in my sight, that I may eat from her hand." Then David sent to the house for Tamar, saying, "Go now to your brother Amnon's house, and prepare food for him." . . . Then Amnon said to Tamar, "Bring the food into the bedroom, that I may eat from your hand." So Tamar took the cakes which she had made and brought

them into the bedroom to her brother Amnon. When she brought them
to him to eat, he took hold of her and said to her, "Come, lie with me,
my sister." But she answered him, "No, my brother, do not violate me,
for such a thing is not done in Israel; do not do this disgraceful thing!
As for me, where could I get rid of my reproach? And as for you, you
will be like one of the fools in Israel. Now therefore, *please speak to the
king, for he will not withhold me from you.*"

2 SAMUEL 13: 6–7, 10–13; emphasis added

What a bizarre thing for Tamar to say! David would have permitted a
marriage between his children? He had either lost his mind or lost any sense
of authority over his family. Unfortunately, Tamar's reasoning wouldn't stop
her half brother's forced advances. He raped her:

However, he would not listen to her; since he was stronger than she,
he violated her and lay with her.

2 SAMUEL 13:14

When he finished satisfying his lust with Tamar, Amnon's great "love"
turned instantly to bitter hatred, and he said to her, "Get up, go away" (v.
15). Then he threw her out onto the street.

Now take note of the reaction of the men in her life:

Then Absalom her brother said to her, "Has Amnon your brother
been with you? But now keep silent, my sister, he is your brother; do
not take this matter to heart." So Tamar remained and was desolate
in her brother Absalom's house. Now when King David heard of all
these matters, he was very angry. But Absalom did not speak to Amnon
either good or bad; for Absalom hated Amnon because he had violated
his sister Tamar.

2 SAMUEL 13:20–22

David was very angry? That's it? That's all? Just angry? According to
the Law, which David knew very well, whoever violated his sister was to

be vomited out of the community. That was the law of a land over which David was king. He was to enforce the Law of God! David should have put him out of the house, out of Jerusalem, out of the land of Israel, thereby making a bold statement to all the community that his son's actions had caused him to be an abomination. But Amnon knew his father. So did all of his children. Amnon knew he could get away with it. Due to his father's past failures, he had no backbone for discipline. That's why Amnon had such gall.

David got very angry . . . but he did *nothing*!

ABSALOM'S CHOICE

Absalom, already embittered toward his father, stewed in his resentment and anger for two long years. He waited in vain for his father to do what was right. Remember our study of Cain in chapter 2? Unresolved sin and anger will eventually lead to tragedy, quite possibly murder. Not surprisingly, that's exactly the plan Absalom put in motion:

> Absalom commanded his servants, saying, "See now, when Amnon's heart is merry with wine, and when I say to you, 'Strike Amnon,' then put him to death. Do not fear; have not I myself commanded you? Be courageous and be valiant." The servants of Absalom did to Amnon just as Absalom had commanded.
>
> —2 SAMUEL 13:28–29

So we have Prince Absalom raised in this unruly, undisciplined, completely dysfunctional home. His half brother raped his sister with no consequences because their father was too weak to uphold the Law of God in his own home. And all of this leads to yet another murder. Absalom killed Amnon, then went into hiding. Don't miss where he went:

> Now Absalom fled and went to Talmai the son of Ammihud, the king of Geshur. And David mourned for his son every day. So Absalom had fled and gone to Geshur, and was there three years. The heart of King

David longed to go out to Absalom; for he was comforted concerning Amnon, since he was dead.

2 SAMUEL 13:37–39

Remember the name Talmai? That's Absalom's maternal grandfather, the ruler of an important city to the north of Jerusalem. He took refuge with his granddad. Apparently Absalom had established a link with him and found something in the home of Grandfather Talmai that he couldn't find in David's. He remained there for three years.

Throughout this time, rather than missing his son, David's attitude seems to be one of relief. He appears to be grateful that he didn't have to carry out justice against his oldest son. In a convoluted sort of way, the situation worked itself out, leaving David little to do, ultimately, but woo his tortured son home. During Absalom's self-imposed exile, that is exactly what David and his commander-in-chief, Joab, did. But I find David's stance to be an odd one:

> So Joab arose and went to Geshur and brought Absalom to Jerusalem. However the king said, "Let him turn to his own house, and let him not see my face." So Absalom turned to his own house and did not see the king's face.

2 SAMUEL 14:23–24

This is just a little bit different than the story of the prodigal son in the gospel of Luke, isn't it? That father said, "This son of mine was dead and has come to life again; he was lost and has been found" (Luke 15:24). This father said, "Yeah, he can come back, but I don't want to see his face! Let him have his own place and raise his own family, but I want nothing to do with him." Though they must have lived fairly close, there was no contact.

ABSALOM'S SCHEME

Both men, it appears, held on to their resentments. David's spirit became increasingly unforgiving while his son lived out his days as a bitter, critical, vengeful man. Being deceptive, he appeared to be something quite different on the outside. Notice that the tone of the historical writer changes from pure facts to introduce a little color:

> Now in all Israel was no one as handsome as Absalom, so highly praised; from the sole of his foot to the crown of his head there was no defect in him. When he cut the hair of his head (and it was at the end of every year that he cut it, for it was heavy on him so he cut it), he weighed the hair of his head at 200 shekels by the king's weight.
>
> 2 SAMUEL 14:25–26

Absalom, though angry and resentful at heart, came across as a winsome Prince Charming. He was not only extremely handsome, but the Bible says that he had not a single physical blemish—not a mark, not a mole, not a pimple, no acne, and certainly no disease. But he did have a distinctive feature: a mane of thick, dark hair that he cut once a year. According to my best commentaries, 200 shekels equaled at least three pounds (1.4 kg)! That's a load of hair!

It occurs to me that Absalom could have cut it more than once per year, if it was a genuine bother. But that unusual amount of hair, combined with his remarkable good looks, must have attracted women from all over the kingdom. So, let's face it, knowing the effect his good looks had on women, it was vanity that kept him out of the barber's chair.

Our prince was as charming as he was handsome. On the inside, his spirit became a tangle of unresolved sin, resentment, bitterness, and hatred. But he maintained a much different facade:

> Now it came about after this that Absalom provided for himself a chariot and horses and fifty men as runners before him. Absalom used to rise early and stand beside the way to the gate; and when any man had a suit to come to the king for judgment, Absalom would call to him and say, "From what city are you?" And he would say, "Your servant is from one of the tribes of Israel." Then Absalom would say to him, "See, your claims are good and right, but no man listens to you

on the part of the king." Moreover, Absalom would say, "Oh that one would appoint me judge in the land, then every man who has any suit or cause could come to me and I would give him justice." And when a man came near to prostrate himself before him, he would put out his hand and take hold of him and kiss him. In this manner Absalom dealt with all Israel who came to the king for judgment; so Absalom stole away the hearts of the men of Israel.

2 Samuel 15:1–6

It seems our Prince Charming was a scheming rebel. But we can't be surprised. The failure of David to hold Amnon accountable for the rape of his sister stood between father and son. And so, just as the prophet Nathan had earlier predicted, the sword never departed from the house of David. When the young man returned, David gave the same attention to him as he did Amnon . . . none. Neither good nor bad. And when the king eventually granted his son an audience, his welcome was very cordial but cool. The text tells us that Absalom bowed before his father and that David kissed him.

While that may sound like a tender reconciliation, we have to remember that this is a different time and culture. In those days, a kiss was the equivalent of our handshake. No tears. No kind words of affirmation and reconciliation. No fatherly embrace. This was a superficial gesture that made official peace between the men, but it did nothing to warm a relationship that chilled with each passing month of pervasive silence. Eventually, Absalom's heart became deadly cold toward his father, and he began a calculated plan to overthrow him.

ABSALOM'S MOTIVES

The details of his long campaign to destroy David are enough to fill a book, so I'll focus instead on the important ones: the reason a son would conspire against his dad.

Absalom bore in his heart a deep, unresolved resentment against his father, which kept him from seeing David for who he was. I wonder how

Absalom might have responded if David had not kept him at a distance but invited him to come close. I wonder if the boy's bitterness would have softened if his father had chosen to be completely transparent, unguarded, willing to bear even pent-up anger and extreme criticism.

We, as parents, have a mistaken notion that our children expect us to be perfect. And we have an uncanny ability to keep them at a distance, thinking that it will conceal the flaws that we hate most about ourselves. In truth, our children want to know us as we are—flaws, hurts, confusion, limitations, scars, the whole truth, warts and all. They want to love us deeply, but that requires unguarded vulnerability and painful authenticity. Too many of us remain focused on making a living and maintaining a reputation that we hope will inspire awe. You might be able to get away with that when they're young, but as they mature, they'll see the cracks in your character. They'll see through all the cover-up. Disillusioned and disappointed, they will pursue authenticity somewhere else.

All Absalom wanted was to know his real dad. If he had seen David's profound sorrow over his sins and heard a heartfelt apology for his poor handling of Amnon's violation of Tamar, what a difference it would have made. Instead, what he got was a sterile, formal relationship sealed by a dutiful kiss.

Another reason for Absalom's rebellion was David's halfhearted expression of forgiveness. The young man wanted resolution so much that he preferred death to living in limbo. Observe his attitude when he originally requested to see his father:

> Why have I come from Geshur? It would be better for me still to be there. Now therefore, let me see the king's face, and if there is iniquity in me, let him put me to death.
>
> 2 SAMUEL 14:32

Tragically, the young man's attempt to connect with his father failed to give him any resolution. His anguish knew no bounds.

Considering all that had happened—David's own sin, his unwillingness to punish Amnon, his refusal to build a bridge back to Absalom, giving him neither justice nor mercy—is it any wonder that Absalom used justice to curry favor with the people and undermine his father? I find great irony in the biblical writer's choice of words:

> Moreover, Absalom would say, "Oh that one would appoint me judge in the land, then every man who has any suit or cause could come to me and I would give him justice." *And when a man came near to prostrate himself before him, he would put out his hand and take hold of him and kiss him.*
>
> —2 Samuel 15:4–5; emphasis added

Absalom's Contempt for David

When Absalom finally was given freedom to roam Jerusalem and the palace, he set up his own little kingdom within David's. Over time, it grew like a cancer, steadily turning loyal subjects into rebels. He started by dispensing judgment to the people so their attitude toward the king would sour. Then he set his sights on one of David's top advisers, a disgruntled member of his cabinet. You may remember his name from earlier in this chapter. It's Ahithophel.

> And Absalom sent for Ahithophel the Gilonite, David's counselor, from his city Giloh, while he was offering the sacrifices. And the conspiracy was strong, for the people increased continually with Absalom.
>
> 2 Samuel 15:12

Winning over Ahithophel was no small victory, but it didn't take much. He was probably just as disillusioned with David as Absalom. This elder statesman was the grandfather of Bathsheba, with whom David committed adultery and for whom David murdered Uriah, a close companion to Ahithophel's son. In this very shrewd move, Absalom turned a strained relationship between Ahitophel and David to his advantage. Winning this respected nobleman gave him enough support among Israel's elite to overthrow the king. To cut to the chase, David had to flee the palace and return to his wilderness life. Only this time, his own son, not Saul, sought to kill him.

To rub salt into David's wound, Ahithophel, the grandfather of Bathsheba, gave Absalom this advice:

> Ahithophel said to Absalom, "Go in to your father's concubines, whom he has left to keep the house; then all Israel will hear that you have made yourself odious to your father. The hands of all who are with you will also be strengthened." So they pitched a tent for Absalom *on the roof*, and Absalom went in to his father's concubines in the sight of all Israel. The advice of Ahithophel, which he gave in those days, was as if one inquired of the word of God; so was all the advice of Ahitho-phel regarded by both David and Absalom.
>
> —2 SAMUEL 16:21–23; emphasis added

Where was David when he first lusted after Bathsheba? Did you notice where Ahithophel said to place the tent? *The roof.* And thus the prophecy was fulfilled. "I will even take your wives before your eyes and give them to your companion, and he will lie with your wives in broad daylight. Indeed you did it secretly, but I will do this thing before all Israel, and under the sun" (2 Samuel 12:11–12). The reenactment of rooftop lust was the ultimate payback, ripping the scabs off his father's old wounds.

ABSALOM'S DEMISE

I wish the story of this Prince Charming ended like a fairy tale. But 2 Samuel 18 tells us the sordid, sad ending of his life. David had rallied loyal troops and was fighting to regain his throne. His army and that of his son were engaged in battle, and David's had gained the upper hand. Joab, David's commander-in-chief, and two other men with whom he had planned his strategy were close by when the king gave strict instructions concerning the battle:

The king charged Joab and Abishai and Ittai, saying, "Deal gently

for my sake with the young man Absalom." And all the people heard
when the king charged all the commanders concerning Absalom.

2 SAMUEL 18:5

Obviously, David bore tremendous guilt over his longstanding neglect of
the boy he kept at arm's length, the young man whom he had never known
or mentored. His fight was to regain his rightful place on the throne of
Israel, not retribution, certainly not to see his son dead. Nevertheless, the
source of Absalom's vanity would prove to be his undoing:

> Now Absalom happened to meet the servants of David. For Absalom
> was riding on his mule, and the mule went under the thick branches of
> a great oak. And his head caught fast in the oak, so he was left hanging
> between heaven and earth, while the mule that was under him kept
> going. When a certain man saw it, he told Joab and said, "Behold, I
> saw Absalom hanging in an oak." Then Joab said to the man who had
> told him, "Now behold, you saw him! Why then did you not strike
> him there to the ground? And I would have given you ten pieces of
> silver and a belt." The man said to Joab, "Even if I should receive a
> thousand pieces of silver in my hand, I would not put out my hand
> against the king's son; for in our hearing the king charged you and
> Abishai and Ittai, saying, 'Protect for me the young man Absalom!'
> Otherwise, if I had dealt treacherously against his life (and there is
> nothing hidden from the king), then you yourself would have stood
> aloof." Then Joab said, "I will not waste time here with you." So he
> took three spears in his hand and thrust them through the heart of
> Absalom while he was yet alive in the midst of the oak. And ten young
> men who carried Joab's armor gathered around and struck Absalom
> and killed him.

2 SAMUEL 18:9–15

This leads to one of the saddest passages in all the Bible. A messenger
brought news of Absalom's death. What follows in very few words reveals
the bottomless depth of David's grief.

The king was deeply moved and went up to the chamber over the gate and wept. And thus he said as he walked, "O my son Absalom, my son, my son Absalom! Would I had died instead of you, O Absalom, my son, my son!"

2 SAMUEL 18:33

As we read those words of utter anguish, we realize that the tragic life of Absalom flashed across David's mind—heartbreaking memories of a thousand fatherly failures. Though he would have given his own life for a chance to erase those many errors, the death of Absalom seared them into his mind, like a white-hot branding iron. Remorse is merely the pointless wish that we had done things differently. Alas, it came too late. The time to make things right with those we love is *before* they die.

ABSALOM'S LESSONS FOR US

In this tragic tale of a king and his wayward son—a rebel Prince Charming—I find no fewer than three lessons that linger to this day. I touched on them as I recounted the story, but they bear repeating.

First, *an unhappy home produces unbalanced children*. However idyllic the kingdom of David, his home was unhappy. He may have built an impressive legacy for Israel and expanded his realm beyond the dream of any other man. He may have been a brilliant battlefield commander, strategizing and mobilizing troops to win impressive victories. And he may have been a man after God's own heart, penning prophetic psalms and composing melodies that prompt others to worship. But he couldn't lead his family in the way that he himself walked. When it came to public accomplishments, he was a success. But when it came to his family, he was a failure. His home was so unhappy and his children so unbalanced, the dysfunctional fallout would keep a modern counselor busy for decades.

Men, I have little doubt that you are successful in building your career and having an impact on the professional world. That's impressive and gratifying. But let me urge you to pause and think: are you cultivating a happy home? Is it a home that will produce fulfilled, well-balanced, godly men and women? Your job as protector and provider is to create a safe and healthy environment for each of the people in your care—your wife and your children—to become anything God might have in mind for them. You don't have to be perfect around the house. You don't have to be flawless. But you do need to be *there*, investing yourself with the same energy and problem-solving skills and ingenuity that you model at work.

Don't lose yourself in business as your children slip through your fingers like tiny grains of sand. Believe the cliché: before you know it, they're gone! You don't want them one day to look back and say, "Who is that man? Why did he ever have me?" Absalom's story lives on. The lengths to which people will go to fill the void left by absentee fathers are recorded every day at the courthouse. Absalom made his own choices, but David couldn't deny the consequences he caused by his neglect, and his grief proved almost too much to bear.

Second, *lack of parental discipline breeds insecurity and resentment in children*. We are living in a day in which children have luxury and leisure heaped upon them, with little or no discipline to balance things out. Sure, they'll beg and whine for more freedom, but that isn't what they really want. Like Absalom, they long for the security of a home where right behavior is rewarded and wrong behavior is acknowledged and firmly dealt with. Children and adults alike need that kind of structure to make sense out of the world. Imagine playing a game where the rules changed without notice, and the very moves that cost you points caused another person to win. Eventually, your insecurity and resentment would require that you either cheat or stop caring about the game.

I can't find one instance in Scripture where David disciplined his children. I only see one example after another where a son flouted the Law of God and David did nothing. In the end, even his most trusted and loyal general, Joab, knew he could disobey a direct order and suffer no consequences. Boundaries were conspicuous by their absence.

Lack of parental rule setting and reinforcement breeds insecurity. I cannot guarantee that if you discipline consistently and fairly that you'll have model children. But I can guarantee that if you discipline them, *you* will be obeying Scripture. I encourage you to be faithful to do what is right and leave the results to the Lord. Your children need your love and affection . . . plenty of both. But with equal passion, they long for boundaries that are set and maintained.

Third, *failure to repair a broken relationship inflicts wounds that never heal.* I once had the unfortunate task of trying to counsel a family very much like David's. The father was extremely busy making a lot of money. His girls and his one boy soon sensed that his business meant more to him than they did. And so they began to live cheap, sensual, compromising lives that they didn't even bother to conceal. The behavior of the children became so notorious that the testimony of the church came under criticism by the community, so I had to visit the family at their home. At one point I had to break up a fistfight between two of the girls after they brought down the dining room chandelier and knocked a shutter off the window. The mother sat there wringing her hands, muttering, "I just don't know what I'm going to do with these children." Obviously the relationships between each member of this family had been broken for a very long time, if ever there were any to begin with.

At the age of forty-two, the father's heart stopped beating long enough to cause significant brain damage. By most standards, he was dead, although his body lingered for some time at the veteran's hospital. As the children visited, hoping for some sign that there might be a chance for reconciliation, the grief mounted as his condition declined. Finally, he died. The dismal atmosphere of remorse and profound heartache that filled the mortuary made it almost impossible to breathe.

This father had departed emotionally long before his tragic end. He left his children with no moral guidance. He left his wife to fill the role of both parents. He left his family with no reason to think that they were important and loved. And he left them with no way to heal the deep, emotional wounds they both suffered and inflicted. Ultimately, he left them to make it on their own.

For years, the lingering wounds have continued to afflict the man's children. I don't know that they will ever enjoy a normal relationship with a mate or their children or anyone intimate.

I urge you to make the effort now to repair those broken relationships.

Trust me, it's worth it. Again, I repeat: It's never too late to start doing what is right! Make contact today. Begin with these words: "I have been wrong. I love you, and I want a close relationship with you. Please forgive me and tell me how we can make it happen."

Tough words, I know. But they're easier than, "If only I had . . ."

I remember memorizing a very short poem by John Greenleaf Wittier in grammar school with all my classmates. It was an assignment required by a very wise teacher. She knew that those in her class were too young for it to make much sense then . . . but someday it would register. I cannot name the times I have repeated these words to myself and others during my adult years. Because they fit so perfectly the tragic story of this well-known father and his rebellious son, I leave them for you to ponder:

> For of all sad words of tongue or pen,
> The saddest are these: "It might have been!"[2]

CHAPTER TEN

Rehoboam: The Reckless Phony

You wouldn't have known it at first, but their home was nothing but a facade. Literally. One side looked like a beautiful, half-million-dollar home with brick and siding on the exterior, while the other side was nothing but a lattice of two-by-fours propped up with pulleys and scaffolding. Tap on the brick and you hear the hollow thump of plaster and chicken wire. Of course, the family who lived there didn't exist, except for thirty minutes each week on television.

I am amazed by the detail that set designers put into a television studio. Look in one direction and you see the outside of a home, complete with bushes and grass, even ivy climbing the brick walls. Look in another, and you see a living room. They even improvised an outdoor camping scene with trees, dirt, and a completely realistic campfire. Everything was created with great attention to detail and with a high value placed on authenticity. That is, unless you looked at it from the wrong side. Behind the scenes, where the camera doesn't go, it's all a messy network of plastic, metal, and wood—a flimsy mask, as it were—held together with cheap, temporary material. It's all built in short order to meet the weekly schedule. From the other side, however, the camera makes it look like the place has been there for years. It's all phony. The bushes, the ivy, the grass, the brick—everything. Fake.

Mark Twain said, "Everyone is a moon and has a dark side which he never shows to anybody."[1] Rehoboam could have sat for that portrait. He had a dark side that only God saw through. In fact, He was pleased to reveal the story of his life to us in the ancient books of 1 Kings and 2 Chronicles. These musty, dusty books are twin witnesses to history, preserving fascinating stories of forgotten lives, with names we can barely pronounce. Yet each one teaches lasting lessons worth learning.

The story of Rehoboam is no exception. Like a television stage, the side that faced the audience—the public man—looked very genuine. The inspired story takes us behind the scenes for a hard and very realistic look at the real Rehoboam . . . a reckless phony.

THE MAKING OF A HYPOCRITE

To understand the man, we must understand what helped make Rehoboam the man he became. Steven Ambrose said it well: "It is through history that we learn who we are and how we got that way, why and how we changed, why the good sometimes prevailed and sometimes did not."[2] First Kings 11 is the story of the fall of Rehoboam's father. You may be surprised to learn that his father was Solomon, a king upon whom God showered wisdom, success, and fabulous wealth. Space doesn't permit me enough room to describe the lavishness of Solomon's kingdom. The surrounding realms sent him tribute, and Israel's import/export business brought in astounding sums of money each month.

Though he was rich, he let his relationship with the Lord slip, and he began to live like a reprobate. The following words describe how the erosion began:

> Now King Solomon loved many foreign women along with the daughter of Pharaoh: Moabite, Ammonite, Edomite, Sidonian, and Hittite women, from the nations concerning which the LORD had said to the sons of Israel, "You shall not associate with them, nor shall they associate with you, for they will surely turn your heart away after their gods." Solomon held fast to these in love. He had seven hundred wives, princesses, and three hundred concubines, and his wives turned his heart away. For when Solomon was old, his wives turned his heart away after other gods; and his heart was not wholly devoted to the

LORD his God, as the heart of David his father had been. For Solomon went after Ashtoreth the goddess of the Sidonians and after Milcom the detestable idol of the Ammonites. Solomon did what was evil in the sight of the LORD, and did not follow the LORD fully, as David his father had done.

1 Kings 11:1–6

In that long list of women, take note especially of one particular nationality of wives and their false god. In verse 1, the writer mentions Ammonite wives, and in verse 5, "Milcom the detestable idol of the Ammonites." Then in verse 7, "Molech, the detestable idol of the sons of Ammon." Most scholars believe that Milcom and Molech were the same idol viewed from different perspectives. Perhaps they were twin gods of the same false religion. In either case, they belonged to the Ammonite people.

Solomon, a man of God, married more than one woman, like his father, David. And he took David's compromise to new depths by marrying women from cultures that God had expressly forbidden. Then he appeased those wives by allowing them to worship their idols on the very soil that God wanted cleansed of all pagan influence. Over time, he compromised further by building them places to worship their false gods. As if that weren't enough, he ultimately fell completely by participating in the idolatry his foreign wives embraced.

During Solomon's forty-year reign, the wealth of the nation continued to climb. David had won peace with an aggressive military campaign, and the tribes were united against any threat. The surrounding kingdoms held Israel in high regard because of David's military might and Solomon's wise diplomacy, not to mention the power of the Hebrews' God. Not surprisingly, the threat to Solomon's kingdom came from within. He chose to worship idols instead of serving the Lord exclusively; he chose to tax the people of God instead of leading them wisely. Women over God, money over people. No wonder a nation that had been unified and strong for more than a century began to collapse under its own weight.

Because of the king's spiritual compromise and his overt abuse of power, influential men began to desert him. One of them was Jeroboam. In order to judge Solomon because of his evil choices, the Lord promised Jeroboam that he would reign over ten of Israel's twelve tribes. He would even build him a dynasty *if* he remained faithful. But Solomon, rather than accepting the rebuke and then repenting, saw Jeroboam as a threat to his kingdom and sought to kill him. So Jeroboam escaped to Egypt and lived under the protection of Shishak, the king of Egypt.

Eventually Solomon died, and his son Rehoboam took his place on the throne of Israel. The Bible tells us in the fourteenth chapter of this same book that he was a forty-one-year-old man at the time Solomon died. So for forty-one years Rehoboam had been living in the palace of the king, though not under the direct tutelage of his father. His primary influence was an idolatrous mother. He did, however, learn by the negative example of his father. From Solomon, he learned how to live a sham before the public, all the while nurturing behind the scenes a phony, failing, and ungodly life . . . as dark as the other side of the moon.

THE RISE OF A PHONY AND THE FALL OF A NATION

Then Rehoboam went to Shechem, for all Israel had come to Shechem to make him king. Now when Jeroboam the son of Nebat heard of it, he was living in Egypt (for he was yet in Egypt, where he had fled from the presence of King Solomon). Then they sent and called him, and Jeroboam and all the assembly of Israel came and spoke to Rehoboam, saying, "Your father made our yoke hard; now therefore lighten the hard service of your father and his heavy yoke which he put on us, and we will serve you."

1 Kings 12:1–4

Take note of who approached Rehoboam: all Israel—the country's most influential leaders representing the people—led by a man who had been in exile for several years. Especially during the latter half of his reign, Solomon, while successful, was not respected by the majority of the nation. With the ascension of his son, they hoped to find relief. Notice how Rehoboam bought a little time to put on a show:

Then he said to them, "Depart for three days, then return to me." So
the people departed. King Rehoboam consulted with the elders who
had served his father Solomon while he was still alive, saying, "How
do you counsel me to answer this people?" Then they spoke to him,
saying, "If you will be a servant to this people today, and will serve
them and grant them their petition, and speak good words to them,
then they will be your servants forever."

1 Kings 12:5–7

He entered the chamber that his father Solomon had developed and put
the question to a council of wrinkled, bearded men who had been tempered
through the years, who had seen the nation decline yet remained faithful.
Their seasoned advice was that he become, truly, a servant-king, unlike his
father. The very next words confirm that this whole exercise was a sham:

But he forsook the counsel of the elders which they had given him, and
consulted with the young men who grew up with him and served him.

1 Kings 12:8

Rehoboam polished his image as he appeared to seek wise counsel while
formulating his domestic policy, but clearly, he had already made up his
mind. He didn't seek advice; he sought justification. This is evident as he
turned from the elders to listen to his peers:

So he said to them, "What counsel do you give that we may answer
this people who have spoken to me, saying, 'Lighten the yoke which
your father put on us'?" The young men who grew up with him spoke
to him, saying, "Thus you shall say to this people who spoke to you,
saying, 'Your father made our yoke heavy, now you make it lighter
for us!' But you shall speak to them, 'My little finger is thicker than
my father's loins! Whereas my father loaded you with a heavy yoke,
I will add to your yoke; my father disciplined you with whips, but I
will discipline you with scorpions.'"

1 Kings 12:9–11

So the new king took three days to receive wise counsel (supposedly) and then summoned Jeroboam and the nation to hear his decision. Observe whose advice he chose:

> The king answered the people harshly, for he forsook the advice of the elders which they had given him, and he spoke to them according to the advice of the young men, saying, "My father made your yoke heavy, but I will add to your yoke; my father disciplined you with whips, but I will discipline you with scorpions."
>
> 1 Kings 12:13–14

Don't miss the imagery that Rehoboam used to characterize his father's regime. A yoke is something you place on a beast of burden in order get work out of it. A scorpion was likely a lash that had a single handle with up to twelve leather straps, each imbedded with pieces of bone or metal, whereas the whip was comprised of a handle with one leather strap. Obviously, he viewed his father's kingdom as one that should be burdened by the yoke and driven by the whip. These were vivid pictures describing forced labor, carrying out a master-slave relationship in which the people served the king.

Why would he go through the motions of seeking counsel from the elders if he had no intention to heed it? In front of the camera, these looked like the actions of a wise, young ruler, but behind the scenes, this was a phony counseling session—a charade to make him look good while flexing for the public. Soon he would find that his position wasn't nearly as secure as he thought. Kings—even powerful, rich kings—need the loyalty of their subjects to keep their crowns.

> When all Israel saw that the king did not listen to them, the people answered the king, saying,
> "What portion do we have in David?
> We have no inheritance in the son of Jesse;
> To your tents, O Israel!
> Now look after your own house, David!"
> So Israel departed to their tents.
>
> 1 Kings 12:16

With the period at the end of verse 16, a terrible civil war broke out. Suddenly a nation that had been unified for more than a century is shattered into a dozen pieces. Ten of the twelve tribes sided with Jeroboam against the arrogant Rehoboam, who retained only the land belonging to Judah and Benjamin, with Jerusalem as his capital. The ten tribes to the north sided with Jeroboam, who formed his own kingdom, calling it Israel (or occasionally, Ephraim). He established his capital in Samaria.

THE POLITICAL POWER OF PRETEND OBEDIENCE

Thanks to the arrogance and the foolishness of the reckless phony, the Promised Land became a divided kingdom for the first time. How tragic! One might have hoped that Rehoboam would learn his lesson and choose to be a genuine, servant-hearted leader, dependent upon God. But he didn't. He merely added a fresh coat of paint to the old facade.

Second Chronicles 10–11 is a parallel account that offers more details about what happened next:

> Now when Rehoboam had come to Jerusalem, he assembled the house of Judah and Benjamin, 180,000 chosen men who were warriors, to fight against Israel to restore the kingdom to Rehoboam. But the word of the LORD came to Shemaiah the man of God, saying, "Speak to Rehoboam the son of Solomon, king of Judah, and to all Israel in Judah and Benjamin, saying, 'Thus says the LORD, "You shall not go up or fight against your relatives; return every man to his house, for this thing is from Me.""
>
> 2 Chronicles 11:1–4

That's not hard to understand. God said, in effect, "Don't fight. Don't plan this assault. Don't train your soldiers. Go back home. This is precisely what I predicted would happen. The sword has come. As I told David, that sword would never depart from his house. And I told Solomon his kingdom would split. This is exactly as I planned it. I'm in control of all that's happening. Go home. Don't fight."

On the surface, Rehoboam appeared to have obeyed the Lord's command. As we'd say today, that act was for the cameras. He merely delayed his plans, like when he sent the people away for three days. Behind the scenes, the king prepared for war:

> Rehoboam lived in Jerusalem and built cities for defense in Judah. Thus he built Bethlehem, Etam, Tekoa, Beth-zur, Soco, Adullam, Gath, Mareshah, Ziph, Adoraim, Lachish, Azekah, Zorah, Aijalon and Hebron, which are fortified cities in Judah and in Benjamin. He also strengthened the fortresses and put officers in them and stores of food, oil and wine. He put shields and spears in every city and strengthened them greatly. So he held Judah and Benjamin.
>
> 2 Chronicles 11:5–12

Did Rehoboam go home and relax and trust God? Not on your life. Without delay, he prepared fifteen cities in his territory for siege—strengthened the walls, stocked them with provisions and weapons, and staffed them with a heavy military presence. Some claim that because all of these cities lie south of Jerusalem, whereas Jeroboam's territory was to the north, that Rehoboam merely wanted to protect his country from attack by Egypt. But do you remember where Jeroboam lived during Solomon's reign? With his friend Shishak, the king of Egypt.

Building fortresses to resist an attack from the south would have been a wise move from a purely human perspective. He probably justified his actions with the words, "Better safe than sorry!" But then a rationalization is always reasonable, isn't it? That's how phonies get away with so much for so long. This was a cover for his true plan, which he put in motion by turning these normally peaceful cities into fortresses.

As World War II raged, I was only a boy living in Houston, Texas. I remember the workmen beginning to fortify the barrier island of Galveston. I'll never forget the uneasy feeling it put in the pit of my stomach. I never felt insecure or vulnerable to attack until I saw the workers pouring huge concrete bunkers along the shore . . . the same shore where we once built sand castles. Before long, the beaches of Galveston were declared off limits. Then the public was denied access to other parts of the island, section by section. It became evident to me, though I was just a lad, that if the war continued, we very well could expect a German fleet to steam right into the Gulf of Mexico. With just a little imagination, I can see the people of Judah and Benjamin sleeping a little less soundly with Rehoboam's defense plan in motion.

Evidently his plan to appear godly had the right effect. Take note of the next section, just after the description of his fortifications:

> Moreover, the priests and the Levites who were in all Israel stood with him from all their districts. For the Levites left their pasture lands and their property and came to Judah and Jerusalem, for Jeroboam and his sons had excluded them from serving as priests to the LORD. He set up priests of his own for the high places, for the satyrs and for the calves which he had made. Those from all the tribes of Israel who set their hearts on seeking the LORD God of Israel followed them to Jerusalem, to sacrifice to the LORD God of their fathers. They strengthened the kingdom of Judah and supported Rehoboam the son of Solomon for three years, for they walked in the way of David and Solomon for three years.
>
> 2 Chronicles 11:13–17

As king of the northern tribes, Jeroboam worried that his people would begin to switch their allegiance to Rehoboam as they continued to worship the Lord at Solomon's temple in Jerusalem. So he established two worship centers to false gods in his own territory in order to give his subjects less reason to travel and to woo them away from the God of David and Solomon. Nevertheless, the people who loved the Lord uprooted their families and moved south. And for three years, Rehoboam's plan worked. He presented a godly figure to the camera, and his fans cheered.

BEHIND THE SCENES OF A PHONY LIFE

Between verses 17 and 18, the camera changes perspective. Verse 17 shows us the public side of Rehoboam. Verse 18 goes behind the scenes for a look at his domestic life. And the first thing we notice is that he was not unlike his wayward father:

> Then Rehoboam took as a wife Mahalath the daughter of Jerimoth the son of David and of Abihail the daughter of Eliab the son of Jesse, and she bore him sons: Jeush, Shemariah and Zaham. After her he took Maacah the daughter of Absalom, and she bore him Abijah, Attai, Ziza and Shelomith. Rehoboam loved Maacah the daughter of Absalom more than all his other wives and concubines. For he had taken eighteen wives and sixty concubines and fathered twenty-eight sons and sixty daughters.
>
> 2 Chronicles 11:18–21

A quick chart of the genealogies (I rarely overlook them) reveals that he married his cousins, which is something we look down upon today but wasn't forbidden by the Law. In fact, he would have been commended for choosing wives within the royal family rather than non-Hebrew, pagan women.

Alas, this too was a sham. Eighteen wives and sixty concubines. Sound familiar? Rehoboam was just like his father and his grandfather in this respect. In nearly all of the biographical sketches in the Old Testament, we see over and over and over that like produces like, a lust for sensuality produces children having lust in their hearts. And within a generation or two, a tiny seed of compromise grew to shameless rebellion in full bloom.

David ignored the Lord's restriction against Hebrew men marrying pagan women, who might lead them into idolatry. He also disregarded the Lord's restriction against kings taking multiple wives. He compromised in that one area, but his heart never turned to idols. His sensuality led him to commit adultery and murder, but he never tolerated a rival religion. His son, Solomon, took after his father and built an enormous harem, perhaps thinking that since David's devotion survived the potential hazard, his would as well. However, as we mentioned earlier, those wives eventually led him to build places of worship to false gods and then enticed him to participate with them.

Rehoboam did as his father and grandfather did behind the scenes while maintaining a public perception that he held a steadfast devotion to the Lord. And while he carefully nursed a public image, he systematically passed on a dark legacy to his own sons:

> Rehoboam appointed Abijah the son of Maacah as head and leader among his brothers, for he intended to make him king. He acted wisely and distributed some of his sons through all the territories of Judah and Benjamin to all the fortified cities, and he gave them food in abundance. And he sought many wives for them.
>
> 2 Chronicles 11:22–23

Amazing! The man was not satisfied to build his own harem; he was out getting wives for his sons. What a reckless, shameless display of royal privilege and power!

At this point, I wish to take issue with the translation of the Hebrew word rendered "wisely." Translated this way, a reader in English might have the impression that the biblical writer approved of Rehoboam's actions as good and honorable. Most often, this form of the Hebrew word *bin* is translated "skillful" or "skillfully." Rehoboam acted shrewdly, skillfully, with discernment, using a specialized training in the art of warfare; nevertheless, it was all done in direct disobedience. This is the way the ancient world built and maintained a kingdom. But Israel represented God's people. They were supposed to be different.

The Real Phony Emerges

The narrative in 1 Kings 14 details the next period in Rehoboam's life. A quick summary is needed. After he was crowned, he pretended to seek counsel but then split the country with his foolishness; he acted as though he trusted the Lord but then built fortresses; he presented himself as a godly man to lure God-fearing families from the north but then filled his harem with idolatrous women. Finally, in this next stage of his life, Rehoboam's facade crumbles to reveal the hypocrisy that propped up his public image.

> Now Rehoboam the son of Solomon reigned in Judah. Rehoboam was forty-one years old when he became king, and he reigned seventeen years in Jerusalem, the city which the LORD had chosen from all the tribes of Israel to put His name there. And his mother's name was Naamah the Ammonitess.
>
> 1 Kings 14:21

This collection of sentences attracts my attention for two reasons. First, they seem like random, unrelated facts. Second, they are closely packed together, which tells me that they are anything but random or unrelated. Rehoboam lived in a city called *Jeru shalom,* "City of Peace." This was the city where God wanted *His* name, Yahweh, to be prominent. Then the writer interjects Rehoboam's mother's name, Naamah the woman from Ammon. Rehoboam wanted his capital to *look* like the city of the Lord, but underneath it was, in fact, quite the opposite. It was the city of Naamah the Ammonitess and her idols, Molech and Milcom.

The name *Naamah* means "sweetness, pleasantness," which probably described her general disposition. This narrative tells us twice, in verses 21 and 31, so that we won't miss its significance, that Rehoboam's mother was "*the* Ammonitess." She was an Ammonite woman with considerable influence. So much so, she convinced her husband to abandon Yahweh for a particularly detestable idol.

Rehoboam was forty-one years old when he became king. We know that Solomon reigned for forty years, so Rehoboam was nurtured by Naamah the Ammonitess, the worshiper of Milcom and Molech. One archaeologist writes,

> Molech was a detestable Semitic deity honored by the sacrifice of children, in which they were caused to pass through or into the fire. Palestinian excavations have uncovered evidences of infant skeletons in burial places around heathen shrines. Ammonites revered Molech as a protecting father. No form of ancient Semitic idolatry was more abhorrent than Molech worship.[1]

His mother, Naamah, reared her son in the worship of Molech, and Solomon consented to the practice by building temples to the false god. The sin that Mom loved and that Dad permitted, ensnared the son. So it should come as no surprise that he led his kingdom into the same deadly trap:

> Judah did evil in the sight of the LORD, and they provoked Him to jealousy more than all that their fathers had done, with the sins which they committed. For they also built for themselves high places and sacred pillars and Asherim on every high hill and beneath every luxuriant tree. There were also male cult prostitutes in the land. They did according to all the abominations of the nations which the LORD dispossessed before the sons of Israel.
>
> 1 Kings 14:22–24

In just two generations, David's compromise had degenerated into complete rebellion. The final sentence stated above captures the irony of Judah's rock-bottom standing before God. The Lord established David's dynasty to be a witness to the surrounding pagan nations, and by the time of his grandson, the Promised Land was polluted with the same filth that Joshua had cleansed earlier. Make no mistake, the people had become exactly like their leader: utterly contemptible and totally decadent from the inside out.

THE SUCCESSFUL PHONY

Rehoboam had been that way all along, you understand. He was reared by his mother to be an idolater, but he kept it hidden from his God-fearing public in order to enlarge his kingdom. He even attracted families who were loyal to the Lord by pretending to worship and obey Him. In truth, he was morally bankrupt. Until the southern cities were fortified and his wealth secured against invasion, he carefully maintained his slick image. But as soon as he felt secure, the real Rehoboam burst forth:

When the kingdom of Rehoboam was established and strong, he and all Israel with him forsook the law of the LORD.

2 Chronicles 12:1

Success. Many would say that success can ruin a man. I say that success reveals who the man was all along. When he needs the help of others, when he's on the way up, he'll be whomever or whatever he must be in order to get where he's going. Once he feels that he has arrived and no longer needs the facade, the true character of the man emerges.

Success doesn't destroy character; it exposes character.

As we should expect, the Lord would not allow this to continue. In an exquisite twist of irony, He chastised Rehoboam with what he feared most:

[Shishak, the king of Egypt] captured the fortified cities of Judah and came as far as Jerusalem. Then Shemaiah the prophet came to Rehoboam and the princes of Judah who had gathered at Jerusalem because of Shishak, and he said to them, "Thus says the LORD, 'You have forsaken Me, so I also have forsaken you to Shishak.'" So the princes of Israel and the king humbled themselves and said, "The LORD is righteous." When the LORD saw that they humbled themselves, the word of the LORD came to Shemaiah, saying, "They have humbled themselves so I will not destroy them, but I will grant them some measure of deliverance, and My wrath shall not be poured out on Jerusalem by means of Shishak. But they will become his slaves so that they may learn the difference between My service and the service of the kingdoms of the countries." So Shishak king of Egypt came up against Jerusalem, and took the treasures of the house of the LORD and the treasures of the king's palace. He took everything; he even took the golden shields which Solomon had made.

2 Chronicles 12:4–9

Seeing his fortresses knocked off one by one shook Rehoboam to his core. He repented of his sin and arrogance at the last minute. In the marines, we called this "foxhole faith." In the heat of battle, lots of guys become very godly . . . until they were safe back at the barracks. Then everything returns to life as usual. But in His mercy, the Lord took the king's plea at face value and promised to spare the kingdom complete destruction, reducing it to a slave state before Egypt. In the process, Rehoboam lost everything that his father had gained.

The opulence of the buildings that Solomon built was second to no other kingdom on earth, including Egypt. Just one example of his prosperity could be seen hanging in one of his public buildings in Jerusalem. He had artisans craft five hundred golden shields to decorate the walls as a symbol of Israel's might. Any visiting dignitary could interpret Solomon's meaning: "I have enough wealth in this building alone to train, feed, equip, and mobilize an army that will destroy you if I so choose."

Based on their description in 2 Chronicles 9:15–16, I estimate that the total value of the gold alone in today's currency would be just under $176,000,000. That was enough to fund a significant military campaign . . . and win. But once the sweep of Judah was complete, everything, including the golden shields, belonged to Shishak.

THE HUMBLE PHONY

The good news is that Rehoboam genuinely humbled himself before God, and, as the Scripture says, "the anger of the LORD turned away from him, so as not to destroy him completely; and also conditions were good in Judah. So King Rehoboam strengthened himself in Jerusalem and reigned" (2 Chronicles 12:12–13).

The bad news is that Rehoboam never really changed. Not deep within. He remained a phony all way to the end. Take an extra moment here. Pay close attention to what he did after the Egyptians marched off with Solomon's golden shields:

> Then King Rehoboam made shields of bronze in their place and committed them to the care of the commanders of the guard who guarded the door of the king's house. As often as the king entered the house of the LORD, the guards came and carried them and then brought them back into the guards' room.
>
> 2 Chronicles 12:10–11

What a charlatan! He made shields of bronze to replace the golden ones but didn't keep them on display. Instead he trotted them out for special functions, but otherwise he kept them under guard, perhaps to keep them shined up! The last thing he wanted was to have the public realize that they weren't gold.

The truth of the matter was that nearly two million dollars' worth of gold had been carted off by the king of Egypt. So Rehoboam went to work behind the scenes to provide a cheap substitute, an imitation, a gold-appearing prop for the cameras to focus on. The image-conscious king carefully hid them in secret so nobody would know the truth . . . that they were bronze—a third-class substitute after a first-class blunder.

Hypocrisy defined the life of Rehoboam. Four specific examples come to mind as I reflect on what transpired.

First, he pretended to seek counsel from the elders, but he already knew what he would do. When the elders didn't give him the answer he wanted, he consulted his boyhood friends, who would naturally agree with him.

Second, he pretended to obey when the Lord told him not to fight, but he spent years preparing his cities for war. Near the end of both accounts of his life, the historians add the note, "And there were wars between Rehoboam and Jeroboam continually" (2 Chronicles 12:15).

Third, he was given a city that was to have the name of Yahweh, but it really bore the name of Naamah, a pagan Molech worshiper.

Fourth, when the golden symbol of the kingdom's wealth and might was pilfered by Egypt due to his apostasy, he replaced it with a bronze imitation. Such a fitting metaphor. A bronze shield, polished to shine like gold but worthless by comparison.

A TOUGH QUESTION

The final verse of the account in 2 Chronicles states, "And Rehoboam slept with his fathers and was buried in the city of David; and his son Abijah became king in his place" (2 Chronicles 12:16). Unfortunately, only one of the world's phonies died back then. Today, we have them living all around us.

Now here's the tough question: *Are you one of them?*

Pause, please. Don't be defensive. Allow me to probe. If we were to pull the cameras behind the scenes of your life, what would we see? What's behind the part of your character that faces the public? Are you someone who speaks the Christian language fluently, but only on Sundays? Is yours a religious mask?

What does your family see? A godly man or woman before the church crowd, who nurtures and rationalizes a pet sin at home? Have you fooled yourself into thinking that you can manage the consequences? Realistically, you might be able to keep that sin contained just enough to keep it from ruining your life, but have you considered the effect of that sin on the people you influence—in particular, your children?

I call it the domino effect. David's compromise weakened Solomon, and in turn, Solomon's sin impacted Rehoboam. In the end, the sin that Mom loved and Dad permitted, entangled the son and taught him to be a reckless, misguided phony.

Tragically, the beat goes on . . . and on . . . and on. Nobody's immune. Phony living could be happening in your house, or my house, or any house . . . even the White House.

CHAPTER ELEVEN

Jabez: The Unknown Who Became Well Known

Take a walk with me. We're strolling through an old cemetery somewhere in the Deep South of the United States. Around the perimeter of two or three acres in the heart of this quiet town dripping with history is an iron fence separating two worlds, the ancient and the modern. This would be prime real estate were it not for the long-forgotten dead. We lift the latch to a rusty gate, and with a hard push, it squeaks open probably for the first time in months. By now the survivors of the deceased have long since died, so visitors are rarely seen.

Gigantic, eerily twisted trees full of thick, hanging moss shield this gloomy realm from the outside. We notice that it's unusually dark and cool for such a sunny day. Despite the layers of decaying leaves and tangled undergrowth, stone grave markers tell us where the dead lie. Clusters of tilting headstones of a dozen varieties tell us who built the surrounding city. Towering monuments tell us who was a "somebody." Humble footstones used to bear the names of those who were "nobodies," although a century of rainfall has all but erased them.

Each tablet marks an entire lifetime with just the basic facts: name, date of birth, date of death, beloved something to someone. With a closer look, we can glean a few more facts. Family names occasionally crisscross, so we can imagine a happy day when a man and a woman joined lives. A tiny marker beside them with just a few months between the dates tells us

187

of the grief they must have endured. Beyond that, though, the details that made these lives fascinating are now secrets, buried in decaying boxes six feet beneath where we're walking.

As we turn toward the gate and meander through the clusters of silent stone chronicles, we glance at the names and dates as they come into view and then pass from our consciousness. They all look the same now. Wilson, born, died . . . Johnson, born, died . . . Anderson, born, died . . . but then, something's different. Etched into an otherwise average headstone, we see an unusual name accompanied by a short narrative. The words are few . . . just three or four sentences. But compared to the hundreds of stones we've seen, this is a mini-history book. We're forced to stop and read.

AN EPITAPH WORTH STUDYING

A stroll through the first nine chapters of 1 Chronicles is a lot like walking through a cemetery—endless genealogies with names we can barely pronounce and having no context to give them relevance to us. I admit with no apology that I frequently find these sections boring, but I also feel compelled to read them since they are a part of God's Word—no less so than the red letters in our New Testament.

> Naarah bore him Ahuzzam, Hepher, Temeni and Haahashtari. These
> were the sons of Naarah. The sons of Helah were Zereth, Izhar and
> Ethnan. Koz became the father of Anub and Zobebah, and the families
> of Aharhel the son of Harum.
>
> 1 Chronicles 4:6–8

See what I mean? Three full chapters just like that, and six more to go. But then, suddenly, we stumble across a short epitaph in chapter 4. Two terse verses. That's not much in light of how much the Bible says about other great men and women, but compared to the hundreds of monotonous memorials in 1 Chronicles 1 through 9, this is hidden treasure waiting to be unearthed and appreciated. Here's a stone worth our time. J. Oswald Sanders, in a fine little book called *A Spiritual Clinic*, writes, "When God troubles to preserve the epitaph of one man out of millions and gives it in such concise and meaningful language, we can be certain that it will repay detailed study."[1] We ask ourselves, as we stand among the silent stones, what might God want us to see in these few words?

Before we pause and ponder the epitaph, let me preface this with a few comments. Much of my study and the principles I discuss in this chapter are not new. I first taught on Jabez back in 1976 and then again in 1990—a full decade before my colleague and longtime friend, Bruce Wilkinson, wrote his widely popular book—and my views have not changed. None of this is meant either to support or refute his work, so if you're looking for a fight, you won't find it here. I will, however, present a different slant on the subject as well as include a few more word studies than usual. Because the character of Jabez has become so controversial in some circles and because I think the extra scrutiny is healthy, I want to be careful to establish a solid basis for the principles I present. With that, let's pause and ponder the man I call "the unknown who became well known."

How the Story of Jabez Is Important

The Lord had a reason for directing the author of the Chronicles to tell us about Jabez. We'll have to do some detective work to understand why. Whenever we do a study of a passage of Scripture, it's helpful to know why the words were written, what causes the author to include them, and, in the case of history, when the events actually took place. One reliable source states,

> The purpose of 1 and 2 Chronicles is to show God's elective and pre-serving grace in His covenant people through David, the messianic king and priest. The genealogies are given to show how David and Judah were chosen by God. That divine selection is traced back to patriarchal and even prepatriarchal times.[2]

The Hebrew people are often called "God's covenant people" because throughout their history, God repeated His promise that they would be a great, prosperous nation in the land of Canaan. He promised it to Abraham, the father of the Hebrew people, and He promised it to the nation when they came out of slavery in Egypt to settle the "Promised Land." In Deuteronomy 28:1–11, the Lord told them that His desire was to make them so wealthy and so powerful and so influential that the world would wonder at their great God and desire to know Him. After all, who would be attracted to a God who delighted in keeping His people poor and oppressed?

His desire for all of His people is to enjoy abundance—though never at the expense of their holiness—for three reasons. First, because He loves us. Second, because it brings Him pleasure. Third, because it brings Him glory. The early church father Irenaeus wrote, "The glory of God is a man fully alive, and the life of man consists in beholding God."

Stay with me as we continue to dig deeper. This book of history was written during a very weak, unstable period in the life of the nation. Like King Saul, God's covenant people peaked and then endured a long, agonizing, embarrassing decline. Finally, the Lord had His fill of their rebellion and implemented the severe consequences. He woke the sleeping giant, Babylon, who invaded and ravaged the land and then carried the Hebrew people into bondage. The Chronicler prepared this literary account not long after returning from seventy years of captivity in Babylon. During this time, the nation was struggling to regain its identity as God's covenant people. They were just learning, again, to have hope in the promises God had made centuries before in Deuteronomy 28.

If we look at the names that fall before and after the name of Jabez, we can discern that he lived around the time of the Joshua and the conquest of Canaan. Perhaps he was born into a family not particularly wealthy or influential during Israel's wandering years. But, as we shall see, he distinguished himself.

Now that we have his historical backdrop in place, let's observe what Scripture records about Jabez:

> Jabez was more honorable than his brothers, and his mother named
> him Jabez saying, "Because I bore him with pain." Now Jabez called
> on the God of Israel, saying, "Oh that You would bless me indeed and

enlarge my border, and that Your hand might be with me, and that You would keep me from harm that it may not pain me!" And God granted him what he requested.

1 Chronicles 4:9–10

That's it. The man is never mentioned again in Scripture. It's not much to go on, but it's enough. In fact, I suggest that you go back and read those words again . . . only slower and preferably aloud.

The Hebrew is remarkably compact and concise. There's a lot going on in these verses if we're careful to observe them. First is his name.

FROM HUMBLE BEGINNINGS TO HIGH HONOR

The English rendering is Jabez, but the Hebrew is pronounced *yah-betz* (the second syllable sounds like the word *baits*.) His mother had the Hebrew word *ah-tzav* in mind when she chose her son's name. The term *ah-tzav* refers to anguish, intense sorrow, or pain. To arrive at his name from the Hebrew word, you transpose two letters. So it's a pun based on sound play. This would be like someone who hates cottage cheese, which is made from milk *curd*, saying, "I don't prefer milk *crud*, thanks." Somehow, his birth was associated with intense pain, though we have no idea how or what that pain might have been.

As a father of four children born into our home, I can recall the intense pain that Cynthia endured during childbirth, but this was to be expected. No one is surprised that giving birth is painful. Nor were the circumstances of life very sorrowful, so I never would have thought to name any one of my children Agony or Pain. However, in the birth of Jabez, his mother chose that name for a reason. We can only speculate.

The family could have endured financial distress. The prayer Jabez offered doesn't sound like something a rich man would pray. Health problems and survival were always major concerns in those days. And caring for children while physically ill as well as handling the rigors of the desert would have been very difficult. Maybe their times were tough. I can imagine lots of children having gloomy names during the Great Depression of the 1930s in

America. Perhaps Jabez's father died during one of Israel's many battles. The nation fought a lot of them during this time in Hebrew history. Single motherhood is never easy, but it would have been borderline impossible during ancient times.

Some children are given pleasant names like Faith, Hope, Joy, Grace, and Charity. Imagine growing up with the name Pain. We can just imagine some neighborhood kid knocking on the door and asking, "Can Pain come out and play today?" At dusk, his mother opens the door and calls out, "Pain! Time for supper, Pain!" Every mention of his name would be a stinging reminder of the sorrow surrounding his birth. Not the joy of a new arrival, not the celebration of new life, not stories of how happy Mom and Dad were when he came into the world, but mourning. "When you came into the world, Pain, life couldn't have been worse."

Can you identify with Jabez? Some of you reading these pages can recall rather vividly the story of your origin, how you weren't even wanted, and no one bothered to keep that a secret. Perhaps you don't know your birth parents, and you wonder how the two people who gave you life could also give you up. Maybe you were born into horrendous circumstances—parents struggling with poverty or substance abuse or out-of-control emotions—and you were almost the straw that broke the family's back. And so you became their verbal punching bag. Or maybe you simply came later in life, long after Mom and Dad had decided on no more children, and you never knew the security of their warmth and affection.

Jabez was born into humble circumstances and was given a name that would never let him forget it. Nevertheless, don't miss the descriptive phrase just behind his name:

> Jabez was more honorable than his brothers.
>
> 1 Chronicles 4:9

The Hebrew word for *honorable* literally means "heavy." We use that same concept in English when we say, "This is a weighty matter." When used of a person, it conveys the idea that he or she is impressive or noteworthy. One insightful resource on Hebrew terms puts it this way:

The reputation of an individual is of central importance in these usages. Thus the person of high social position and accompanying wealth was automatically an honored, or weighty, person in the society (Numbers 22:15, etc.). Such a position, its riches, and long life were commonly assumed to be the just rewards of a righteous life (1 Chronicles 29:28, etc.). While one would be honored automatically if one attained this stature, it is also clear that one was expected to merit the honor and the glory.[3]

Remember that these words were written, not during Jabez's lifetime, but after it had ended. The tree is down, so the measurement is trustworthy. Whatever the sorrowful circumstances that surrounded the beginning of his life, he ended his days with more honor, higher status, and greater influence than any and all of his brothers. In fact, the first sentence of verse 9 points to the contrast. After studying the Hebrew carefully, here is what is often called a nuanced translation, taking the complexity of the word usage and grammar into account. I placed my amplified portions in brackets:

> Jabez was [one who was more noteworthy, more impressive, more weighty in his community] than his brothers, [ironically, though,] his mother [had] named him Jabez, [which is a sound play on the word for "pain,"] saying, "[I am giving him this name] because I bore him [in anguish]."

Take note of how his epitaph unfolds. Jabez was a great man, though he had humble beginnings. This is like saying, "Abraham Lincoln was one of America's greatest presidents, but he was born in a log cabin." What you would expect next is an explanation of how he made the transition. Verse 10 tells us how Jabez rose from the sorrow and anguish of his birth to such influential greatness in his later years.

THE AMBITIOUS PRAYER OF A HUMBLE MAN

How did his significance emerge? We're told it came as the result of a bold, earnest prayer that God chose to honor. Here is my nuanced translation of his prayer:

Now Jabez called out to the God of Israel, [this prayer:] "Oh [the deep longing I have] that You would [exceedingly bless me], and [You would cause the increase of] my [sphere of responsibility, prosperity, and means], and that Your [continual presence and power] might be with me, and that You would [act to protect] me from harm [so] that it may not [be sorrowful to me] [as my name implies]!"

Clearly, Jabez made four specific requests. Let's examine each in turn.

Divine Ennoblement

First, he asked for God to bless him . . . but this was no cliché, no ordinary request. The Hebrew reveals the deep emotion of his prayer with what scholars call a particle of wishing. This very rare expression combined with the intense form of the verb reveals a man desperately wanting something. As a result, the request "bless me" is doubly intensified so that it becomes "bless me with overwhelming blessing."

He asked for what we might call divine ennoblement. The Hebrew blessing is no insignificant matter, as it is very closely connected with God's covenant with Israel, which will become clearer in the next section. All Hebrew people desired this covenant blessing, but the request by Jabez was different. In effect, he petitioned the Lord with, "Bless me with uncommon blessing. Lord, break through the cloud that has covered my life, from the sorrow that surrounded my birth to the limitations that I have endured all these years. Make my future a contrast to my past. Give me a giant stake in Your covenant with my people."

Divine Expansion

Next, "enlarge my border." At first glance, this looks like raw ambition, a prayer the health-and-wealth, name-it-and-claim-it, word-of-faith preacher might want us to send up. Janis Joplin used to sing with biting sarcasm, "Lord, won't you buy me a Mercedes Benz?" If we stop with "enlarge my border" and fail to dig deeper for the full meaning, we might reduce prayer to a "gimme" list. And we're probably too close to that as it is.

Make no mistake, though, enlarged borders in the ancient world meant greater wealth, higher standing in the community, more power, and increased responsibility to the Lord and the community. Land was wealth . . . and much more. Jabez called out to the God of Israel to make him rich and powerful. This was an over-the-top prayer by a man with a genuinely sanctified ambition and great hope.

Please understand, ambition in the right context is not wrong. Praying for wealth for the sake of getting rich is not what the Lord desires, and I must underscore, becoming rich is *not* what Jabez longed for! In the context of Hebrew culture, and as it related to the promises of Deuteronomy 28, increased acreage involved a greater stake in the plan of God for Israel. Asking the Lord for more land was asking for a greater share in the covenant, which also brought with it all of its conditions—including the curses for disobedience. His was an honorable ambition.

Divine Empowerment

Next, Jabez prayed for divine empowerment: "and that Your [continual presence and power] might be with me." The New American Standard Bible renders the Hebrew faithfully: "and that Your hand might be with me." In the Old Testament culture and literary world, the hand was a symbol of power, strength, control, or skill. Throughout the Bible, God's sovereign intervention and the exercise of His omnipotence are associated with "the hand of the Lord."

In effect, Jabez prayed, "Lord, I'm counting on You to do these things in Your time and in Your way. But when You do, I don't want to go it alone. I want You to go with me. I want You to guide each step I take with Your mighty hand. I don't want to feel less and less of Your hand on my life as I taste more and more of a successful life. Therefore, I humbly ask that You will be with me."

Throughout the Scriptures, we see this pattern: those whom God blesses and uses in order to have the greatest impact are those who live in submission to His authority, seeking only His glory.

I can only wonder who might be reading these pages or what your future holds. For all I know you may be the future president of a corporation or a future congressman or a future high-ranking officer at the Pentagon or an influential minister of the gospel in the making or an insightful teacher of many or a gifted artist in great demand. God only knows. To you I offer this solemn advice: when the time comes for you to accept that high calling with tremendous responsibility and greater prosperity, be sure that your prayer includes, "May Your hand be with me, Lord. Keep me from arrogance and pride. Guide me so that I will remain faithfully submitted to You despite the illusion of power all around me. Remind me often of the perils that accompany success."

In the previous chapter, I said that success doesn't ruin the character of a person; it exposes the character he or she already had. Nevertheless, we can ask the Lord to use success to shape our character as we progressively grow in Christlikeness. Jabez didn't want success if it meant distance from his God, so he immediately and humbly requested that the Lord stay close.

Divine Enablement

His last request is closely related with the third. The simple, word-for-word translation reads: "and that You would keep me from harm that it may not pain me!" My own amplified version is "and that You would [act to protect] me from harm [so] that it may not [be sorrowful to me] [as my name implies]!"

The hand of God is not only a guiding presence, but it's also a protective power. The request of Jabez is not far from being exactly what the Lord promised to give Israel in Deuteronomy 28. He promised that He would not only give His people prosperity, but also protect them from invasion. It's a natural thing for anyone to request, but the closing phrase suggests that this request is much more personal for Jabez. He used the word his mother had in mind when she named him.

This is good reason to suggest that he wasn't merely asking for the Lord to guard him from future harm. He was likely asking to be unshackled from an existence of sorrow and anguish that characterized his life. He probably felt like he had a better chance of escaping his own name than the pain that followed him. He as much as said, "Help me not to live up to my name! Set me free from the ball and chain that is my past as You release me to a great and glorious future."

The final sentence of this eloquent epitaph tells us the result of his prayer. "And God [brought about for him] [altogether] what he had asked."

How I render the Hebrew description of what God did for Jabez captures the subtlety of the verb. "God granted" is direct enough, but it leaves the impression that somehow the Lord waved His hand, and Jabez instantaneously found himself dressed in fine clothing, suddenly standing on his new estate. God brought about what Jabez desired, not miraculously (though He could have), but by sovereignly acting through human interactions and everyday circumstances. He caused Jabez to prosper, most likely not overnight, but over a number of years. He guided and protected him through the years.

Jabez took a bold step of faith, and God honored it. The Lord smiled upon his requests and then walked with him, developing his faith through each victory and setback. Ultimately, He gave him everything he asked for.

May I offer one last observation? As we observe the verses before and after this two-verse narrative about Jabez, we see repeatedly the phrases "father of" and "son of" and "brother of." But we find none of those words about this humble man who prayed such an extraordinary prayer. He had a mother and he had brothers, but he was otherwise disconnected from any of the hundreds of names in this book. If anybody ever qualified as a "nobody," it would have to be Jabez.

It's quite possible you have little trouble identifying with him. For years you may have thought of yourself as a "nobody." Your beginning in this world may have been sorrowful, and your past may be littered with a series of tragic circumstances. All of that may have resulted in your telling yourself that the only impact you'll ever have is on someone's car door in the parking lot. You may look at where you came from and where you've been as living proof that small, narrow borders are all God intends for you.

This is not to say that filling a small space well is necessarily wrong, but let's be careful to examine our perspective. Complacency is the dark side of contentment. God calls us to surrender our wills to Him. He strongly desires our submission . . . but neither of those involves having a defeatist attitude. If you sincerely believe that your world is as big as God has planned for you, by His grace, then accept it and fill it well. Your reward will be great both on this planet and in eternity.

On the other hand, if you simply haven't taken the time to look to the heavens and allow yourself to think beyond your present limitations, what are you waiting for? What makes us so hesitant to ask God for a grand place in the world, for a position having vast responsibilities? Of course it's a surprise when He lifts someone to a position of authority and responsibility. Most of the people I know who rise to such heights tell me that they feel surprised to have such authority. Most often, they feel unprepared and often extremely undeserving. Notice that I said undeserving, which is a healthy sign of humility.

I have two questions for you that only you can answer: Could it be that the Lord has planned for you a position having much responsibility, high privilege, and great authority? Could it be that the role He has in mind for you is far beyond what you have ever imagined, where He would have you making decisions that impact society in a significant way? Admittedly, those are unenviable positions involving lots of limelight and flak, but the reward for obedience would be worth the trouble. Now here's a third question that may frighten you, but I urge you to consider it: what's keeping you from praying for an expanded vision and enlarged borders? I cannot help but wonder if God preserved this brief but powerful story to cause the reader to come to terms with questions like those I have just asked.

THREE PRINCIPLES

In the story of Jabez, I'm not only prompted to ask you those questions, but I also find three principles worth keeping in mind as you examine your current limitations.

First, *a small, struggling start doesn't necessitate a limited life.* If you're not careful, the adversary will convince you that, because of your struggling start and limited past, your future can never be anything more. The enemy of your soul is trying to convince you that you were born into the restrictions that govern your life and you're condemned to live there from now on. No! Remember Jabez, the unknown who began his life in sorrow but the Lord led him to a place of honor, because he dared to pray boldly with devotion for God. The Lord granted Jabez what he requested. Why wouldn't He do the same for you?

Second, *no measure of success is safe without God's presence and power.* In the previous chapter, we examined the life of Rehoboam. The wealth and power that his father, Solomon, left behind should have been enough to protect the Hebrew nation from enemy invaders. Rehoboam had enough gold in one public building to fund an army large enough to destroy Egypt, yet because God removed His protection, nothing stopped the king of Egypt from conquering the Hebrews and simply making the gold his own. Never doubt it: success on your own is a perilous existence.

Third, *when God prospers and blesses a life, no place for guilt remains.* God's gifts are always appropriate, always righteous, and never to be considered a source of embarrassment or shame. Privileged rank or status, and the blessings that go with it, are small compensation for the responsibility that people in large places bear. With great responsibility comes an equal load of stress. Occasionally, I've studied a photograph of the president of the United States shortly after his inauguration. Eight years later, I've looked closely at one taken near the end of his second term. The contrast is always amazing. The stress of eight years in office has aged the president by decades.

Never apologize for blessings the Lord gives you. Life has enough sorrow without our attaching guilt to the good things He gives us. If you happen to be one whom God has chosen to fill a high-profile role that included the blessings of material abundance, gratefully accept it. Determine to use all that He gives you for His purposes, and give generously for the advancement of His kingdom. Enjoy God's goodness to the fullest.

THE CHALLENGE: DREAM GOD-SIZED DREAMS

Let me make all of this personal. Could it be that your current vision, your present paradigm has been shaped by the restrictive demands and limitations of your original setting? Could it be that the influences that give your life order and comfort are the very things that hold you hostage, bound to a certain way of life or a certain way of thinking? Could it be that you have not broken free simply because the thought of breaking free hasn't occurred to you? Have you asked the Lord to give you a vision far beyond your current borders? Why not?

One of my very closest friends in the ministry, Dr. Mark Young, was born and raised in Putnam County, West Virginia, just like seven generations of Youngs before him. Now, I don't want to play into any stereotypes with his story. His father was a banker and provided a normal, middle-class income for his family, but he hoped that Mark would be the first Young in seven generations to earn a college degree. A noble ambition. And very reasonable. But, in retrospect, a somewhat limited one.

Not only did Mark graduate from Marshall University, but he went on to earn his master of theology degree at Dallas Theological Seminary. Later He completed his PhD at Trinity Evangelical Divinity School. Prior to finishing the program, he and his wife had moved to Poland—then still behind the iron curtain—where Mark helped begin and establish an evangelical seminary. After many years of ministry, experiencing the transition from the Soviet regime to democracy and seeing the seminary flourish, Dr. Mark Young now serves as Professor of World Missions and Intercultural Studies at Dallas Seminary. He's also our senior executive pastor of strategic planning and ministry training at Stonebriar Community Church.

Amazingly, it all started in the tiny town of Hurricane, West Virginia, where his father merely hoped his boy would go to college. The Lord has blessed him, indeed . . . and he would be the first to acknowledge that fact.

Now, *that's* what I call enlarged borders! Trust me, Mark would tell you, this was nothing he could have pulled off by merely dreaming big and "reaching for the stars." This remarkable journey, one he's still on, was God's doing. Jabez and Mark had these in common: a limited life, a desire to see more, and a gracious God who was more than willing to demonstrate His power through them. Both handled it beautifully.

If you don't at least hold out the possibility that you could be a part of a much larger world, you are doomed to remain an ignorantly blissful prisoner of the one you live in today.

Don't stay there.

CHAPTER TWELVE

Naaman: The Officer Whose Leprosy Was Cleansed

Second Kings 5 contains the story of a miracle and a mystery. The account is very well crafted in the way that it's recorded. The writer uses what literary experts call dramatic or situational irony, where the reader knows something that the character does not. As a result, the character's actions take on a different meaning for the reader. Writers often use this device to force a reader to reexamine his or her own values or opinions, which is certainly not a bad idea in this case!

In order to prepare our minds to appreciate this story, we need a fresh perspective. Isaiah 55 will help:

> Ho! Every one who thirsts, come to the waters;
> And you who have no money come, buy and eat.
> Come, buy wine and milk
> Without money and without cost. . . .
> Incline your ear and come to Me. . . .
>
> Seek the LORD while He may be found;
> Call upon Him while He is near.
> Let the wicked forsake his way
> And the unrighteous man his thoughts;
> And let him return to the LORD,

And He will have compassion on him,
And to our God,
For He will abundantly pardon.
"For My thoughts are not your thoughts,
Nor are your ways My ways," declares the LORD.
"For as the heavens are higher than the earth,
So are My ways higher than your ways
And My thoughts than your thoughts."

Isaiah 55:1, 3, 6–9

SEEK THE LORD

Effective and insightful Bible study always begins with very careful observations. First, please notice that these words are written to those who do not know the Lord. They would be what we call "seekers," those who are on a search for God (whether they realize it or not) because something has sparked their interest. Peter Marshall, the greatly beloved Presbyterian chaplain of the U.S. Senate during the late 1940s, called this "the tap on the shoulder":

> If you were walking down the street, and someone came up behind you and tapped you on the shoulder . . . what would you do? Naturally, you would turn around. Well, that is exactly what happens in the spiritual world. A man walks on through life—with the external call ringing in his ears, but with no response stirring in his heart, and then suddenly, without any warning, the Spirit taps him on the shoulder. The tap on the shoulder is the almighty power of God acting without help or hindrance . . . so as to produce a new creature, and to lead him into the particular work which God has for him.[1]

This "tap" begins with a command: "Seek the Lord."
Second, also notice that this command to seek involves an invitation, a warning, and two promises. The invitation is to call upon the Lord. The warning is for this unrighteous seeker to abandon his current way of think-

ing and turn—repent—from the direction he or she is heading and move toward God. The tone and context carries an implied warning, much like a mother might say to her child, "You'd better listen!" Fail to abandon that old way of thinking and the seeker will have a price to pay, serious consequences to face. And the promises include the Lord's compassion and the offer of complete pardon.

Third—and crucial to understanding our story—don't overlook the fact that the Lord has a surprise in store for anyone coming to Him. Carefully observe verses 8 and 9. Read them slowly. This is important, not only to the miracle story of 2 Kings 5, but also to understanding how the Lord wants to write *your* story:

> "For My thoughts are not your thoughts,
> Nor are your ways My ways," declares the LORD.
> "For as the heavens are higher than the earth,
> So are My ways higher than your ways
> And My thoughts than your thoughts."
>
> Isaiah 55:8–9

You may remember in the earlier chapter on Abigail, we saw this principle in action. After the Lord brought justice down on Nabal, otherwise known as Fool, His plan to bless David and Abigail could clearly be seen. It was there all the while, standing just behind the door of obedience.

The Lord delights to surprise us with His goodness, if only we will unlock the door of obedience with the key of faith—which He has given us—and then push it open and walk through.

You may think you have already reached the pinnacle of God's goodness in your life. If that describes you, are you ever in for a surprise! As long as you have breath in your lungs, the Lord wants to surprise you with His ways. He is infinitely creative and inexhaustibly resourceful. His ways don't conform to our way of thinking, and we make Him less when we expect that they should. Furthermore, His plan is much higher than ours. His goal is not to bring us down, but to lift us up. Contrary to popular opinion, He has no desire to bury us, but to raise us for His use and His glory.

But it's a lengthy and arduous process. Once we turn from our way to pursue Him, we have a long journey ahead. I made that turn as a boy, and my surprising adventure of traveling with God began on that day. It continues to this very moment. Just about the time I think, *That was it. This past year was the ultimate. How could the Lord possibly arrange more surprises for Chuck Swindoll?* Then, sure enough, the next year amazes me with the twists and turns no one could have predicted, including *me*!

As we turn to the miracle story of 2 Kings 5, keep Isaiah 55:6–9 in mind. Remember what we've observed: the invitation, the warning, the promises . . . and especially the surprise.

THE SEEKER

Like exquisite jewelry, a story needs a setting. And this one is a bit unusual for what we normally see in the Old Testament. You may remember from the chapter on Rehoboam that the Hebrew nation split as a result of his foolishness. The ten tribes of the northern kingdom called themselves Israel, while the two tribes in the southern kingdom were called Judah. Not surprisingly, they fought regularly. This was a civil war not unlike the War between the States from 1861 to 1865. This was a tumultuous time—a time of confusion and upheaval, a time when enemies may suddenly join forces to fight an invader, then return to hate and distrust one another after the crisis.

During this confusing time in Hebrew history, God worked primarily through His prophets, who served as His spokesmen. The Bible was not yet complete, so the words of a genuine prophet were those of the Lord. True prophets made no mistakes in their announcements and predictions. If the declaration of someone claiming to be a prophet turned out to be incorrect in any way, that person was to be taken to the outskirts of the city and stoned immediately. Often the messages of a prophet were delivered in written form. These were preserved along with the recorded utterances of other prophets whose words proved to be authentically from God, and they have been preserved in our Bible. Prophets played an all-important role prior to the completion of the written Word of God. They were God's mouthpiece.

This story occurred during a lull in the fighting between the northern and southern kingdoms. Syria (or Aram, as it was called by the Hebrews) was a growing civilization to the north of Israel and had begun to take an interest in Palestine. One particular prophet didn't find much favor with anyone. Elisha, like his mentor, Elijah, remained at odds with his society. Very few kings of his era followed the Lord, and the one who did merely tolerated Elisha's presence. Perhaps we could say, Elisha had no friends in high places. What the prophet Elisha did have, they feared: supernatural power. As a result, most everyone left him alone.

The main character in this episode of Elisha's ministry is a man called Naaman. (His name is pronounced *Nah-ah-man,* with all three a's sounding the same.) Of all the people Elisha dealt with in his ministry, none of them was of Naaman's caliber as a man. Check out his resume:

> Now Naaman, captain of the army of the king of Aram, was a great man with his master, and highly respected, because by him the Lord had given victory to Aram. The man was also a valiant warrior, but he was a leper.
>
> 2 Kings 5:1

In just a few phrases, we learn that Naaman was a remarkable man. He was neither of the northern nor southern kingdoms. In fact, he wasn't even a Hebrew. He was a high-ranking officer in the Syrian army—what we might call a field marshal or a four-star general. Scripture calls him "a great man with his master," so he obviously enjoyed the trust and friendship of the king of Syria, Benhadad. Furthermore, his bravery gained him the respect of everyone around him. He would be considered a responsible, honorable, and distinguished military man in our day. But for all of his wealth, power, respect, and success that his courageous achievements and noble character brought him, he suffered with the disease of peasants.

In Hebrew, the sentence strings these accolades together in rapid succession so that the ending shocks the reader. In effect, it reads, "He's esteemed, he's respected, the Lord made him successful, he's noble, he's valiant, he's a leper." A what? A leper. Someone normally feared and completely shunned by the general public because this dreaded disease killed its victims slowly and painfully.

The term *leprosy* was used to describe a number of skin ailments, everything from foot fungus to the horrible Hansen's disease. As a result, some commentators would suggest that it wasn't the terminal form we normally associate with rotting flesh, missing fingers, and bloody bandages. But, as we'll see later in the story, the lengths to which Naaman went to find a cure showed him to be a desperate man.

Nevertheless, had he been Hebrew, Naaman would have been cast out of society once any chronic skin condition presented itself, especially something as bad as Hansen's disease. But he's Syrian, remember. The venerable German scholar C. F. Keil offers this observation in his commentary on 2 Kings:

> There is an allusion here to the difference between the Syrians and the Israelites in their view of leprosy. Whereas in Israel lepers were excluded from human society, in Syria a man afflicted with leprosy could hold a very high state office in the closest association with the king.[2]

In Israel, no leper could keep his position of authority. God instituted laws concerning leprosy to protect the general population from epidemic disease, but pagan influence had twisted their meaning. Leprosy came to be seen as an indication of God's displeasure and the outward mark of inward sin. This is ironic considering the state of morality in Israel during this era. But not in Syria. By their culture, a leper could remain active, involved with other people, even guiding the important affairs of state.

The day Naaman noticed the first spot on his skin must have come as a shock, much like the sudden blow at the end of verse 1. Let's imagine what happened. He rolled out of bed one morning, began to put on his clothes, and looked down to see what irritated his skin. To the man's total shock . . . it had all the characteristics of *leprosy!* Suddenly other words probably came to mind. *Pain. Hopeless. Terminal. Unfair.* And just as quickly, the medals that hung from his chest, the pomp and prestige following a hundred victories, the string of impressive accolades all withered. The momentous proof of his approaching mortality made him dizzy. Everything he once thought important seemed utterly insipid. Patients who face the very real possibility of death will testify to its power to clarify things. My own heart attack back in October 2000 immediately resulted in a wake-up call. A different list of priorities filled my mind.

While we have applied a little imagination, let's not forget that Naaman wasn't a fictional character. He was a man. And no man wanted to waste away with a terminal disease any more then than now. However, keep in mind that this is a miracle story.

THE WAY OF THE LORD

Now the Arameans had gone out in bands and had taken captive a little girl from the land of Israel; and she waited on Naaman's wife. She said to her mistress, "I wish that my master were with the prophet who is in Samaria! Then he would cure him of his leprosy."

2 Kings 5:2–3

Isn't God's way fascinating to watch? Do you recall the invitation of Isaiah 55?

Seek the LORD while He may be found . . .
Let the wicked forsake his way . . .
And [the Lord] will have compassion on him . . .
"For My thoughts are not your thoughts,
Nor are your ways My ways," declares the LORD.

Isaiah 55:6–8

In plain and simple terms, this was Naaman's tap on the shoulder. The Lord began working in his life to offer him healing. Of course, the prophet he heard about was Elisha, but this man's world was Syria. As far as he was concerned, Elisha was just another hocus-pocus holy man blindly engaged in one of many worthless religions. Look at this from his perspective. What had the Syrian gods done for Naaman? He also must have concluded that if the God of Israel was so powerful, why did His kings worship the gods of other nations?

His general attitude toward the Lord on any other day would have been dismissive at best. On this day, however, something was very different. On this day, news of a prophet in Israel had great significance because Naaman had a grave need. Take note of his reaction:

> Naaman went in and told his master, saying, "Thus and thus spoke the girl who is from the land of Israel."
>
> 2 Kings 5:4

Naaman must have sounded desperate to King Benhadad. To appreciate the significance of this, let's put it into a modern-day setting. Imagine the secretary of state to be a man diagnosed with ALS, the terminal, degenerative disease that took the life of Lou Gehrig. His body is already beginning to twist and contort so that everyone notices how difficult walking has become for him. He's fought bravely, and he has won the respect and admiration of his peers, but soon he will be unable to walk, or talk . . . or even move. Finally, he will die. And with the smell of desperation on him, he steps into the Oval Office and says, "Mr. President, a housekeeper that my wife hired told me about a voodoo medicine man down in Honduras. She says he can cure my disease."

Frankly, my initial impression is that Naaman's response represents the impulse of a man trying to seize onto anything that might save his life, even if it sounds ridiculous. I will quickly add, I wouldn't blame him. And the words I would choose to redirect his steps would be laced with sensitive tenderness. Someone that desperate and in that kind of pain needs gentle compassion, not cold logic.

Missteps of an Earnest Seeker

King Benhadad immediately wrote a letter to the king of Israel requesting permission for Naaman to see Elisha. So, with the little girl's sketchy information, the four-star general began a desperate search for the prophet. But his actions reflect the thinking of a nonbeliever. Observe in the following verses some errors common to unsaved people who respond to the tap on their shoulder.

Then the king of Aram said, "Go now, and I will send a letter to the
king of Israel." He departed and took with him ten talents of silver
and six thousand shekels of gold and ten changes of clothes.

2 Kings 5:5

The natural order of things on Planet Earth says that nothing's free.
A man with the power to heal terminal diseases must be in great demand
and hard to reach, so bribes will be necessary. And once someone gains an
audience, he'd better be ready to put up a lot of cash. Healers don't come
cheap. Authentic ones could charge whatever they wish.

Naaman's first error: he thought he could purchase his healing.

This still goes on today. Too many people are willing to pay for something as wonderful and significant as heaven. Unfortunately more are willing
to *pay* their way into heaven than those willing to *believe* their way in. Yet
the invitation is clear: "Ho! Every one who thirsts, come to the waters; and
you who have no money come, buy and eat. Come, buy wine and milk
without money and without cost" (Isaiah 55:1)

The idea that we must come to the Lord with gifts and offerings of
money in order to receive His grace is reinforced every day by the so-called
word-of-faith message that crowds the airwaves and television channels. We
are told that we must sow seeds of faith in order to reap a harvest of God's
blessings. The discerning know what they mean. The "seed" is money, the
"ground" is their pocket, and the "blessing" is whatever ails you. And this
brings us to another mistake the unsaved often make.

Naaman's second error: he thought he would be healed by another
sinner.

He brought the letter to the king of Israel, saying, "And now as this letter
comes to you, behold, I have sent Naaman my servant to you, that you
may cure him of his leprosy." When the king of Israel read the letter, he
tore his clothes and said, "Am I God, to kill and to make alive, that this
man is sending word to me to cure a man of his leprosy? But consider
now, and see how he is seeking a quarrel against me."

2 Kings 5:6–7

The letter by the king of Syria was considered standard protocol in those days. In pagan cultures, the priests kept the people mystified, and they answered to the king, the deity's physical presence among humans. Naaman expected that the king would direct his holy men to perform the right incantations to heal his leprosy.

Beware any human being who even hints at having special power from God or secret knowledge of His ways. During Old Testament times, the Lord held both prophets and priests especially accountable so that no one would ever mistake who had the power. Unfortunately, many so-called Christian leaders behave more like pagan priests. To gain healing, you have to attend their rallies and give money to their organizations in order to receive specially "anointed" devices.

Let's not forget the invitation in Isaiah 55:3, 6: "Incline your ear and come to Me" and "Seek the Lord while He may be found; call on Him while He is near." Notice the Bible never says, "Seek My prophet and let him heal you. Call on My priests while they may be found." That's because the relationship is between you and God. In the Old Testament, the priest merely served as a go-between, a messenger. Now, in this New Testament age, Jesus Christ is our High Priest. And because He is God, we (as individual believer-priests) have direct access to the Almighty through our Savior.

I'll be blunt. Let no man, no woman pretend to be the Lord's sole representative in terms of proclaiming His message of miraculous deliverance or His power to cleanse your sin and/or heal your life. God, alone, does that personally. Go directly to Him.

The king of Israel was right to be frightened. He knew that he could not heal Naaman, nor could he order Elisha to do it. The God of the Hebrews doesn't operate that way. He's reasonably sure that Benhadad knew it as well and was using this opportunity to put him at odds with the military commander:

> It happened when Elisha the man of God heard that the king of Israel had torn his clothes, that he sent word to the king, saying, "Why have you torn your clothes? Now let him come to me, and he shall know that there is a prophet in Israel."
>
> 2 Kings 5:8

God was at work. His ways are mysterious and higher than our ability to understand. We can only wonder how Elisha heard about this. In whatever way that happened, he sent orders to the king of Israel (see the pecking order here?) to have Naaman visit him. On the surface, it would seem that Elisha was violating the very principle I mentioned earlier. As the story unfolds, however, we'll see that this was merely his way of preparing this seeker for an introduction to the Lord.

All of this leads to Naaman's third error: he came with a list of his own expectations.

> So Naaman came with his horses and his chariots and stood at the doorway of the house of Elisha. Elisha sent a messenger to him, saying, "Go and wash in the Jordan seven times, and your flesh will be restored to you and you will be clean."
>
> 2 Kings 5:9–10

That was it. No long, drawn-out ceremony. No hocus-pocus. No smoke or bloodletting or lengthy prayer vigil or even a face-to-face meeting. A man of great dignity had crossed diplomatic bridges and a number of miles. He brought with him the equivalent of multiple thousands of dollars, in the hopes of gaining an audience with a powerful shaman who would call upon the mysterious forces of the universe to make him whole again. What a letdown!

Can you imagine the scene? As General Naaman stands outside the prophet's house with his entourage of chariots and mounted soldiers looking on, an unknown household servant creaks the door open, quietly steps outside, and gives him a message. He says, in effect, "Elisha says to go dip in the river seven times and you'll be fine. Have a nice day." The door shuts and the bolt slides into place. The seasoned soldier in full-dress uniform stands there speechless. The prophet didn't even bother to come to the door, nor did he make one remark over all the nice things the man had brought with him. And what a humiliating, silly set of instructions! "Doesn't this prophet know who he's dealing with?"

But Naaman was furious and went away and said, "Behold, I thought, 'He will surely come out to me and stand and call on the name of the LORD his God, and wave his hand over the place and cure the leper.'"

2 Kings 5:11

"Naaman was furious." Of the six primary Hebrew words referring to anger, this is perhaps the strongest. It usually describes God's righteous wrath toward sin. Naaman was angry because his encounter with God met with none of his personal expectations. (That still happens.)

He expected to be taken seriously by the prophet. Naaman was a man who commanded armies. When he spoke, people jumped to action. His mere presence brought others to their knees. He was important and probably thought that the prophet ought to be impressed to think a man of his rank and authority would even show up at his obscure little village.

He expected his illness to be taken seriously. He would have felt better if Elisha had met with him and then said something like, "Well, this is going to take some doing, but I think we can motivate God to do something extra with the piles of money you brought." All of that would feed his pride and make him feel (and look!) important. He expected the cure to be elaborate, or at least dignified. Take note of his reasoning:

"Are not Abanah and Pharpar, the rivers of Damascus, better than all the waters of Israel? Could I not wash in them and be clean?" So he turned and went away in a rage.

2 Kings 5:12

In effect, he said, "If bathing is the answer, why would I wash my body in some sorry little river in Israel when we've got our own great rivers back home? Syrian rivers are better than all the waters put together in the land of Israel. This is downright stupid!"

Sound familiar? You're witnessing pride on parade. "I want cleansing on *my* terms, in *my* way, earned by *my* merit. I will have no part in such humiliating actions!" But as we learned in Isaiah 55:

"For My thoughts are not your thoughts,
Nor are your ways My ways," declares the LORD.
"For as the heavens are higher than the earth,
So are My ways higher than your ways
And My thoughts than your thoughts."

Isaiah 55:8–9

GOD'S FAITHFULNESS TO THE SEEKER

Naaman felt like he was getting the runaround. Nothing was what he expected. Yet, by virtue of the author's use of dramatic irony, we see the Lord guiding this seeker every step on his journey to cleansing. God first used a servant girl, then the king of Syria, the king of Israel, a soft-spoken messenger of Elisha, and, finally, Naaman's own servants in order to keep him on the right path:

> Then his servants came near and spoke to him and said, "My father, had the prophet told you to do some great thing, would you not have done it? How much more then, when he says to you, 'Wash, and be clean'?"

2 Kings 5:13

Naaman came dangerously close to going back home to die. And it would have been his own stinking pride that killed him—his own stubborn unwillingness to abandon his way for the Lord's. We see the same scenario all too often today. People are told the good news of salvation by grace alone, only to respond with, "That's too simple. Where's the dignity? Where's the effort? If it's all that life changing, surely something sacrificial is required of me!"

Fortunately, Naaman's servants were able to convince him otherwise. Perhaps desperation got his attention and kept him teachable. As he listened, he probably realized he was out of options. Slowly, his pride melted as he pondered the simple set of instructions. Finally . . .

He went down and dipped himself seven times in the Jordan, according to the word of the man of God; and his flesh was restored like the flesh of a little child and he was clean.

2 Kings 5:14

What a miracle! Don't miss the simplicity of it. Elisha arranged the healing so that the Lord, not himself, would be seen as the cleansing power. And he included just enough complexity—seven dippings—to ensure complete obedience. Beyond the surprising procedure he was to follow, this was nothing more than ordinary water in an ordinary river. No angels sang. No trumpets, fire, or smoke. Nothing glowed. The only extraordinary element in this miracle story is the invisible, invincible Lord—His invitation, His ways, His grace, all for His glory. As the man's flesh was restored, only One was deserving of his praise. How grateful he must have been to look down and see that he'd been cleansed!

LESSONS FOR THE SEEKER

Four lessons for any and all seekers arise from Naaman's experience:

First, *only when we acknowledge our own sin-sick state will we seek cleansing.* Jesus Christ didn't come to Planet Earth to call the righteous to repentance, but sinners. Once someone acknowledges his or her sinfulness, the journey to salvation is over halfway traveled.

Second, *only when we hear the truth will we discover the path to cleansing.* The Lord tapped Naaman on the shoulder and then whispered the truth in his ear using a slave girl. Then He put people in the leper's path to bring him closer, step by step. Without those reliable messages of truth, he would never have been cleansed.

Third, *only when we reach the end of our own way will we be ready to follow the Lord's.* His way doesn't involve a lot of money or sacrificial effort or secret knowledge or good behavior. His way is nonnegotiable. It violates our normal, earthly sensibilities and requires the absence of pride. As soon as we abandon our own way, we're capable of following His.

Fourth, *only when we do as God requires will we receive His cleansing.*

Merely knowing where to find the Jordan River and what to when he got there was not enough. He had to put actions to his faith by stripping down, actually getting wet in the river, and immersing himself precisely seven times. Nothing more, nothing less, and nothing else. God's way is like that. Just as leprosy is not cleansed by your homemade prescription, salvation is not cut by your homemade pattern.

The powerful, pleading words of a Scottish preacher provide a fitting conclusion:

> I advise you to get over your temper, and to try that very way that you have up till now been so hot and so loud against. It will humble you to do it, and you are not a humble man; but if you ever come back from Jordan with your flesh like the flesh of a little child, you'll be the foremost to confess that you had almost been lost through your pride, and your prejudice, and your ill-nature. . . .
>
> You all know, surely, what the true leprosy is. You all know what the leprosy of your own soul is. It is sin; yes, it is sin . . . it is yourself. . . . O leper! leper! go out with thy loathsome and deadly heart . . . Go wash in Jordan. Go in God's name. Go in God's strength. Go in God's pity, and patience, and mercy. . . . Go this moment.[3]

> There is a fountain filled with blood
> Drawn from Emmanuel's veins,
> And sinners plunged beneath that flood
> Lose all their guilty stains.[4]

CHAPTER THIRTEEN

Gehazi: The Servant Who Got Greedy

Greed is a disease that will consume a minister from the inside out if it's not detected early and treated aggressively. And greedy people will do the same to a thriving ministry. That's because greed is everything that ministry is not.

Ministry serves others; greed serves self. Ministry calls a woman or a man to set aside selfish gain in order to assist another. Greed is an excessive or reprehensible desire to acquire something for the benefit of self. A minister must live by the highest ethical standard, especially in regard to wealth and material possessions. A greedy person will sacrifice his or her ethical standard when it blocks the path to an object of desire. Whereas ministry uses things to serve people, greed uses people to obtain things.

Greed is never acceptable. Some work hard to rationalize it, sanctify it, even attempt to build a theology around it. Still, greed is a deadly enemy of genuine service to others.

Early on in my own ministry, I learned that greed often begins as covetousness. Fortunately, a wise mentor pointed out the danger before it could become an issue. When I first began serving in ministry, I enjoyed the privilege of working closely with a very gifted man of God. He was all the things I was not: scholarly, extremely knowledgeable of the Scriptures, seasoned as a preacher, and profound as a teacher. Naturally, his number of speaking engagements grew with his reputation. He attracted both Christians and non-Christians, and, though great crowds gathered to hear him, I never saw him attempt to draw attention to himself. Mine was an enviable position as his assistant, his ministerial helper, on staff at the church where he served as pastor. I had complete access to him, and he shared much of his life with me, especially when we traveled together. I counted it an incredible privilege to be near him and serve him.

I might add that this was a very heady opportunity. For example, when I preached in his absence, I enjoyed the crowds that *his* reputation had earned. Because I worked with him at the hub of this large ministry, I had influence that *his* position warranted. Mine was a borrowed popularity that *his* prolific writing and profound thinking had gained. I enjoyed immense blessings as a result of serving this man as a ministry partner, and, to this very day, I have sustained a deep sense of gratitude.

One day, a good friend who was not in ministry gave me a tough yet tender word of warning. He had seen me work in tandem with this great man and how my senior colleague loved and trusted me. He saw a healthy, wholesome mentor-protégé relationship that easily could have become tainted if I failed to guard it. "Watch out for the enemy," he said. "From my vantage point in the congregation, as an officer in the church, and as a friend of both of you, I see your position as the more precarious of the two. Avoid the temptation to drop his name or use any other means to gain attention because of your association. You enjoy many benefits that you have not earned over the years. He has earned them, and *his* is the role of significance. Yours is a role of assistance." He was absolutely correct. To this day I vividly remember the man's timely warning.

Another of my early mentors heard that I had taken on the role of personal assistant to this very prominent man. He, too, gave me wise advice: "Your purpose is to help make that man you serve far more successful than he ever would be without you."

Both of these men approached me with a genuine desire to see me become successful in ministry, not to knock me down a peg or two. They gave me strong, necessary, valuable words of counsel. They reminded me that ministry is all about service, and they steered me clear of what could have become covetousness, leading to greed.

THE MANY FACES OF GREED

That experience taught me to keep a close check on my motives. It also taught me that greed isn't always associated with money. One can become greedy in at least four very common ways.

Money

We're most familiar with this realm of greed. This is a hunger for more money, even at the expense of relationships and personal integrity. The insatiable drive for more leads easily to outright greed.

Possessions

This is closely related to money-greed, but it differs slightly. Misers die with money hidden in mattresses and buried coffee cans, but they possess nothing. However, thanks to little plastic cards, we don't need a huge income to become greedy for possessions. We can feed our greed for more possessions on credit. Watch out, though. When the lust for toys surpasses one's ability to afford them, that's greed.

Fame

This is an inordinate desire for attention—to be known, to be quoted, to be seen, to be popular, to be recognized in public, to be influential, to be sought after for photographs and autographs.

I knew a young man who couldn't rest until he hit it big on the political stage. At first, he begged the Lord to give him the right opportunities and the best contacts. He saw each political office as a means to the one above it. By and by, relationships became mere stepping stones. His longing for notoriety overshadowed any genuine desire for personal friendship or public service. He was greedy for fame.

Pleasure

A natural by-product of an affluent society is hedonism. At its extreme, this is the playboy's lifestyle, an existence that seeks to satisfy one's sensual desires above all else. Those who are greedy for pleasure try to distract themselves from the growing emptiness with even more pleasure. Before long, they find themselves tortured by what should be deeply satisfying.

I need to caution all of us at this point to beware the temptation to feel smug. You might think, *Well, that's not me. I don't have a lot of money, or possessions, or fame, and my lifestyle is not only simple, it's barely even comfortable. I'm in no danger.* I caution you, don't look for signs of raw greed. If you're greedy, you will have already rationalized them. Instead, be on the lookout for the early stages: envy and covetousness. Greed hides itself behind excessive and inordinate desires for the good things of life, often because of another's achievement.

This book began with a discussion about the behind-the-scenes people we sadly regard as "nobodies"—those people who impact the world by means of their assistance to others. In that chapter, I sang their praise, hopefully encouraging those who serve without recognition and admonishing all of us to appreciate their work and affirm them as significant in God's estimation.

If you are someone whose primary role is to assist another, this chapter is for you. Just like my friend helped me see a danger, I want to do the same for you who work alongside a more visible figure. I write this for the benefit of you who serve as helpers, as vice presidents, as associates in a ministry, as assistant managers in business, as administrative assistants, interns in any specific career, or any other (if I may use the word in a dignified sense) servant role. I write this to remind you and encourage you. Don't underestimate the power of your impact as a servant. Your actions either support or undermine the work of the person you serve. The future implications of your motives and choices can be staggering at times. I'll use the story of Gehazi, the servant who got greedy, to expose both the dangers and the opportunities you have, as well as illustrate the potential impact of your faithfulness.

THE STORY OF THE GREEDY SERVANT

This story is a continuation of the tale of Naaman, the officer whose leprosy was cleansed. As you will recall, the proud general of the Syrian army thought he needed money to purchase his healing but found that the Lord's ways are higher than ours. He discovered God's grace, which is free for the asking. The prophet Elisha refused the bribe, sending him on his own to dip himself seven times in the Jordan River. When Naaman emerged from the river, he found his skin completely healed of leprosy. But his cleansing was not merely external. His heart, like his skin, was transformed.

> When [Naaman] returned to the man of God [Elisha] with all his company, and came and stood before him, he said, "Behold now, I know that there is no God in all the earth, but in Israel; so please take a present from your servant now."
>
> 2 Kings 5:15

This and the verses that follow reveal a man whose heart and direction had been changed by the free grace of God, but he was still ignorant. While he accepted the one true God and vowed to sacrifice to the Lord alone, he was still guided by superstition. I love Elisha's response. He didn't rebuke Naaman or make his thinking thoroughly orthodox before he sent him home. The wise prophet dismissed him in peace, trusting that this was merely the beginning of the general's long journey to becoming a devout, mature worshiper of the one true God.

When someone becomes a brand-new believer, the next few days are crucial. The information he or she receives during that brief period may either confirm grace or steal it. "OK, you have received the free gift of salvation in Christ and your place in heaven is secure. Now you must be baptized. Now you must start tithing. Now you must clean up your life. Now you must give up cigarettes, and alcohol, and your foul language, and . . . Now you must . . . now you must . . . now you must . . ." The poor, new Christian is left to wonder, "But you said I was free! What happened?"

When Naaman found he had been cleansed, he wanted to give the prophet a gift—not a bribe, like before, but a gift of thanksgiving. Observe Elisha's noble and unselfish reaction:

> But [Elisha] said, "As the LORD lives, before whom I stand, I will take nothing." And [Naaman] urged him to take it, but he refused.
>
> 2 Kings 5:16

What Elisha refused was no small sum. We don't trade in talents and shekels, so let me convert the gift into today's currency. Naaman offered this humble servant of God 750 pounds of silver and 150 pounds of gold. That comes to roughly $1.1 million dollars. (The clothes were by no means cheap, but they were probably included as a gesture of friendship with the original payback.)

Imagine the ministry potential of a sum like that in the hands of an honest prophet of God. And, let's face it, if you were the one living on a prophet's salary, that would be enough money to make your eyes tear up. You'd be fixed for life. So why did Elisha refuse the gifts? The Bible doesn't tell us, but we can put enough clues together from the story to conclude that it was to reinforce the lesson that Naaman had learned. The Lord cannot be charmed. His salvation is freely given by grace, through faith. Taking Naaman's money would compromise that message.

Perhaps the man on his way back would think, *Interesting, that Elisha took a couple of the very best suits and some of the silver and gold. I wonder if he didn't want that all along.* A compromised message leads to cloudy thoughts like that. But Elisha kept his ministry clearly in focus and would not allow even the slightest hint of greed to taint it.

"But Gehazi, the servant."

With those few words, the story turns. Standing alongside Elisha through this whole series of events is a servant, the prophet's assistant. Gehazi was a man who had been working alongside Elisha much like Elisha had served Elijah. We know from 2 Kings 4 that he had been with his master for a number of years, working very closely with him, even going on his behalf to perform miracles. He had been serving in the limelight created by Elisha's amazing, awe-inspiring ministry. His was a borrowed popularity. He enjoyed influence because Elisha's anointing was so powerful, so spiritually significant. Gehazi lives in the shadow of greatness.

THE SUBTLE, TRANSFORMING POWER OF RATIONALIZATION

Somewhere along the journey at Elisha's side, something twisted Gehazi's thinking. The next verse reveals a remarkable feat in ethical gymnastics—the kind of rationalization that becomes this easy only after lots of practice.

> But Gehazi, the servant of Elisha the man of God, thought, "Behold, my master has spared this Naaman the Aramean, by not receiving from his hands what he brought. As the LORD lives, I will run after him and take something from him."
>
> 2 Kings 5:20

A couple of phrases jump out at me. First, "my master has spared this Naaman." The Hebrew word for "spared" is better translated "denied" or "restrained." In other places in Scripture, the word carries the idea of holding something back. Gehazi said, in essence, "My master held this general back from expressing his gratitude. He merely wanted to say thank you. Isn't saying thank you the right thing to do? Besides, refusing his gift could seem discourteous. The grateful general even urged us. Why, Elisha kept him from doing what was *right*!"

Another phrase: "as the LORD lives." These same words appear several times throughout the books of Samuel and Kings. The phrase forms a solemn vow that invokes the sacred name of Yahweh in a very serious and specific way. This is tantamount to saying, "I guarantee that this deed will be accomplished because it's the Lord's will, and I cannot fail because He's enabling me." Take note of the words Elisha spoke just a few moments earlier:

> But he said, "As the LORD lives, before whom I stand, I will take nothing."
>
> 2 Kings 5:16

Gehazi's rationalization transformed his greed into God's will for his life! He had just heard his master say, in effect, "In accordance with the Lord's will and by His power, I will not receive your money." Once Naaman's caravan disappeared over the horizon, however, the greedy servant's mind began the very creative process of turning wrong into right. With a little imagination, we can guess what else Gehazi might have been thinking:

The man has millions. Now, if he didn't have plenty, he wouldn't offer such lavish gifts. It's only right that we accept something of what he brought. Elisha shouldn't have held him back from doing what his heart led him to do. The Lord has led this general to make us this offer!

It's amazing how God leads. Who would have thought that such an abundant and much-needed provision would come through the hands of a converted Syrian? Praise the Lord for His miraculous gift to us!

It got even worse . . .

My master has plenty, but I have virtually nothing. And Elisha hasn't given me a raise for years. I've served him faithfully and diligently. Maybe he doesn't have a need for these God-given provisions, but I have a family to provide for.

See how rationalization accompanies greed? Understand, these thoughts are not always evil. In some circumstances, they might be absolutely correct. But that's the power of a rationalization. It takes truth out of context and forces it into perfectly valid conclusions at the wrong time, the wrong place, with the wrong motive, and in the wrong situation. A good rationalization scrubs away the guilt in order to provide the necessary permission to act inappropriately. In the end, the greedy person gets to pocket his or her cash with no sin to acknowledge.

Amazingly, greedy people become such masters of self-deceit, so blinded to their own evil that they are genuinely surprised, often offended, when someone dares to call them dishonest.

So what's wrong with Gehazi's rationalization? First, his role as Elisha's assistant was to make the prophet more successful in his ministry. He was to follow Elisha's lead and model the choices (as it related to the ministry) after those of his master. Elisha had said essentially, "The Lord's will is that I *not* receive any money for your cleansing." If Gehazi could no longer support the ministry of his mentor, his responsibility was to say so, separate himself, establish his own ministry, or attach himself to one whom he could support.

Another flaw in Gehazi's thinking: he, personally, was never offered anything. Naaman offered the gifts to Elisha. The provisions were not Gehazi's to receive.

Furthermore, Gehazi obviously knew that his actions were dishonest because he deliberately chose to conceal his plan from his superior. It's clear that he didn't pull Elisha aside to say, "Master, I have a different opinion than you regarding this offer. I understand that you are convinced the Lord would not have you receive anything, but I feel the Lord is leading me otherwise. Would it be permissible for me to receive a small portion of his offer? What is your response to that? May I do so with your blessing?"

GREED IN FULL BLOOM

Gehazi's greed had grown imperceptibly and been kept a secret. It started with covetousness until, like a disease of the soul, it rotted his loyalty and twisted his perspective. I repeat, greed is the enemy of ministry. Unlike his mentor, the protégé had self-interest in first place, not the best interest of his master, or even the good of Naaman. The fruit of his secret greed can be seen in no fewer than five self-serving acts in the rest of the story:

> So Gehazi pursued Naaman [*he pursued*]. When Naaman saw one running after him, he came down from the chariot to meet him and said, "Is all well?" He said, "All is well. My master has sent me [*he lied*], saying, 'Behold, just now two young men of the sons of the prophets have come to me from the hill country of Ephraim. Please give them a talent of silver and two changes of clothes.'" Naaman said, "Be pleased to take two talents." And he urged him, and bound two talents of silver in two bags with two changes of clothes and gave them to two of his servants; and they carried them before him [*he stole*]. When he came to the hill, he took them from their hand and deposited them in the house [*he concealed*], and he sent the men away, and they departed. But he went in and stood before his master. And Elisha said to him, "Where have you been, Gehazi?" And he said, "Your servant went nowhere [*he lied*]."
>
> 2 Kings 5:21–25; comments added

First, Gehazi *pursued the goods* without a single word of prayer, with no thought given to how it might harm the Syrian's spiritual growth, and with no concern for how it would compromise the ministry or reputation of his master. Start to finish, it was selfishness in action.

Second, *he crafted an elaborate lie* to swindle Naaman out of his money and even leave him feeling more spiritual for it. (Sounds like the work of today's religious hucksters.) In fact, all was not well. His master had not sent him. There were no needy sons of prophets. The gifts were not intended for anyone other than Gehazi. He used his office, his spiritual role, his association with a great, godly man to manipulate this secular mind to do a very unspiritual thing: pay for the Lord's free healing.

Third, *he received* from Naaman *what did not belong to him.* Any gift received would have rightfully belonged to Elisha, to whom it was offered. Furthermore, Naaman intended the gifts for two starving seminary students. That would be like someone asking you to support oversees orphanages that didn't exist, only to pocket the money you gave in good faith. Any way you look at it, Gehazi shamelessly stole.

Fourth, *he concealed his actions* from Elisha. He had Naaman's servants carry the loot as far as the ridge in front of the village where Gehazi and Elisha lived. In case his master happened to look out his window, the greedy servant said to the delivery crew, "I'll take it from here. Go in peace." He took the cash out of their hands, pronounced a pious-sounding blessing, sent the men off, and deposited the stolen property in his house where no one would be the wiser. His sins were deliberately hidden from his master.

Fifth, when asked by his mentor where he had been, *he lied without hesitation.* Don't miss the spiritual gloss he added to the outright fabrication in verse 25: "*Your servant* went nowhere." How sickening.

Serving another man or woman as an assistant, especially someone whose influence is widespread, demands absolute loyalty. Yes, the word is *absolute.* Even when he or she is absent, there should be no reason to suspect you of deception or taking unfair advantage of your position. Because trust is essential, your integrity must remain steadfast. If you discover reasons you cannot be loyal, leave. Otherwise, stay on the team giving full support! Maintain a high level of accountability—more than expected. Nurture your relationship with the one you serve so that you not only *know* his or her desires, but you *care* about them and can defend them. Constantly examine you motives to be sure your actions carry out the interests of the one you serve and not your own.

The Disfiguring Effects of Greed and the Hope of Repentance

Not surprisingly, Elisha was not fooled, and the consequences were tragic:

> Then he said to him, "Did not my heart go with you, when the man turned from his chariot to meet you? Is it a time to receive money and to receive clothes and olive groves and vineyards and sheep and oxen and male and female servants? Therefore, the leprosy of Naaman shall cling to you and to your descendants forever." So he went out from his presence a leper as white as snow.
>
> 2 Kings 5:26–27

Try to imagine how Gehazi must have felt. Imagine how foolish; Elisha was a powerful seer. Imagine how exposed and embarrassed; the sin he had worked so hard to conceal was like an open book to the man he admired most. Imagine how disappointed; he was to Elisha what Elisha had been to his master, Elijah. Gehazi forfeited his future ministry. Imagine how frightened; he now had the very disease that another man was willing to pay millions to have cleansed. Imagine how shamed; Elisha's rebuke reflected an innocent quality that Gehazi had lost a long time ago. The greedy servant had forgotten that ministry serves others, never self.

Four Compelling Challenges

After studying this passage and pondering the humanity of this tragic story, I find at least four compelling challenges that apply to everyone . . . but especially those who serve in an assisting role. My hope is that you who serve in a ministry capacity will take special heed.

First, *guard your imagination.* An active imagination is fertile ground for covetousness to sprout into greed and for greed to produce its poisonous fruit. Webster's defines imagination this way: "The act or power of forming a mental image of something not present to the senses or never before wholly perceived in reality."[1] More intriguing is the last definition: "A creation of the mind; especially: an idealized or poetic creation ... fanciful or empty assumption."[2]

Creative people have remarkable imaginations. But that fact has a dark side. The same creativity that helps us dream wonderful dreams can also fantasize destructive fantasies. That's what Gehazi did. On the surface, he served Elisha and even referred to himself as his servant. But in the secret world of his lurid imagination, he forgot his role. He allowed greed to displace ministry.

Second, *rationalization makes all sin less objectionable, especially greed.* Rationalization is providing plausible, right-sounding motives for poor conduct, which encourages us to act upon our fantasies. Like most things, practice makes perfect. In my years in ministry, I've heard the most inventive rationalizations for living a licentious lifestyle, even rationalizations that appeal to the Bible for support in walking away from one's longstanding marital commitment to pursue an illicit affair. These people had become experts in the art of self-delusion as a result of constant practice so that outright sin could be seen as something good, even beneficial. Money is a morally neutral issue, which gives rationalization an even greater opportunity.

The antidote to this poisonous thinking is the discipline of accountability. I call it a discipline because your emotions will work against you. It takes mental toughness to do what is right when you much prefer to do wrong. Develop the habit of running your ideas past a trusted, mature, Christian friend. Trust me on this: it will make a *major* difference. Whereas rationalization will blur the lines between right and wrong, accountability has a remarkable way of keeping them sharp. Chances are good, the more you don't want to discuss your plans with this friend, the more you need to.

Third, *determine to keep all of your business dealings out in the open.* Leave no room for deception by remaining completely transparent in all of your transactions. This will discourage self-deception and the resulting temptation to deceive others. Those things only stimulate greed to keep our motives secret.

A practical example of this is how Insight for Living conducts its business. Our radio ministry voluntarily participates as a member of the Evangelical Council for Financial Accountability. This independent organization has established specific standards of conduct considered to be ethical, and it conducts routine audits of our accounting and business practices to be certain that we remain in complete compliance. Knowing that we are being watched helps keep everyone who occupies a decision-making, leadership position from self-delusion and even a hint of dishonesty.

Fourth, *examine your motives, call it greed when you see it, and confess it.* Confession usually brings sin to a necessary and abrupt end. Never doubt, it can also be the most difficult thing you do. Realizing that you are guilty of something as ugly as avarice, sometimes having to acknowledge that you covered it with a spiritual veneer, takes remarkable self-awareness and gut-wrenching strength. Nevertheless, I can think of no other way to deal with the sin of greed than to name it, openly confess it, find forgiveness based on the free grace of Jesus Christ, and then claim God's power to choose a different path.

Apparently Gehazi repented, though he was never cleansed of the consequence, his leprosy. According to Hebrew law, he was able to continue serving as Elisha's assistant because his skin had turned completely white (Leviticus 13:12–13). Later, he would stand before King Jehoram as the servant of Elisha. He had been restored to ministry, but his white, flaking skin would forever remind him of three mental images: the face of the Syrian, whose faith he compromised; the disappointed look of his master, whom he had undermined; and the awful day when he gave in to greed.

A final word is to all my colleagues serving in ministry. Let's forever remember what Gehazi forgot: greed is the enemy of ministry.

CHAPTER FOURTEEN

Uzziah: The Leader Who Became a Loser

We're near the end of our study of very significant "nobodies." My desire in this book is the same as in my life: to finish well. So, I've chosen to end with Uzziah, a remarkable man for a lot of reasons. My purpose will become more evident as his story unfolds.

Uzziah was born during a tumultuous period in the history of the Hebrew people. One hundred years prior to Uzziah's reign, the foolishness of Rehoboam (remember him?) had torn the kingdom into two bitter enemies: Israel in the north and Judah in the south. In the century that followed, the nations routinely warred against one another, as progressively evil kings occupied their thrones and dominated their people. Israel's kings were all reprobate, violent pagans, while many of the kings in Judah were at least somewhat godly. But eventually the violence of the north became commonplace in Judah.

Bear with me through a quick 'n' dirty bit of history; it's important. Uzziah's father, Amaziah, was assassinated. Amaziah's father, Joash, fell victim to a conspiracy by his officers. Joash's father, Ahaziah, sat on the throne for only one year before he was murdered. Ahaziah's mother, Athaliah, reigned in his place until she was executed. So the last four monarchs to sit on the throne of Judah had all been killed prior to Uzziah's coronation. Welcome to an ugly, violent world, young man.

This was a bloody, wicked era for Judah. Her bad kings were thoroughly godless. The nation would have despaired were it not for the presence of faithful prophets and priests. Her good kings brought periods of relative stability and peace, though they never worshiped and obeyed God with the kind of passionate devotion that David and Solomon had displayed. After nine kings, Uzziah promised to be different. A close look at his history tells us that he may have reigned toward the final years of his father. A curious statement appears in the text that prompts us to think that probably occurred:

> And all the people of Judah took Uzziah, who was sixteen years old, and made him king *in the place of his father Amaziah.* . . . Uzziah was sixteen years old when he became king, and he reigned fifty-two years in Jerusalem; and his mother's name was Jechiliah of Jerusalem.

> 2 Chronicles 26:1, 3; emphasis added

Based on a careful chronology of Judah's kings, it appears that Amaziah was king for only six years when the people installed his sixteen-year-old son as coregent. Why? Scripture says of the older man's leadership, "He did right in the sight of the LORD, yet not with a whole heart" (2 Chronicles 25:2). Another translation puts it this way: "Amaziah did what the LORD said was right, but he did not really want to obey him" (NCV). In other words, Amaziah was a fence rider, an unstable man who could not be counted upon to remain consistent.

Amaziah started out well, relying upon the Lord's strength to defeat Judah's enemy, Edom. Then he made a compromising decision to set up their idols and begin worshiping them instead of the one and only true God of Judah, who gave him victory. He paid a huge sum of money to buy mercenaries, only to send them home with the money without using their services. He picked a pointless fight with the king of Israel, only to lead Judah into a humiliating loss. Fed up, the people crowned his sixteen-year-old son to rule as vice regent. Eventually, though, the people could tolerate Amaziah no longer and killed him, leaving the much younger Uzziah to lead the nation.

Unfortunately, young men from such sordid roots ultimately become old men who look a lot like their fathers. He began well, and the good he did was reminiscent of his father's early start:

> He did right in the sight of the LORD according to all that his father Amaziah had done.
>
> 2 Chronicles 26:4

Before we continue, allow me to make this personal by asking you a probing question. If your children follow in your steps, will they do what is right in the sight of the Lord? If your children emulate you—*and they will*—will you be able to say that their adult years were God-honoring?

Imagine walking over snow-covered ground a few paces ahead of your child. Each step you take leaves an imprint he or she can clearly see. Now imagine that little person following you stretching those short legs to place his or her feet in the footprints you left behind. That's exactly what your children will do in life. In fact, that's what we see Uzziah doing. He made good tracks early on, just like his father, but he made them with a reluctant heart, also like his father:

> He continued to seek God in the days of Zechariah, who had understanding through the vision of God; and as long as he sought the LORD, God prospered him.
>
> 2 Chronicles 26:5

Don't rush too quickly past those last ten words. They point to a principle: seek the Lord and He will prosper you. That doesn't mean you'll necessarily enjoy great financial gain or material wealth or widespread fame or anything that the world considers a sign of prosperity and success. It means the Lord, in His own inimitable way, will use you and honor your efforts and, in that sense, prosper you. You may have to rethink your definition of prosperity to grasp the true spiritual meaning of the concept. It's worth the effort to do so.

THE WORK OF A GOOD KING

Because of grace, God prospered Uzziah in many of the ways we would expect a king to enjoy success.

Military Conquest

> Now he went out and warred against the Philistines, and broke down the wall of Gath and the wall of Jabneh and the wall of Ashdod; and he built cities in the area of Ashdod and among the Philistines. God helped him against the Philistines, and against the Arabians who lived in Gur-baal, and the Meunites.
>
> 2 Chronicles 26:6–7

Uzziah was not only a capable general, but he was a wise and compassionate statesman. He didn't merely pillage his enemy after conquering them. He subdued these potentially dangerous nations and then turned them into peaceful neighbors by treating them with compassion. More importantly, however, are the words in verse 7: "God helped him."

Notoriety and Respect

> The Ammonites also gave tribute to Uzziah, and his fame extended to the border of Egypt, for he became very strong.
>
> 2 Chronicles 26:8

In the ancient world, tribute was appeasement money. It said, "We respect your power over us. Please accept this gift as a token of our loyalty to you . . . and our gratitude for not wiping us out."

Prosperity

> Moreover, Uzziah built towers in Jerusalem at the Corner Gate and at the Valley Gate and at the corner buttress and fortified them. He

built towers in the wilderness and hewed many cisterns, for he had much livestock, both in the lowland and in the plain. He also had plowmen and vinedressers in the hill country and the fertile fields, for he loved the soil.

2 Chronicles 26:9–10

Uzziah made wise plans, carried them out, and in keeping with the principle of grace pointed out earlier, the Lord gave him favorable results. As the psalm goes, "Unless the LORD builds the house, they labor in vain who build it" (Psalm 127:1). Kings not only ran nations, but they also built personal estates.

This particular king was a farmer at heart. He loved to work the soil. If you and I were to have visited Uzziah's Jerusalem, we would have seen a bountiful landscape covering the slopes of Judea. The land known as wilderness became known as a fertile field. Uzziah had a talent for making anything he touched bloom and bear fruit. (Unlike me. I love the soil, but it doesn't like me at all. Honestly, I could kill a dead plant deader!)

Power

Moreover, Uzziah had an army ready for battle, which entered combat by divisions according to the number of their muster, prepared by Jeiel the scribe and Maaseiah the official, under the direction of Hananiah, one of the king's officers. The total number of the heads of the households, of valiant warriors, was 2,600. Under their direction was an elite army of 307,500, who could wage war with great power, to help the king against the enemy.

2 Chronicles 26:11–13

Uzziah was a very capable warrior—a creative, strategic thinker. We have already seen how he was ready to take the offensive when strategy called for it, but unlike his father, he wasn't looking for a fight. Virtually everything he did was to ensure the prosperity and safety of the kingdom.

Security

> Moreover, Uzziah prepared for all the army shields, spears, helmets,
> body armor, bows and sling stones. In Jerusalem he made engines of
> war invented by skillful men to be on the towers and on the corners
> for the purpose of shooting arrows and great stones. Hence his fame
> spread afar, for he was marvelously helped until he was strong.
>
> 2 Chronicles 26:14–15

I'm impressed by the inventiveness and ingenuity of this man. He didn't rely entirely upon brute force—weapons, helmets, and shields—for defense. Uzziah put together an ingenious array of machines to augment his towers and strengthen the walls. Along with the impressive army he had assembled were all these cutting-edge inventions that put Judah far ahead of other nations. Before long, the country Uzziah led bristled with defense-ready cities, surrounded by a vast, lush, produce-rich countryside. Anyone even thinking of attacking Judah would be smart to change his mind.

The Pride

Uzziah's impressive reputation as a creative, prosperous, strong king spread rapidly. His neighbors both feared and admired him. His subjects praised him and pledged their loyalty. And with all of this success surrounding the man Uzziah, everyone quite naturally supposed that the credit belonged to him.

This is to be expected in human nature. When people admire a public figure, they think, *My, isn't that person great?* There's really nothing wrong with that. The danger isn't in what the public thinks, but in what the admired person thinks. And in case you're wondering about Uzziah, check out the last four words of verse 15: "He was marvelously helped until he was strong."

For many years, Uzziah acted wisely, and the Lord multiplied his efforts. It could have just as easily gone the other way. Uzziah acted wisely and the Lord let it come to nothing. Farmers seem to have an instinctive understanding of this. They can prepare the ground, plant, water, fertilize, and protect the crop from bugs, but it's always the Lord who is responsible for the increase.

As soon as a public figure begins to believe the press about him or her, everyone's in for trouble. While pondering that truth, another name comes to mind. We studied him earlier. His name is Saul.

Remember him? He was another "nobody." He originally thought so little of himself that when God put His hand on him and said, "You will be the king of My kingdom," he hid among the baggage. He doubted his ability to do the job and had no desire to be in the public eye. But what a change once the Lord prospered him! After a few victories on the battlefield, he saw himself as a big shot, so he began to strut around the kingdom as though he had built it. People snapped to attention when he barked orders, and he began throwing his weight around as his fame spread. Before long, he believed the great press he received.

Remember what happened next? He gave himself a promotion. No longer satisfied with the position as merely supreme commander of Israel, he decided to become high priest. He slipped a priestly robe over his battle armor and prepared for sacrifices. That's when Samuel, the man of God, confronted him, saying, in effect, "Saul, when you were little in your own eyes, God could use you, but now that you are great in your own eyes, you are useless to Him."

These thoughts give us reason to pause and ponder. Take a few moments to put yourself in Uzziah's sandals. You may or may not be a public figure, so let's look at this more in terms of blessing and success. Perhaps you're on the way up right now. You're implementing plans that are paying off. You're creative and competent. You're reaping the harvest of hard work. Things are going well for you. You can justifiably say that the success you're enjoying is the direct result of applying good strategy or wise leadership or creative thinking or uncommon perseverance or, perhaps, a combination of those things. If that's you, I say, "Good for you!" I mean that sincerely. No hint of sarcasm in that at all. Why should there be? The Lord has chosen to bless and prosper you. How gracious of Him to do so!

Uzziah was a remarkable man in many ways. The Hebrew in verse 15 reads, literally, "and his name went out to a distant place, for he did extraordinarily to be helped until he was strong."[1] He deserved a great deal of credit for his accomplishments, and kept in the right perspective, so do you. Giving all the glory to God doesn't mean that you should deny your role. (Read that again, please.) The danger lies in diminishing the Lord's role.

THE FALL

Linger over the first word in verse 16. "But . . ." Amazing what that one word does to your spirit, isn't it? How eloquent a role it plays in many a life! We've seen that repeatedly in this book.

> But when he became strong, his heart was so proud that he acted corruptly.
>
> 2 Chronicles 26:16

This can happen to anyone, not just kings and public figures. You can be a minister of the gospel or a business professional or an artist, a teacher, a salesperson, a homemaker, a waiter, a construction worker, a musician, a mathematician . . . any role. When you recognize the necessity of God's power and the futility of your efforts apart from Him, He wants to "marvelously help you until you are strong."

But . . . there's that awful word again. But, when you become strong in your own eyes, things change. Uzziah didn't read history, so he was doomed to repeat it. Driven by self-importance, nothing remained sacred. If you're like me, you see Saul in the next verse:

> But when he became strong, his heart was so proud that he acted corruptly, and he was unfaithful to the LORD his God, for he entered the temple of the LORD to burn incense on the altar of incense.
>
> 2 Chronicles 26:16

As Christians—those of us who know the Lord Jesus as Savior—our first area of faithfulness is not the workplace and not even the home. Our primary realm of faithfulness to the Lord is our hearts. We won't struggle to remain humble publicly if we keep a proper perspective inwardly. After all, we merely behave the way we think.

Uzziah began to think, *My, I'm really something. Those Egyptians are right. There's never been a king like me. Why, look at those inventions. There's never been anyone that's come up with something like that. Look at the prosperity I have brought the kingdom. These citizens haven't had it this good since Solomon. Am I great, or what?* Eventually, his conceit convinced him that his sovereign rule included the Lord's temple. He probably thought, *I don't need priests to worship the Lord. I'm in charge here! Who are they to say that I can't do something if I want to?* So he grabbed the censer, and he stepped into a place where he had no right to enter. Blinded by pride, he lost all restraint. In doing so, he stepped far beyond the bounds of safety:

> Then Azariah the priest entered after him and with him eighty priests
> of the LORD, valiant men. They opposed Uzziah the king and said to
> him, "It is not for you, Uzziah, to burn incense to the LORD, but for
> the priests, the sons of Aaron who are consecrated to burn incense.
> Get out of the sanctuary, for you have been unfaithful and will have
> no honor from the LORD God."
>
> 2 Chronicles 26:17–18

Some people would call this "a moment of clarity." Moments like this have a remarkable way of crystallizing the truth. In this explosive collision of wills, everyone could see Uzziah's conceit, his pride, his disrespect for the Lord, what he thought of his role and the role of the priests. Everything is exposed. If anyone had missed it before, the truth about Uzziah's attitude was unmistakable. And what happened next helped to clarify reality for the king as well:

> But Uzziah, with a censer in his hand for burning incense, was enraged;
> and while he was enraged with the priests, the leprosy broke out on
> his forehead before the priests in the house of the LORD, beside the
> altar of incense. Azariah the chief priest and all the priests looked at
> him, and behold, he was leprous on his forehead; and they hurried

him out of there, and he himself also hastened to get out because the
LORD had smitten him.

2 Chronicles 26:19–20

Can you picture it? Uzziah, clad in his royal finery along with the flowing priestly robe, censer in his hand, eyes blazing with furious indignation,
commands the priests to move aside. Just as he begins to remind them of
his "divine authority" as the king of Judah, a small, leprous sore forms above
his eyes. Then the flesh of his face, neck, and arms begins to decay far too
quickly to be natural. Within a few minutes his body is covered with the
most dreaded disease of his day. Nothing reduces a person to ground zero
like leprosy.

In 1958, I had just enough exposure to see why leprosy caused such fear
in the ancient world. While I was a marine stationed on Okinawa, I had the
privilege of playing in the Third Marine Division band. On one occasion,
we were invited to play a concert for a leper colony in the northern part
of the island. We played a number of selections, using various ensembles,
giving our very best performance for these dear, wonderful, albeit forgotten
people. While we felt sure they enjoyed the music, we heard only muted
applause. When we finished the concert, the victims of this awful disease
did their best to clap for us, but they did so with disfigured hands and
arms—many having only stubs because of the necessary amputations.

After we packed our instruments, we did our best to mingle with them
and say a few kind words before leaving. But that proved awkward. They
hid their disfigured faces with their mutilated hands and arms, moving away
from us because they felt ashamed of the "unclean" disease that made them so
undesirable. I noticed the absence of one quality more than any other. Pride.
There wasn't an ounce of it anywhere in that colony of broken souls.

THE IMPORTANCE OF FINISHING WELL

Considering Uzziah's long, impressive career—fifty-two years in all—this
was a tragic end. A just end, but tragic nonetheless. The Lord helped him.
The Lord prospered him. But when this remarkable and greatly gifted

leader presumed to extend his authority to the temple, God's holy place, the Lord struck him down. Enough was enough. And Uzziah the leader became Uzziah the loser.

Read his epitaph with a sigh:

> King Uzziah was a leper to the day of his death; and he lived in a separate house, being a leper, for he was cut off from the house of the LORD. And Jotham his son was over the king's house judging the people of the land.
>
> 2 Chronicles 26:21

I mentioned before that I played in the Third Marine Division band. Something I learned as a musician is that the most important notes you play are often those in the last few bars of the piece. You can recover from a rough beginning. You still have time to settle down and find yourself in the middle. But there's nothing to follow those last notes except silence. The quality of those final notes on the final page of the finale will usually be the ones that shape the audience's memory of your performance.

Without question, Uzziah started well. The majority of his career provided a godly, safe, prosperous environment for God's people. But the final notes of his performance spoiled the whole concert. Observe what his audience remembered:

> So Uzziah slept with his fathers, and they buried him with his fathers in the field of the grave which belonged to the kings, *for they said, "He is a leper."* And Jotham his son became king in his place.
>
> 2 Chronicles 26:23; emphasis added

Because he was a leper, he lived out the rest of his days all alone. Think of it! When he died, they buried him in a field adjacent to the royal cemetery—not within it—because he was still considered unclean. They didn't mark his gravestone with "He was a king." They didn't even say, "He was a king who became a leper." By the end, his greatness was forgotten. They wrote what they remembered: "He was a leper."

UZZIAH'S IMPACT ON US

Here are three powerful principles we can glean from this fascinating story:

First, *there is no genuine success apart from the Lord God.* The psalmist got it right: "Unless the LORD builds the house, they labor in vain who build it" (Psalm 127:1). Uzziah started strong, but it was the Lord who gave his efforts success. If you're enjoying prosperity, give God all the credit and all your thanks. Even though it came as a result of careful planning and strong commitment and honest labor, the harvest was only possible because the Lord gave your labor success. Never forget that, please!

Second, *few tests reveal the character of a person like success.* I said in an earlier chapter that success doesn't ruin a person; success reveals a person. Curiously, most people can handle adversity with grace, but very few can handle life at the top. If you're enjoying great success, don't fool yourself into thinking that it's your reward for being God's favored child. Better to consider it a trial. Do with success what you do during any other difficult time. Pray. Hold it loosely. Seek wise counsel. Don't be afraid of it . . . but regularly ask the Lord to keep you safe and aware. Look for the lessons. This trial, just like any other, is an opportunity to grow. Furthermore, it's temporary. It may have taken you years to get here, but it can vanish in a flash. As Solomon wrote, "Riches make themselves wings; they fly away" (Proverbs 23:5 KJV).

Third, *the God who blesses is also the God who can break.* Remember the old adage: don't bite the hand that feeds you. Uzziah's father defeated the Edomites by the power of the Lord God, then he brought the impotent gods of his defeated enemy home and began worshiping them. So the Lord disciplined him. Like his father, Uzziah became strong because the Lord prospered him, but when he tried to use his power to flout God's law in God's temple, the Lord disciplined him. That cause-and-effect principle still occurs.

God is a God of grace, so we must not come away with the idea that we have to be good to enjoy God's blessing. He will always give us better than we deserve. However, God is far more concerned with our holiness than our happiness, so He will send us whatever will make us holy. If blessing won't get the job done, then He has little choice but to send chastisement.

Let's face it: the Lord wants to bless us beyond all we can imagine. The Lord that helped and prospered Uzziah is the same Lord who said, "Let him have leprosy." Does that sound harsh? Consider this: because God is perfectly right, infinitely loving, absolutely holy, inexhaustibly patient, and inexplicably merciful, we can be sure that leprosy was the very least He could do to get the attention of the king He loved. It worked.

A FINAL THOUGHT

Uzziah was a someboy who ended up as a "nobody." As we have seen all the way through this book, God loves "nobodies." When God walked the earth as a man, He said, "It is not those who are healthy who need a physician, but those who are sick; I did not come to call the righteous, but sinners" (Mark 2:17). The exquisite irony of this story is that the proud king merely discovered what he really was from the very beginning. The uncleanness of his sores and his status as an unclean outcast alerted him to the uncleanness that had been in his soul all along.

When he finally accepted his status as a "nobody," he took his place alongside the rest of humanity. Then, and only then, was he prepared to meet the only real Somebody. My hope is that Uzziah, quarantined from society at large and permanently barred from public service, allowed the Lord to make him somebody worth emulating. It's quite possible. After a long string of outright evil kings and good kings gone bad, Uzziah's son, Jotham, became the only king of Judah in 130 years to be listed as exclusively good. I would like to think that it was the seven years Jotham spent in coregency with his father, perhaps learning from his mistakes.

If so, that's the kind of impact every "nobody" should have, including you . . . and me.

CONCLUSION

This safari through the Scriptures has been quite a trip. It's been like a journey through a jungle of humanity. Talk about variety! We've met people who are not only obscure; they could not have been more different.

For instance, there's the son who couldn't find a way to win with his parents. And the older brother whose rage against his younger brother was so severe it resulted in murder. Then there was the father whose love for his son was so adoring, he went all the way to the brink proving that his commitment to God was even greater. And speaking of commitment, we met a woman whose loyalty to her undeserving husband was so strong, she was willing to stand in the gap for him as she softened the heart of a man who was on his way to kill him.

And how about that king who was his own worst enemy? Or the charming young prince who wound up hanging by his hair from a tree with three spears in his chest . . . or the gifted and creative king who started so well as a leader on his way to greatness, but ended so poorly as a loser covered with leprosy? It's hard to know whether his story of uncontrolled pride is worse than the servant whose greed got to best of him or the soldier whose hidden sin resulted in a national disaster.

And those are only *some* of those whose lives we uncovered together. Thankfully, not all have been studies in tragedy. One man's prayers were so honored by the Lord, he grew up to be the exact opposite of what he had been as a little boy. And how about that general who had such a struggle following simple orders? And the child, all alone and away from his mother, who heard God's voice time and again in the middle of the night? And I haven't even mentioned the long list of courageous men whom a king named as his "mighty men" when he came to the end of his life . . . men whose names we not only can't remember, but we can hardly even pronounce!

These fascinating stories of forgotten lives are woven like threads through the fabric of God's tapestry. Though ancient, they are forever relevant. They remain preserved like etchings in the timeless stones of His Book, waiting to be read and imagined, appreciated and applied. We have done that through these chapters.

Is it any wonder why Paul wrote what he did in his letter to the Romans?

> Even if it was written in Scripture long ago,
> you can be sure it's written for *us.*
> God wants the combination of His steady, constant calling,
> and warm personal counsel in Scripture
> to come to characterize *us,*
> keeping us alert for whatever He will do next.
>
> 15:4 MSG; emphasis added

You have patiently worked your way through these pages, acquainting yourself with any number of people and situations, most of which have probably been unfamiliar to you. I commend you for staying with it. And I thank you.

You have finished the book, but you're not through—not really. Now comes the real challenge. Having traveled through these stories, you're better prepared to have them travel through you.

You see, that's what is important to the One who preserved them for us. His concern is not simply that we learn about others, whether they are obscure or familiar, well known or unknown, but that we learn about *ourselves.* That explains why Paul emphasized that they were "written for *us.*" These people and their stories have been kept in the treasury of truth to serve as carefully preserved mirrors, revealing to *us* things about ourselves that dare not be overlooked or ignored.

I urge you to go back and reread those points of application that were drawn at the end of each chapter. The second time around, rather than seeing them as principles related only to the one whose life we examined in that chapter, consider them as precepts ready to be taken personally—in your life—today.

The wide variety ought to encourage you. It's saying to all of us that God has room in His plan for you, for me. No one is excluded. That's right, no one.

And the more you glean from God's "warm personal counsel in Scripture," the more those important truths will "come to characterize" your life. What better goal could you and I possibly have?

Who knows? In the years to come, long after we have drawn our final breaths, God may choose to use the fascinating stories of our lives to encourage others in future generations. Even though you and I may be tempted to think that we'll soon be gone and quickly forgotten, that's not so. If we've learned nothing else from these pages, it's this:

**No life is insignificant when God chooses to use it
to teach His truth to others.**

That's enough to "keep us alert for whatever He will do next." Exciting, isn't it?

ENDNOTES

Chapter 1

1. Richard Matheson, *The Incredible Shrinking Man* (New York: Tom Doherty Associates, LLC, 1994), 202.

Chapter 2

1. Charles W. Colson, *Faith on the Line* (Colorado Springs: Victor Books, a division of Cook Communications, 1985), 24–25. Used by permission.
2. Jay Adams, *Competent to Counsel* (Grand Rapids, MI: Baker, 1970), 147.
3. Anna Russell, *Jolly Old Sigmund Freud*, BR Music Publications Inc./APRA. www.apra.com.au.

Chapter 3

1. A.W. Tozer, *The Pursuit of God* (Harrisburg, PA: Christian Publications, Inc., 1982, 1993), 21–22, 30. Used by permission of Christian Publications, Inc., 800-233-4443, www.christianpublications.com.
2. This material is taken from *My Utmost for His Highest* by Oswald Chambers, copyright ©1935 by Dodd Mead & Co., renewed 1963 by the Oswald Chambers Publications Assn., Ltd. Used by permission of Discovery House Publishers, Box 3566, Grand Rapids, MI 49501. All rights reserved.
3. Eileen Guder, *God, But I'm Bored* (New York: Random House, 1971), 55.
4. A.W. Tozer, *The Pursuit of God* (Harrisburg, PA: Christian Publications, Inc., 1982, 1993), 31. Used by permission of Christian Publications, Inc., 800-233-4443, www.christianpublications.com.

Chapter 4

1. James Hastings, ed., *The Greater Men and Women of the Bible*, vol. 1 (Edinburgh: T & T Clark, 1913), 451.

Chapter 5

1. Alexander Whyte, *Bible Characters*, vol. 1 (London: Oliphants Ltd., 1952), 173, 175.

Chapter 6

1. Alexander Whyte, *Bible Characters*, vol. 1 (London: Oliphants Ltd., 1952), 74–75.
2. Ibid, 75–76.

Chapter 7

1. J. Sidlow Baxter, *Mark These Men* (Grand Rapids, MI.: Zondervan, 1960), 25.
2. Merriam-Webster's Collegiate Dictionary, 10th ed., s.v. "rationalize."

Chapter 9

1. Alexander Whyte, *Bible Characters*, vol. 1 (London: Oliphants Ltd., 1952), 309.
2. John Greenleaf Whittier, *The Complete Poetical Works of John Greenleaf Whittier* (Boston: Houghton, Mifflin and Company, 1884), 151.

Chapter 10

1. Mark Twain, *Following the Equator: A Journey Around the World*, Vol. 2 (New York: P. F. Collier & Son, 1899), 237.
2. Stephen Ambrose, *To America* (New York: Simon & Schuster, 2002), xvi. Used by permission. All rights reserved.
3. Merrill F. Unger, *Unger's Bible Dictionary* (Chicago: Moody Press, 1957), 416.

Chapter 11

1. J. Oswald Sanders, *A Spiritual Clinic: A Suggestive Diagnosis and Prescription for Problems in Christian Life and Service* (Chicago: Moody Press, 1958), 120.
2. John F. Walvoord, Roy B. Zuck, and Dallas Theological Seminary, *The Bible Knowledge Commentary: An Exposition of the Scriptures* (Colorado Springs: Victor Books, a division of Cook Communications, 1985), 591–592. Used by permission.

3. R. Laird Harris, Gleason Leonard Archer, and Bruce K. Waltke, *Theological Wordbook of the Old Testament* (Chicago: Moody Press, 1980), 426-427.

Chapter 12

1. Peter Marshall, *Mister Jones, Meet the Master*, ed. Catherine Marshall (New York: Fleming H. Revell, a division of Baker Books, 1950), 135–36.
2. C. F. Keil and F. Delitzsch, *Biblical Commentary on The Old Testament* (Grand Rapids, MI: Wm. Eerdmans, 1982), 317.
3. Alexander Whyte, *Bible Characters*, vol. 1, (London: Oliphants Ltd., 1952), 374–75.
4. William Cowper, "There Is a Fountain Filled with Blood," Public Domain.

Chapter 13

1. *Merriam-Webster's Collegiate Dictionary*, 10th ed., s.v. "imagination."
2. Ibid.

Chapter 14

1. Biblical Studies Press, *The NET Bible Notes*, 2 Ch 26:15 (Dallas: Biblical Studies Press, 2003), 696.

GRACE AWAKENING
ISBN 0-8499-1805-7

The Grace Awakening calls all Christians to wake up and reject living in such legalistic, performance-oriented bondage. The God of the universe has given us an amazing, revolutionary gift of grace and freedom. This freedom and grace set us apart from every other "religion" on the face of the earth. In this best-selling classic, Charles Swindoll urges you not to miss living a grace-filled life. Freedom and joy—not lists and demands and duties—await all who believe in the Lord Jesus Christ.

DAY BY DAY WITH CHARLES SWINDOLL
ISBN 08499-0546-X
Daily Insights from a Master Communicator

We all need to spend quiet time in communication with God . . . and guidance from a leader with Charles Swindoll's wisdom and insight can make that time productive, rewarding, and inspiring.

LIVING ON THE RAGGED EDGE
0-8499-4540-2

In contrast to a life of meaningless work and empty living, *Living on the Ragged Edge* offers hope for satisfaction and significance. Here is an intimate glimpse into Solomon's ancient journal, Ecclesiastes, in which the young king's desperate quest for satisfaction—in work, in sexual conquest, in all the trappings afforded by his fabulous wealth—was as futile as trying to "catch the wind." For those struggling with the anxieties and frustrations of our modern era, the good news is that you can find perspective and joy amid the struggle.

THOMAS NELSON
Since 1798

thomasnelson.com

STRENGTHENING YOUR GRIP
0-8499-4399-X

The all-time favorite book of one of America's favorite authors, *Strengthening Your Grip* will impart spiritual courage and stamina to all who desire a well-aimed life. This is a spiritual classic that refreshes souls and changes lives. Here it is in a revised edition that will bless another generation of readers. Realizing that disillusionment and loss of personal resolve have created an aura of apathy in this age, best-selling author, pastor, and radio minister Charles Swindoll calls on his readers to trade in their half-hearted attitudes for fresh vigor in their souls. In this aimless world, Dr. Swindoll tells people how to live with confidence and purpose.

SIMPLE FAITH
0-8499-4419-8

Must we run at a pace between maddening and insane to prove we're among the faithful? Is this really how the Prince of Peace would have us live? In this best-selling, classic work, Swindoll answers with a resounding, "No!" showing how Christians can break free from exhausting, performance-based faith. He call us back to the simplicity of the Sermon on the Mount.

THE MYSTERY OF GOD'S WILL
0-8499-4326-4

Best-selling author Charles Swindoll tackles one of life's most misunderstood issues: the will of God.

We all face difficult decisions. How can we know that the decisions we make are in God's will? Even popular author, pastor, and Dallas Seminary President Charles Swindoll says at times he's not been so sure. In *The Mystery of God's Will*, Swindoll examines this long-debated subject from a balanced, biblical perspective regarding his own doubts and experiences. For anyone who's ever doubted God's will, or for those who are convinced of it in every situation, this book will be a real eye-opener.

THOMAS NELSON
Since 1798

thomasnelson.com

HAND ME ANOTHER BRICK
ISBN 0-8499-3709-4

Most of us could benefit from wise advice on how to be a more effective leader at work and at home. In this revised edition, Charles Swindoll delves deep into the life of Nehemiah to show how to handle the issues of motivation, discouragement and adversity with integrity.

THREE STEPS FORWARD, TWO STEPS BACK
0-8499-4098-2

\ Charles Swindoll reminds readers that our problems are not solved by simple answers or all-too-easy clichés. Instead, he offers practical ways to walk with God through the realities of life, including times of fear, stress, anger, and temptation.

YOU AND YOUR CHILD
0-8499-3710-8

Best-selling author and veteran parent and grandparent Charles Swindoll believes that the key to successful parenting lies in becoming a "student" of your children—learning the distinct bent and blueprint of each child. Here is practical advice for parents wishing to launch confidenct, capable young adults in today's ever-changing world.

THOMAS NELSON
Since 1798

thomasnelson.com

HOPE AGAIN
ISBN 0-8499-4088-5

Combining the New Testament teachings of Peter and the insights
of Charles Swindoll, one of the most popular authors of our day,
Hope Again is an encouraging, enlivening and refreshing look at
why we can dare to hope, no matter who we are, no matter what
we face.

LAUGH AGAIN
0-8499-3679-9

Discover outrageous joy in this modern classic. Chuck Swindoll
shows how we can live in the present, say no to negativism, and
realize that while no one's life is perfect, joy is always available.
Applying scriptural truths in a practical way, Swindoll shows
readers how to laugh again.

THOMAS NELSON
Since 1798

thomasnelson.com

The Great Lives Series

In his Great Lives from God's Word series, Charles R. Swindoll
shows us how the great heroes of the faith offer a model of
courage, hope, and triumph in the face of adversity.

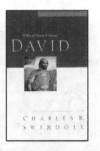

DAVID
A Man of
Passion and
Destiny

ESTHER
A Woman of
Strength and
Dignity

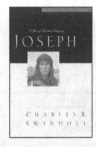

JOSEPH
A Man of
Integrity and
Forgiveness

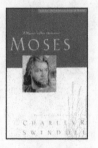

MOSES
A Man of
Selfless
Dedication

ELIJAH
A Man of
Heroism and
Humility

PAUL
A Man of
Grace and Grit

JOB
A Man of
Heroic
Endurance

THOMAS NELSON
Since 1798
thomasnelson.com